THE HISTORY AND THEORY OF INTERNATIONAL LAW

# Sovereignty

# THE HISTORY AND THEORY OF INTERNATIONAL LAW

*General Editors*

NEHAL BHUTA

*Chair in International Law, University of Edinburgh*

ANTHONY PAGDEN

*Distinguished Professor, University of California Los Angeles*

BENJAMIN STRAUMANN

*Alberico Gentili Senior Fellow, New York University School of Law*

In the past few decades the understanding of the relationship between nations has undergone a radical transformation. The role of the traditional nation-state is diminishing, along with many of the traditional vocabularies that were once used to describe what has been called, ever since Jeremy Bentham coined the phrase in 1780, 'international law.' The older boundaries between states are growing ever more fluid, new conceptions and new languages have emerged which are slowly coming to replace the image of a world of sovereign independent nation states which has dominated the study of international relations since the early nineteenth century. This redefinition of the international arena demands a new understanding of classical and contemporary questions in international and legal theory. It is the editors' conviction that the best way to achieve this is by bridging the traditional divide between international legal theory, intellectual history, and legal and political history. The aim of the series, therefore, is to provide a forum for historical studies, from classical antiquity to the twenty-first century, that are theoretically-informed and for philosophical work that is historically conscious, in the hope that a new vision of the rapidly evolving international world, its past and its possible future, may emerge.

PREVIOUSLY PUBLISHED IN THIS SERIES

**Law and the Political Economy of Hunger**
Anna Chadwick

**Nineteenth-Century Perspectives on Private International Law**
Roxana Banu

Hermann Heller (1891–1933), c.1920

Reproduced with the kind permission of the Archiv der sozialen Demokratie der Friedrich-Ebert-Stiftung, Bonn (6/FOTA023312)

# Sovereignty

*A Contribution to the Theory of Public and International Law*

HERMANN HELLER

*Edited and Introduced by*

DAVID DYZENHAUS

*Translated by*

BELINDA COOPER

The translation of this work was supported by a grant from the Goethe-Institut which is funded by the German Ministry of Foreign Affairs

GOETHE INSTITUT

OXFORD
UNIVERSITY PRESS

**OXFORD**
UNIVERSITY PRESS

Great Clarendon Street, Oxford, OX2 6DP,
United Kingdom

Oxford University Press is a department of the University of Oxford.
It furthers the University's objective of excellence in research, scholarship,
and education by publishing worldwide. Oxford is a registered trade mark of
Oxford University Press in the UK and in certain other countries



First Edition published in 2019



Published in the United States of America by Oxford University Press
198 Madison Avenue, New York, NY 10016, United States of America

British Library Cataloguing in Publication Data
Data available

Library of Congress Control Number: 2018961578

ISBN 978–0–19–881054–4

I dedicate this book to VICTOR BRUNS, the founder of the Institute for Comparative Public Law and International Law

# *Series Editor's Preface*

Hermann Heller (1891–1933) has a fair claim to being the most interesting political, constitutional and international legal thinker of the Weimar era, but his work has remained largely obscure, especially in English-language scholarship and as compared to his contemporaries and antagonists Hans Kelsen and Carl Schmitt. A Google Ngram Viewer search confirms this intuition and reveals that mentions of Heller, both in German and in English books, have remained negligible compared to Kelsen and in particular to Schmitt—a case where unfortunately intellectual weight seems inversely proportional to impact. David Dyzenhaus's present edition of Heller's *Sovereignty* (1927), in a lucid translation by Belinda Cooper, seeks to change this.

Heller anticipates current debates about the nature of public reason and its presuppositions, and he shows that Jean Bodin had already anticipated them in the late sixteenth century. Heller points out that Bodin had justified his conception of sovereignty by showing the necessity of giving a binding interpretation of what natural reason demands—the necessity of a referee. For Bodin, the "reason which we call natural is not always so clear and manifest, but that it finds impugners." Hobbes certainly agreed: "no one man's reason, nor the reason of any one number of men, makes the certainty." The necessity of a referee itself, however, is revealed by reason in a sufficiently clear and manifest way, for Bodin and Hobbes no less than for Heller; this makes their theories expressible, transparent—enlightened—and prevents them from being self-defeating. Private reason is prone not only to being wrong, but also to disagreement, which may lead to dangerous conflict. The sovereign referee provides public reason and thus allows for common, binding interpretations of natural reason. This solves practical coordination problems and prevents civil strife. However, and here Heller is again in broad agreement with Bodin and Hobbes, public reason does not just provide an arbitrary solution to coordination problems, but can be right or wrong. It seeks to be correct—it is reason after all. This makes Heller a normative constitutional thinker about sovereignty: sovereignty serves the practical goal to coordinate the behavior of many people through law, but does this by fleshing out an underlying conception of higher-order legal principles.

Heller's sovereign referee produces legislation (statutes or *leges*) but, as Heller reminds us, such legislation is to be sharply distinguished, with Bodin, from higher-order legal principles (*ius*, i.e. Heller's *Rechtsgrundsätze*). These fundamental legal principles provide a normative yardstick for the sovereign's legislation, and can in extreme cases be appealed to by subjects. Partly they are principles of legality, inherent in what legal form requires; partly they are substantive moral principles. Fundamental legal principles cannot, however, replace positive statutes. Rather, they stand in need of concretization and have to be positivized. This is what sovereignty is for. But sovereign legislation also requires a normative ideal to aim at, an ideal that represents the normative purposes of the state, is reasonable and binding on all subject to it. It is because Heller's overall view of sovereignty seeks to capture both the normative ideal and the positive legislation, not denying the tension, that his theory of sovereignty is neither utopian nor simply tied to the factual contingencies that happen to obtain.

For Heller, Kelsen's positivism is the necessary result of Kelsen's moral relativism and provides a congenial stepping stone for a fascist writer like Schmitt to celebrate an irrational decisionism. Heller himself acknowledges what he calls the individuality of states and the contingency within which politics inevitably play out, but this contingency in Heller's thought is accounted for in terms of a body of "highest legal principles," principles which are presupposed by the sovereign's positive legislation. Legislation is adapted to contingencies, but the underlying, more fundamental legal principles are not. They encompass, interestingly, the rules of contract law, as they did for Bodin, which results in a view of the sovereign being bound, not by his own legislation, but by the norms of contract law. This has the important consequence that the state's constitutional architecture, held together by contractual relationships between sovereign and magistrates, is not at the sovereign's disposition. It also entails that the sovereign's dealings with other sovereigns, which is contractual in nature too, has more solidity than legislation does. The sovereign is bound by contracts with its own subjects, because having been established as interpreter- and enforcer-in-chief, it would be self-undermining and irrational for the sovereign not to acknowledge its own contractual duties.

There are several ramifications of Heller's thought that are as interesting as they are topical. Heller was prescient in pointing out the difficulties of a political and legal theory which aims at a conceptualization of European federation without sovereignty and argued for the necessity of mitigating the dangers of the "political individualism" of European nation-states by way of a European federation—but such a federation, Heller believed, would itself need to have *all* the attributes of sovereignty at its disposal. Furthermore, on the domestic plane, Heller diagnosed a displacement of legitimacy "by the surrogate of formalist legality," and he localized this displacement in the denial, by the nineteenth-century bourgeoisie, of the *substantive* ideas of liberty and equality which had been formulated by early modern natural law. Heller's historical diagnosis provided the foundation of his anti-Marxist, Hobbesian, social-democratic take on what substantive legitimacy required in the circumstances of industrialized Europe. Heller thought that there was a dangerous possibility that the corrosion of sovereignty could entail the prospect of a world which "will in future replace state sovereignty with feudal capitalism, for example, which would once again dissolve political rule into a bundle of private-law use rights."

Heller agreed with Hobbes about the causal power of ideas and knew that in the last resort, as Hobbes had put it, sovereignty "hath no foundation but in the opinion and beleefe of the people." This requires a certain optimism about the convergence of private reason on a however limited set of beliefs as well as an optimism about the possibility of justifying these beliefs, given that "they cannot be maintained by any Civill Law, or terrour of legal punishment." With *Sovereignty*, Heller sought to justify certain fundamental normative claims and thereby to provide a foundation "in the opinion and beleefe" of his readers. In his substantial Introduction, David

Dyzenhaus argues that we, as individual legal subjects, cannot avoid taking a stance vis-à-vis those normative claims: Heller's sovereign *Rechtsstaat* requires the subjects of the law not only to authorize the law, but also to check public reason when it diverges from its promise to express fundamental ethical principles of law. Professor Dyzenhaus thus shows why we should return to Heller's arguments about the legal idea of sovereignty, and why this idea deserves to be preserved.

Benjamin Straumann
New York City
November 2018

# *Preface and Acknowledgments*

A sense of political urgency motivated the interwar debate in Europe about sovereignty, as legal scholars and political theorists sought to understand the new legal order that the League of Nations had attempted to create, whether out of a determination to make the international rule of law succeed or to undermine it. As we know, the attempt failed and in our own era we are also faced with an urgent question: whether the renewed attempt after the Second World War to create an international order that had learned from the mistakes of the earlier experiment is also on the brink of failure. It is hardly surprising, then, that there is a renewed interest in the work of these interwar scholars, in particular in those who worked in Weimar Germany where the sense of political urgency was most palpable.

The Oxford University Press publication of a translation of Hermann Heller's *Sovereignty: A Contribution to the Theory of Public and International Law* (1927) makes available in English the work of one of the major players in that interwar debate who is hardly known in English. It is distinctive in that, like the approach set out by his rightwing rival Carl Schmitt, Heller wished to emphasize the political nature of all conceptions of sovereignty. But, like his main foil the great legal positivist philosopher Hans Kelsen, Heller wished to defend a legal idea of sovereignty, one that would explain why sovereignty and the rule of law or *Rechtsstaat* are part of one juridical package. The introductory chapter, "The Politics of Sovereignty," tries both to provide a context for the work and to help the reader navigate Heller's complex argument. I also try to provide some detail about a number of the figures with whom Heller engages in the book and about several of the examples he discusses without providing the reader with much or any context. (To provide detail on all the figures and examples would not only have been a mammoth undertaking, but also would, in my view, have overwhelmed the text.)

In the first two chapters, Heller relies heavily on the work of Jean Bodin and quotes extensively from him, nearly always using the Latin original. I have relied on the 1606 English translation by Richard Knolles, sometimes adapted a little, in rendering the Latin into English—Jean Bodin, *The Six Bookes of a Commonweale*, Kenneth Douglas McRea, ed. and intro. (Cambridge, Mass.: Harvard University Press, 1962). I indicate the pagination of the English translation in square brackets. I have done the same for the translation from the Latin text of Hobbes's *De Cive*, where I have relied on the edition of Richard Tuck and Michael Silverthorne: Thomas Hobbes, *On the Citizen* (Cambridge: Cambridge University Press, 1998).

When Heller uses Latin or French terms, I have supplied the English equivalent in quotation marks and, with the first-time use, put the original in square brackets. Thereafter the terms are marked by double quotation marks. I have erred on the side of caution and so have translated some terms that will seem obvious to most readers. If no square brackets are evident with the first-time use, it is because Heller used the term in English. Heller's use of "*Rechtsstaat*"—the term for a state committed to the rule of law—is retained but the adjective "*rechtstaatlich*" has been translated as "rule of law." (There is a considerable literature on whether there is a distinction between the meaning of *Rechtsstaat* and the rule of law, but this debate does not directly affect either Heller's text or my Introduction.) Translations from the French are my own. The text preserves Heller's original footnotes and no attempt has been made (with one exception) to check them. Heller uses double quotation marks for direct quotations from cited texts and single quotation marks for a variety of purposes: to denote terms of art in a body of work but not as a direct quotation, for emphasis, and to indicate a tone of sarcasm or irony. I have corrected some of these in places where he seems to have slipped. The notes to Heller's text run from 1 to 530 as in the edition of *Sovereignty* in Heller's collected works.

Heller is not the easiest person to read. His ideas are presented in great torrents of often highly polemical argument. With *Sovereignty*, one has the impression even more than usual of a man in a hurry to make his mark in a debate that had already been shaped by interventions in the 1920s by Kelsen, Schmitt, and many others. The translation tries to remain faithful to Heller's mode of argument at the same time as being as clear as possible. For this, I have to thank Belinda Cooper who undertook that very difficult task. I also thank her for her patience as we worked closely together in trying to tease out meaning without departing from Heller's intentions.

The Goethe Institute generously funded part of the cost of the translation and the University of Toronto the remainder. The German publisher of Heller's collected works, Mohr Siebeck, not only agreed to have the book translated, but also warmly encouraged the project and in particular I thank the very helpful Foreign Rights Manager, Elisabeth Wener. Heller's family kindly gave Oxford University Press their permission to publish.

I have been working on Heller for many years, but the suggestion that I should preside over a translation of the book and provide an introduction to it came from Benjamin Straumann, one of the editors of the series in which it appears. I am grateful to Benjamin for setting me off on this path and for much encouragement and help along the way.

The initial work on the translation and a lot of the research for the introductory chapter were done while I was a Fellow at the Wissenschaftskolleg zu Berlin in 2017/18. In my end of year report to the Kolleg, I highlighted that it had provided an ideal environment for this work. First, there was the serendipity that Heller wrote the book in Schlachtensee, just a few kilometers from Grunewald where the Kolleg is located. Second, the incomparable librarians were able to supply me with the often very hard to find material I from time to time needed. Third, Heller assumed that his many quotations—Latin, Greek, French, and Italian—needed no translation, and I could call on my fellow fellows and their partners (Barbara Kowalzig, Giacomo Todeschini, and Jim Zetzel) for help with translation, and on a theologian (Michael Moxter) and an historian of the church (Hubert Wolf) for help with some of his allusions.

That leave would not have been possible without the encouragement of my two homes at the University of Toronto, the Law Faculty and the Philosophy

Department. My thanks go to them as well, including the Law librarians who do in fact compare to the otherwise incomparable librarians of the Wissenschaftskolleg.

For providing comments on the Introduction at short notice, I am very grateful to my friends and colleagues Jutta Brunnée and Karen Knop. I am equally grateful to Daniel Lee for his comments on Heller's reliance on Bodin, some of which pointed out several problems with Heller's own interpretation of Bodin. But as these problems do not affect the main theme that Heller takes from Bodin—that the sovereign's freedom from law is from positive or enacted law not freedom from higher legal principles—I do not address these problems in the Introduction.

Finally, I would like to dedicate the work as a whole to Christoph Müller. Without Professor Müller's commitment to preserving the thought of the liberal-left (often Jewish) public lawyers of Weimar, we would not have Heller's collected works, which he edited in the 1970s, nor more recently the collected works of Hugo Preuss, the "father" of the Weimar Constitution. In a time when the fascistic thought of Carl Schmitt seems all the rage, we will find, I hope, that our debt to Professor Müller is considerable.

# *Contents*

# Introduction

## The Politics of Sovereignty

*David Dyzenhaus*

Hermann Heller published *Sovereignty: A Contribution to the Theory of Public and International Law* [*Sovereignty*][1] in 1927 as an intervention in the interwar debate about the nature of sovereignty. In large part it is a response to the most important legal philosopher of the last century, Hans Kelsen, and in particular to his work of 1920, *The Problem of Sovereignty and the Theory of International Law: A Contribution to a Pure Theory of Law.*[2] It is also in small part a response to one of the most controversial figures in the political and legal thought of the last century, Carl Schmitt and his 1922 book *Political Theology: Four Chapters on the Concept of Sovereignty.*[3] Of the three, Heller's book is the least known, in fact virtually unknown.

This debate remains pertinent today, as Martti Koskenniemi observes in saying that if the "terms of the interwar debate are applied" to contemporary challenges to the jurisdiction of international courts such as the European Court of Justice and the European Court of Human Rights, it is "possible to see that behind the apparently conceptual problem of the limits of the 'political' vis-à-vis the 'legal' there is a more pragmatic concern about who should have the final say about foreign policy—and thus occupy the place political theory has been accustomed to calling 'sovereignty'."[4] This claim is made in Koskenniemi's "Introduction" to another work of the interwar period, by the foremost international lawyer of the last century, Hersch Lauterpacht's *The Function of Law in the International Community* (1933). Koskenniemi continues: "Kelsen, Schmitt, and Lauterpacht all had much to say

[1] Hermann Heller, *Die Souveränität: Ein Beitrag zur Theorie des Staats- und Völkkerrechts* in Heller, *Gesammelte Schriften* (Tübingen: J.C.B. Mohr, Christoph Müller ed.), Volume 2, 31.

[2] Hans Kelsen, *Das Problem der Souveränität und die Theorie des Völkerrechts: Beitrag zu Einer Reinen Rechtslehre* (Aalen: Scientia Verlag, 1981, reprint of the second edition of 1928). See Hans Kelsen, *The Problem of Sovereignty and the Theory of International Law*, (Oxford: Oxford University Press, forthcoming, Paul Silverman, trans.).

[3] Carl Schmitt, *Political Theology: Four Chapters on the Concept of Sovereignty*, (Chicago: University of Chicago Press, 2005, George Schwab, trans.).

[4] Martti Koskenniemi, "Introduction" to Hersch Lauterpacht, *The Function of Law in the International Community* [1933] (Oxford: Oxford University Press, 2011), xxviii, at xlvi

about this, and very little that would have been both new and intelligent has been added to the topic thereafter."[5]

But what Koskenniemi gives with one hand, he takes away with the other. He immediately suggests that in today's "pluralist" world, there is simply no such "ultimate place from which authoritative direction could be received for any and all disputes."[6] He concludes that we should turn away from abstract theory to questions about the politics of international law and institutions, in which the legalist vision of those like Lauterpacht, who believed that "international lawyers, in particular international judges, should rule the world," should be understood as a "political project" in competition with others, each imposing its own set of advantages and disadvantages on participants.[7] More recently, in a collection on sovereignty, Koskenniemi has said that "sovereignty" is "just a word" and that if there is "historical sense to a notion such as 'sovereignty of the law'" it is perhaps "shorthand for the power of the juristic class."[8]

Heller does not figure on Koskenniemi's list though he does get a mention in his magisterial book *The Gentle Civilizer of Nations: The Rise and Fall of International Law, 1870–1960*. There he is described as the "socialist constitutional lawyer" who pointed out that "many of the numerous critiques of sovereignty after the First World War engaged a straw man—no political theorist had ever espoused the absolute conception they attacked. Without a concept of sovereignty in a concretely existing community . . ., they continued to move in an abstract conceptual heaven."[9] "Yet," Koskenniemi continues, "there was force to the argument that the attempt to square the circle of statehood and international law was doomed to fail on logical grounds. Either the State was sovereign—and there was no really binding international order. Or there was a binding international order—in which case no state could truly be sovereign."[10]

Koskenniemi's attribution of a conception of sovereignty to Heller as that which exists in a concrete community seems to put Heller on the sovereignty side of the tension between sovereignty and international law he just sketched. He is not alone in this judgment. In *The Function of Law in the International Community*, Lauterpacht grouped Heller's *Sovereignty* among those works of the time that argued that the relation of the state to international law is "based on the voluntary acceptance of legal obligations" and said that, "in fact," Heller's "able monograph is a somewhat intolerant denial of international law as a system of law, and an affirmation of the absolute sovereignty of the state."[11] But if that judgment is right, it would have been odd for Heller to have argued that "no political theorist had ever espoused the absolute conception."

[5] Ibid. [6] Ibid. [7] Ibid., xlvii.

[8] Martti Koskenniemi, "Conclusion: Vocabularies of Sovereignty – Powers of a Paradox" in Hent Kalmo and Quentin Skinner, eds, *Sovereignty in Fragments: The Past, Present and Future of a Contested Concept* (Cambridge: Cambridge University Press, 2010) 222, at 229 and 241.

[9] Marrti Koskenniemi, *The Gentle Civilizer of Nations: The Rise and Fall of International Law, 1870-1960* (Cambridge: Cambridge University Press, 2001), 239–40.

[10] Ibid., 240.

[11] Lauterpacht, *The Function of Law in the International Community*, note 2 at 416–17.

Heller's book does defend an absolutist conception of sovereignty. But it does so by articulating the complexity of such a conception in a way that explains why so many critics do in fact attack a straw man. Heller sees that conception as both legal and part of a political project, as Koskenniemi claims one should understand Lauterpacht's own legalist vision. But in exposing the politics of a legal or juridical idea of sovereignty, Heller hoped to address sovereignty so as to clarify the space in which pragmatic decisions had to be made. That clarification would preserve the spirit of legalism in a way denied to Kelsen's legal positivist approach and against Schmitt's attempt to show that the rule of law is a liberal sham.

In doing so, Heller approached the understanding of international law that Lauterpacht set out six years later in *The Function of Law in the International Community* because, despite Lauterpacht's own view of Heller, they shared the goal of injecting substance into Kelsen's Pure Theory of Law precisely to square the circle of sovereignty and international law. The major difference between the two is, as I just suggested, that Heller conceived this project as political as well as legal. But he did so in a way that would have led him to resist Koskenniemi's invitation to turn away from abstract theory to an account immersed in the concrete politics of the moment.

Writing in 1968, the distinguished social theorist Wolfgang Schluchter concluded a book on Heller by saying that contemporary political and social theory should not "decline Heller's legacy." Heller's account of progress from a skeptical, pragmatic perspective meant, Schluchter said, that hardly any other theorist had set out as clearly as Heller did the predicament that results from the necessity to make political decisions from a stance of internal uncertainty, while barring any retreat to a past world or to a future salvation, and without engaging in crude simplifications or one-sided treatments of important problems.[12] In this Introduction, I will explain not only why the interwar debate remains relevant today on its own terms, but also why we should pay special attention to Heller's contribution within it, precisely because his argument about the place of sovereignty in the international legal order has the characteristics that Schluchter so nicely describes.[13]

## Paradigms of Sovereignty

Heller died in 1933 aged forty-two and to this day remains at best an obscure figure in the English-speaking world.[14] Kelsen's status in that same world is assured. But he

[12] Wolfgang Schluchter, *Entscheidung für den Sozialen Rechtsstaat: Hermann Heller und die Staatstheoretische Diskussion in der Weimarer Republik* (Baden-Baden, Nomos, 1983), 290. The most comprehensive work on Heller's thought is Michael Henkel, *Hermann Hellers Theorie der Politik und der Staates* (Tübingen: Mohr Siebeck, 2011).

[13] Parts of the following two sections are adapted from my "Kelsen, Heller and Schmitt: Paradigms of Sovereignty Thought" (2015) 16 *Theoretical Inquiries in Law* 337 and I am grateful to the journal for permission to repurpose these parts.

[14] *Sovereignty* was, however, reviewed quite favorably in (1928) 22 *American Journal of International Law* 706 by Francis Deák. For some signs of a revival of interest in Heller, see (2015) 21 *European Law Journal*, issue 3, a collection devoted to the theme of "authoritarian liberalism," a term coined by Heller

is little read even by specialists in legal philosophy and his Weimar-era work, most of which remains untranslated, is almost as unknown as Heller's entire corpus.

Kelsen and Heller were both Jews who had grown up in the Austro-Hungarian empire. Both were committed to democracy, parliamentary government, and were on the social democratic left. Kelsen and Heller were forced out of their positions in Germany in 1933 after the Nazi seizure of power and the enactment of the law that required the elimination of Jews from public positions—The Law for the Restoration of the Professional Civil Service. Heller was at that time a professor in the Frankfurt Law Faculty, where the dismissal of Jewish professors opened the way for the appointment of Ernst Forsthoff, a committed Nazi and a disciple of Schmitt, who as one of Germany's leading public lawyers after the war was instrumental in ensuring Schmitt's lasting influence. Heller's last significant public intervention was his appearance against Schmitt in the *Preussenschlag*. In this case, the Prussian government—the major bastion of social democracy in Germany—contested the seizure of the Prussian state machinery by Schmitt's political masters in the federal government under the pretext that the political situation in Prussia represented an emergency in terms of Article 48 of the Weimar Constitution.

Kelsen was at that time at the Cologne Law Faculty, where as acting dean he had recruited Schmitt to the Law Faculty the year before. Schmitt alone among Kelsen's colleagues refused to sign the Faculty's letter of protest. Heller died in exile in Madrid that year of a heart condition, a relic of his war time service, while Kelsen made his way via Geneva and Prague to the USA. In 1942, he took a visiting position in Political Science at Berkeley, which became a full position in 1945. He remained there for the rest of his long career in relative obscurity.

Carl Schmitt, in contrast, has become in our century one of the central figures in political and legal theory despite the fact, or perhaps because of the fact, that his work is a sustained polemic against liberal democracy and the liberal commitment to the rule of law, an intellectual commitment that had significant practical implications. In the early 1930s, he was in the inner circle of the conservative politicians who were determined to turn the clock back on Germany's first experiment with democracy at the same time as they attempted to contain Hitler. He jumped onto the Nazi bandwagon as soon as Hitler had not only bested these politicians, but also ordered the murder of General Schleicher, the politician to whom Schmitt was closest, along with the murder of Hitler's rivals within his own ranks. Schmitt's public reaction to these murders on the "Night of the Long Knives," and to the enactment of the legislation that retroactively legalized the murders, was an article celebrating this event entitled "The Führer as the Guardian of our Law"[15]—his first major step in

in the last paper he published before leaving Germany. (The collection begins with his essay of 1933, "Authoritarian Liberalism?," translated at 295 by Bonnie Litchewski Paulson, Stanley L. Paulson, and Alexander Somek.) See also Anthoula Malkopoulou and Ludvig Norman, "Three Models of Democratic Self-Defence: Militant Democracy and its Alternatives" (2018) 66 *Political Studies* 442, which revives against Schmittean decisionist and Kelsenian formalist accounts of democracy in contemporary debates Heller's idea of "social homogeneity" as the basis of democracy.

[15] Carl Schmitt, "Der Führer schützt das Recht" in Schmitt, *Positionen und Begriffe in Kampf mit Weimar-Genf-Versailles 1923–1939* (Berlin: Duncker & Humblot, 1988) 199.

ingratiating himself with the Nazis. His involvement with them was sufficient for him to be interned after the war while the Allies considered putting him on trial at Nuremberg. He was not in the event tried, but was prohibited from having an academic position, which did not prevent him from exerting a baleful influence on postwar German public law.[16]

Oxford University Press's publication of Heller's *Sovereignty* as well as Kelsen's work on the same topic in the same year is important at a time when Schmitt has become central to Anglo-American political and legal thought to the extent that essays in the mainstream press will occasionally refer to him as providing insight into our current situation.[17] At the same time, there is an explosion of books about sovereignty, many of which strike a pessimistic note[18] and in which often Schmitt figures prominently and always more prominently than Kelsen, while references to Heller are extremely rare.[19]

The reason for the explosion is that our situation is an eerie echo of the tensions and concerns that came to the fore in Weimar. Sovereignty, in the sense of national sovereignty, is often perceived in liberal democracies today as being under threat, or at least "in transition," as power devolves from nation states to international bodies. Some scholars conclude that we are living in a "post-sovereign order," though perhaps "disorder" would be more accurate, as the loss of control by individual states to bodies which do not have the characteristics of states—for example, a defined territory over which they wield a monopoly of effective lawmaking power—leads to the fragmentation of political power. This threat to national sovereignty is at the same time considered a threat to a rather different idea of sovereignty, popular sovereignty—the sovereignty of "the people"—as, increasingly, important decisions appear to be made by institutions outside of a country's political system or by elite-dominated institutions within.

16 See Reinhard Mehring, *Carl Schmitt: A Biography* (Cambridge: Polity, 2014, Daniel Steur, trans.) and Jan-Werner Müller, *A Dangerous Mind: Carl Schmitt in Post-War European Thought* (New Haven: Yale University Press, 2003).

17 As a search of, for example, *The New York Times*, *The Guardian*, and *The Washington Post* will show.

18 Perhaps the most dramatic title in recent years is George Edmonson and Klaus Mladek, eds, *Sovereignty in Ruins: A Politics of Crisis* (Durham: Duke University Press, 2017) in which the extent of the ruin is confirmed by the fact that sovereignty is hardly discussed by any of the contributors to the book.

19 Compare, for example, the index citations in Richard Bourke and Quentin Skinner, eds, *Popular Sovereignty in Historical Perspective* (Cambridge: Cambridge University Press, 2016); Richard Rawlings, Peter Leyland, and Alyson L. Young, eds, *Sovereignty and the Law: Domestic, European, and International Experiences* (Oxford: Oxford University Press, 2013); Kalmo and Skinner, eds, *Sovereignty in Fragments*, and Neil Walker, ed., *Sovereignty in Transition* (Oxford: Hart Publishing, 2003). The last contains one of the rare discussions of Heller—see Miriam Aziz, "Sovereignty Über Alles: (Re)Configuring the German Legal Order," 279, especially 295–6, as well as a reference in Bardo Fassbender, "Sovereignty and Constitutionalism in International Law," 115, at 124–5. For a more balanced approach to Schmitt and Kelsen, see Jean L. Cohen, *Globalization and Sovereignty: Rethinking Legality, Legitimacy and Constitutionalism* (Cambridge: Cambridge University Press, 2012) and Andrew Arato, *Post Sovereign Constitution Making: Learning and Legitimacy* (Oxford: Oxford University Press, 2016). It is significant that in a recent book on the history and theory of sovereignty, as eminent a scholar as Dieter Grimm refers to Heller only once in a footnote, and refers more often to Schmitt than to Kelsen: see Grimm, *Sovereignty: The Origin and Future of a Political and Legal Concept* (New York: Columbia University Press, 2009, Belinda Cooper, trans.).

Indeed, "sovereignty" has become a kind of catchword in politics for a stance that may include hostility to some or all of the following: the role of international organizations and supra- national organizations in making decisions that have a domestic impact, international law itself, immigrants and refugees, a judicial role in upholding constitutionally entrenched rights and elite expertise, most notably in the scientific fields that concern themselves with the environment and climate change. Those who hold this kind of stance seem intent on eradicating these elements in a bid to restore their countries to a perceived lost "greatness," predicated on an idea of a political community in which the condition of entry is satisfaction of vague criteria of substantive homogeneity.[20]

In the 1920s, a similar sense of loss of control was pervasive. People wondered about their place in a world during a time when new countries and national identities were being formed on terms dictated by the victorious nations at the Paris Peace Conference that ended the First World War. At the same time, these nations attempted to forge a new international order by entering into the Covenant that led in 1920 to the creation of the League of Nations, an association confined to the victors at its inception,[21] and of the Permanent Court of International Justice that was attached to the League and which began operation in 1922.

These tensions and concerns were not unique to Weimar Germany; but they had an existential quality there. Germany was a signatory to the Treaty of Versailles, which ended the war between herself and the Allied Powers in 1919. However, as the principal vanquished country, she had no choice but to sign an agreement that imposed an economic stranglehold on her as well as foreign control over important aspects of international and domestic policy, and which required her explicitly to accept a humiliating statement of responsibility for the aggression that led to the war.

This national humiliation coincided with the birth of the Weimar Republic, which replaced the pre-war political system of a monarch in whom power was concentrated with a democratic system in which the Constitution assigned power principally to an elected parliament. But commitment to the Constitution did not prevail among either the elites or the masses and that made its political and legal institutions most fragile. Indeed, until 1923 there were several violent attempts by the extreme right and left to overthrow the Republic.

In this context, legal scholars on the right regarded the Weimar Constitution as itself a threat to sovereignty, given that it diluted the power of the pre-war sovereign—the Kaiser—by introducing the checks and balances of democratic, parliamentary government. Their concern about sovereignty was, however, much more radical than that of contemporary figures in the Anglo-American tradition of opposition to judicial review who claim that such review undermines parliamentary supremacy and so the authority of the representatives of the people. For these rightwing Weimar

[20] Although in groups that remain for the moment on the political margins, the criteria are often frighteningly precise; and these groups have become less marginal with the election of Donald Trump, the move toward illiberal democracy in Central and Eastern Europe, and so on.

[21] Except for the USA, which decided not to join despite the fact that President Wilson had been its main proponent.

scholars opposed root and branch what they regarded as the too pluralistic party political system of parliamentary democracy; because they thought that, like the judicial system, it was prone to capture by special interest groups and thus contributed to the problem of fragmentation. On their view, popular sovereignty is national sovereignty, with national sovereignty understood as the sovereignty of a substantively homogeneous people. This is a quintessentially political power located outside of legal order. As such, it cannot be constrained by the legal limits that liberals and democrats desire to impose on an authentic sovereign, one who is capable of making the kinds of decisions necessary to solve the fundamental conflicts of a society.

Their position gave rise to one of the three leading paradigms of sovereignty in Weimar. Schmitt, its leading exponent, set out his conception of sovereignty in 1922 in the opening sentence of one of his two most influential works, *Political Theology*: "Sovereign is he who decides on the exception."[22] Schmitt's customarily succinct and enigmatic formulation becomes clearer when paired with his claim in an essay of 1927 "The Concept of the Political,"[23] which he elaborated in his other most influential work as a book in 1932, that the primary distinction of "the political" is the distinction between friend and enemy.[24] It follows, he supposed, that the political sovereign is the person who is able to make that distinction, is indeed revealed in the making of that distinction, and that he decides both that there is an exception and how best to respond to it.

Schmitt argued that liberal democratic institutions with their commitment to the legal regulation of political power, that is, to the rule of law or the *Rechtsstaat*, are incapable of making the distinction, hence, incapable of being sovereign, hence, cannot be the guardian of the Constitution. He took this flaw to be manifested in Article 48 of the Weimar Constitution—the emergency powers provision—since that article recognized the need for the presidential exercise of sovereign authority on existential questions, though it also sought in a liberal-legalist fashion to set limits to an exercise of executive discretion that cannot, in his view, be legally circumscribed.

Kelsen provided the second, legal positivist paradigm, one which opposed the classical idea that each state is sovereign in that it is subject to no legal limits, either internal or external. Indeed, it might be more accurate to say that Kelsen accepted the claim that sovereignty is best understood as the absence of legal limits on ultimate political power, but as a result argued that one has reason to eradicate the idea from theory and practice. Thus, he concluded his 1920 work on sovereignty by advocating the radical suppression of the concept of sovereignty in legal thought if, as he thought desirable, states were to conceive of each other as equal actors within an international legal system.[25]

[22] Schmitt, *Political Theology*, 5.

[23] Carl Schmitt, "Der Begriff des Politischen" (1927) 58 *Archiv für Sozialwissenschaft und Sozialpolitik* 1. This article was not available to Heller at the time he was finishing *Sovereignty*. For his 1928 response to it, see Hermann Heller, "Political Democracy and Social Homogeneity," David Dyzenhaus trans., in Arthur J. Jacobson and Bernard Schlink, eds, *Weimar: A Jurisprudence of Crisis* (Berkeley: University of California Press, 2000) 256.

[24] Carl Schmitt, *The Concept of the Political*, (Chicago: University of Chicago Press, 1996, George Schwab trans.).

[25] Kelsen, *Das Problem der Souveränität*, 320.

In work after publication of his book on sovereignty, Kelsen elaborated his "Pure Theory" of law, according to which a legal system is a hierarchy of norms, where the validity of each norm is traceable to a higher-order norm, until one reaches the *Grundnorm* or basic norm of the system.[26] Such an order is free of contradictions since any apparent contradiction between two norms will be resolved by a higher order norm, which gives an official the power to make a binding decision. The validity of the basic or constitutional norm cannot, however, be traced to any other norm and, Kelsen asserts, its validity has therefore to be assumed. Sovereignty is not a kind of freedom from law, as in the classical conception, since it is a legally constituted property, pertaining to the identity of a particular legal system. Kelsen does not, then, provide a paradigm for understanding sovereignty so much as a paradigm for understanding legal order in a way that does not regard sovereignty as an organizing concept for legal theory.

Kelsen is Schmitt's main foil in *Political Theology* because he understood the Pure Theory of law as the culmination of the attempt by liberalism to impose a legal rationality on political order that would rid it of the personal exercise of sovereign power, which introduces arbitrariness into political life. As he put it, in Kelsen's theory: "Now the machine runs itself." But in Schmitt's view, sovereignty will always assert itself in moments when the public law of a legal order cannot provide an answer to a political question, or where the answer provided is considered by those who wield sovereign power to be inadequate to preserving the substantive basis of the political order in which the legal order is nested. At any moment, the sovereign can break free of the torpor of legal life and assert his pre-legal authority, an assertion whose success depends not on its compliance with legality or the rule of law, but on whether it works.[27]

Heller provides the third paradigm in *Sovereignty*, a book remarkable for its range. He starts by locating his argument in an account of the history of ideas with the founders of the modern conception of sovereignty, in which the principal figure is Bodin (1530–96), the French jurist and philosopher who crafted the first modern "absolutist" conception of sovereignty, which has been both highly influential and, according to Heller, badly misinterpreted. Heller proceeds to discuss contemporary theories in light of his account of Bodin, and then seeks to demonstrate the resources that his account provides for an analysis of sovereignty in both nation states and in international law. Along the way, he illustrates his arguments by reference to examples drawn from domestic public law and public international law. He also engages deeply in the methodological disputes of his day, so that the text and especially the footnotes are populated by issues that are often abstruse and figures that are often either obscure or wholly unknown to readers today.[28]

[26] For a complete statement of his view, see his *Reine Rechtslehre* of 1934, translated as Kelsen, *Introduction to the Problems of Legal Theory*, (Oxford: Clarendon Press 1992, Bonnie Litchewski Paulson and Stanley L. Paulson trans.).

[27] Schmitt, *Political Theology*, 15, 48. Translation at 48 amended.

[28] In the late nineteenth century, philosophers and social theorists in Germany were deeply interested in the problem of the objectivity of the social sciences as well as the relationship between causal explanations of behavior and normative explanations that took seriously the participants' own understanding. Heller refers most often to Max Weber, one of the founders of modern social theory

The trajectory of Heller's argument requires that he vindicates the view that a retrieval of ideas from some of the classics of early modern thought, which are often referred to but hardly read, can throw much needed light on the debates of his time. That light makes worthwhile what he refers to as the end of chapter one as the "ponderous literature review" he undertakes there. It thus resonates with recent work on early modern classics, including Bodin, Hobbes (whom Heller esteemed along with Bodin), and Grotius.[29] In this Introduction, I hope to return the compliment by indicating how a retrieval of Heller's thought might help to respond to pressing problems that coalesce around the topic of sovereignty today.

In my view, the most striking feature of Heller's work is the promise of what we might think of as his *political*-legal theory. It is political in two respects. First, it is a theory of law that takes seriously the idea that the modern legal state enables a kind of political community, a jural community in which the relationships between ruler and ruled are mediated by law. It is this mediation that makes possible the transformation of might into legal right. Second, it is political in that it is explicit about its defense of this kind of community as politically valuable. In other words, there is no pretense of value neutrality, although Heller claimed that the theory is firmly grounded in the reality of the modern, legal state and that legal theory must account for the sociological conditions in which such a state could come to be considered legitimate by those subject to its power.

In putting forward a theory that seeks to show both the value and the actuality of the modern legal state—of the *Rechtsstaat* or rule of law state—Heller joined a group of public law theorists of Weimar who were quite optimistic about law's potential for conditioning the exercise of state power in ways that would serve the interests of those subject to that power. As I have indicated, such optimism is in short supply these days. However, pessimism does not reign everywhere.

"Fragmentation," a kind of Hobbesian worry about anarchy in international affairs in the eyes of one scholar, may amount to a "pluralism" to be celebrated in the eyes of another. And just as liberals argue that there is no loss to the sovereignty of the people when a country entrenches a bill of rights, thus subjecting the decisions of the legislature to constitutional review by judges, so they can argue that an international constitution is emerging and that the subjection of states to the norms of that constitution enhances democracy. One can even combine the pluralist position with the constitutionalist position by arguing that the era of Westphalian sovereignty of

(1864–1920) and sometimes to Heinrich Rickert (1863–1936), a neo-Kantian philosopher whose work influenced Weber. Heller does not state an allegiance to any particular school in this methodological debate but instead picks and chooses what he finds useful to his own position, which combines causal and normative explanation. For a most illuminating account of the methodological debate see Guy Oakes, *Weber and Rickert: Concept Formation in the Cultural Sciences* (Cambridge, Mass.: MIT Press, 1988) and for an equally illuminating account of that debate set in the context of the political and legal theory of the time, see Duncan Kelly, *The State of the Political: Conceptions of Politics and the State in the Thought of Max Weber, Carl Schmitt and Franz Neumann* (Oxford: The British Academy, 2008).

[29] For notable examples, see Daniel Lee, *Popular Sovereignty in Early Modern Thought* (Oxford: Oxford University Press, 2016) and Benjamin Straumann, *Roman Law in the State of Nature: The Classical Foundations of Hugo Grotius' Natural Law* (Cambridge: Cambridge University Press, 2015).

individual states has been replaced by a kind of constitutional pluralism in which all states are bound together in a quasi-federal structure in which there is no sovereign or overarching state.[30]

Heller would have regarded this combination as naïve, as he rejected a version of this view that he found in Kelsen in which the international legal order is conceived, much like a national legal order, a *civitas maxima* or "world state," and thus as a system of legal rules underpinned by a constitution. But he did not think that such rejection drove him into the arms of those who are profoundly pessimistic about law's potential, let alone those like Schmitt who celebrated the idea that a sovereign political decision would break through the facade of the liberal rule of law and permit the restoration of the substantively homogeneous basis of a successful nation state.

Heller was always clear about the dangers of Schmitt's position. However, as we shall see, he shared with Schmitt the idea that sovereignty had to have a central role in legal theory and that the role of sovereignty includes a place for a final legal decision. It might even be more accurate to say that Schmitt shares these ideas with Heller, as there is a plausible case to be made that Schmitt's legal theory was profoundly influenced by the argument of Heller's *Sovereignty*, perhaps the best evidence being that he never refers to Heller.[31] Indeed, while Schmitt liked to claim that he was a dispassionate, scientific diagnostician of politics and law, as I have indicated, Heller regarded all accounts of sovereignty as inherently political.

Given the centrality of Schmitt these days, readers may find it surprising that Heller spends so little time on Schmitt and so much attacking Kelsen. For in *Sovereignty* Schmitt makes only a kind of cameo appearance over the course of a few pages in

[30] See Cohen, *Globalization and Sovereignty*. For different optimistic takes, see, first, Evan J. Criddle and Evan Fox-Decent, *Fiduciaries of Humanity: How International Law Constitutes Authority* (Oxford: Oxford University Press, 2016), arguing that sovereignty should be reconceived along the lines of the private law fiduciary relationship, so that sovereigns are "an entrusted power" or "trustees for humanity" at large; and, second, Oona A. Hathaway and Scott J. Shapiro, *The Internationalists: How a Radical Plan to Outlaw War Remade the World* (New York: Simon and Schuster, 2017) arguing that the twentieth-century pacifist international lawyers such as Kelsen and Lauterpacht succeeded against Schmitt in bringing about the "outlawry" of war.

[31] Pasquale Paquino has given me permission to report the following anecdote, which I first heard him relate at a conference on the work of Ernst-Wolfgang Böckenförde, the public law scholar and Constitutional Court judge who, with Ernst Forsthoff, worked after the war to preserve and extend Schmitt's place in German public law thought. In the early 1980s, Pasquino, who was working on state theory in Weimar, had a conversation with Schmitt about his project. Schmitt said: "Do you want to write yet another stupid book about me? You should much rather work on Hermann Heller; he was the best mind in Germany." ("Wollen Sie noch ein dummes Buch über mich schreiben? Sie sollten eher über Hermann Heller arbeiten; er war der beste Kopf in Deutschland.")

Forsthoff had been a Nazi by conviction in the 1930s and was appointed to the Frankfurt Law Faculty in 1933 as a replacement for Heller and the other purged Jewish professors. After the war he became one of Germany's leading public lawyers and was firmly on the conservative right. See Peter C. Caldwell, in "Ernst Forsthoff in Frankfurt:Political Mobilization and the Abandonment of Scholarly Responsibility," in Moritz Epple, Johannes Fried, Raphael Gross, and Janus Gudian, eds, *"Politisierung der Wissenschaft". Jüdische Wissenschaftler und ihre Gegner an der Universität Frankfurt vor und nach 1933* (Göttingen: Wallstein Verlag, 2015) 249. Böckenförde is a social democrat who claimed that Heller was also one of his "intellectual roots"; see Dieter Gösewinkel, "Interview with Ernst-Wolfgang Böckenförde" in Ernst-Wolfgang Böckenförde, *Constitutional and Political Theory: Selected Writings* (Oxford: Oxford University Press, 2017; Mirjam Künkler and Tine Stein, eds) 369.

which Heller says that he should be given "great credit" for having shown that the dominant theory—the rationalist legalism that culminates in Kelsen—cannot get rid of the problem posed for the *Rechtsstaat* by sovereignty, namely, that legal theory cannot eliminate the moment of personal decision from the legal order.[32] But Heller is clear that Schmitt's attempt to bring the decision back into legal theory is part of a wider political agenda, inevitable in the circumstances of Weimar, to replace democracy and its separation of powers with a dictatorship of the Reich President.

Schmitt's argument is based on his understanding of the role of the President in the circumstances of emergency foreseen in Article 48 of the Weimar Constitution. As Heller points out, Schmitt is correct that the role sketched there is, as Schmitt terms it, "commissarial": The President is subject to constitutional limits and acts under supervision of the Reichstag. But Heller highlights something that remains strangely hard to this day for interpreters of Schmitt to grasp that Schmitt from the start wished to elevate the "commissarial dictatorship" of the President into a "sovereign dictatorship," one in which the President has the extra-legal right to remake the Constitution. [33] He concludes that Schmitt not only analogizes the place of the state of exception or emergency in legal order to the place of miracles in theology, but also wishes to replace legal theory with a "political theology" in which the President is endowed with magical powers. Schmitt wishes, that is, to substitute for the legal idea of sovereignty a relentlessly political idea, and in doing so distorts Bodin's conception of sovereignty in his bid to find historical support for his claims.[34]

In contrast to his quick disposal of Schmitt, Heller's critique of Kelsen is persistent, to the extent that he begins *Sovereignty* by stating in his brief Foreword that the Kelsenian method must "be destroyed at its roots"[35] so that the state can be restored to the center of political and legal theory and Kelsen together with others in the Vienna school of legal positivism—for example, Adolf Merkl and Alfred Verdross—are his constant foils. As Timothy Stanton explains in an astute discussion of the debate between Kelsen and Schmitt in the 1920s, Kelsen was "by far the better known and more eminent figure in jurisprudence. To take him as one's opponent, as Schmitt did, was by implication to place oneself on his level."[36]

This remark applies with equal force to Heller. Moreover, when Stanton lists the sins of which Schmitt accused Kelsen in the 1920s, these are hardly different from the list one could compile of Heller's accusations.[37] For example, in an article published the year before *Sovereignty*—"The Crisis of State Theory"[38]—Heller said that it was his view, "without any irony," that "Kelsen's greatest contribution was to have elaborated logical legal positivism without making any concessions and with

[32] See below 104.

[33] Heller anticipates Kelsen's devastating critique of Schmitt in the exchange between Schmitt and Kelsen in the 1930s about who was the "guardian" of the Constitution. See Lars Vinx, ed. and trans., *The Guardian of the Constitution: Hans Kelsen and Carl Schmitt on the Limits of Constitutional Law* (Cambridge: Cambridge University Press, 2015).

[34] See below 103-4. [35] See below 60.

[36] Stanton, "Popular Sovereignty in the Age of Mass Democracy" in Bourke and Skinner, eds, *Popular Sovereignty in Historical Perspective*, 320, 339, note 88.

[37] Ibid. [38] "Die Krisis der Staatslehre" in Heller, *Gesammelte Schriften*, volume 2, 5.

great vigour and excellent acuity; and so have driven it to its ultimate absurdity,"[39] which was to produce a "theory of state without a state" and a "positivism without positivity."[40]

What does not apply to Heller is Stanton's further observation, that "[d]ifferent purposes were served for Schmitt by the facts that Kelsen was, notwithstanding his eminence, an 'outsider', coming from Prague and owing his intellectual formation to the Austro-Hungarian Empire, and a converted Jew";[41] for Heller shared Kelsen's outsider status in each respect (though did not convert to Christianity). Significant in this regard is that in *Sovereignty* Heller twice refers to Bodin as "the Huguenot,"[42] which is inaccurate, as later scholarship agrees, but revealing about the stance from which Heller wrote.

In "Religion in the Life of Jean Bodin,"[43] Marion Kuntz explains that Bodin was during his life "accused of being a Jew, a Calvinist, a heretical Catholic, an atheist." But, she says, he was none of these. Rather, he was a profoundly religious Catholic who argued for religious tolerance (though not tolerance of atheism).[44] However, Heller's insistence that Bodin was a Huguenot, while mistaken, is not gratuitous in a work of political and legal theory. As a thoroughly assimilated Jew in an anti-Semitic milieu, his project was to make sense of the modern legal state and its institutions as providing the conditions for religious and other kinds of pluralism. He took inspiration from Bodin because of what he regarded as Bodin's fundamental insight that the absolutism of the modern legal state with its monopoly on legitimate violence—to use Weber's term—and its unity of effective decision-making in its legal institutions is a precondition of a pluralistic, tolerant polity.

The claim that absolutism is necessary for toleration will seem at best paradoxical, more likely utterly mistaken, in an era in which individuals are thought to have inalienable rights, including freedom of religion, expression, association, and conscience, that limit the authority of the state. Indeed, Rainer Forst has recently argued that Bodin's political writings on sovereignty give rise only to a "permission conception" of toleration, one in which an absolute sovereign who has an independence from the political and religious conflicts of the day has the ability to prescribe religious tolerance and should do so, but for purely prudential reasons—to avoid

[39] Ibid., 24.

[40] Ibid., 21. (For the same thought, see below 93-4.) In the only reference I have found to Heller's work in one of the major Anglophone figures in philosophy of law of the last century, Lon L. Fuller said of this observation in 1940 that "[i]n this article—which one cannot read today without some sense of the doom which then hung over the German social structure—Heller comments on the extent to which in Germany public law and political science had become passively positivistic. He remarks that the foreign writings most esteemed abroad were unacceptable in Germany because, being tainted by ethics and natural law, they were not deemed sufficiently 'scientific'." Fuller, *The Law in Quest of Itself* (Beacon Press: Boston, 1940) 72.

[41] Ibid. [42] See 62 and 103 below.

[43] This is her introduction to her translation of Bodin's *Heptaplomeres*—Marion Leathers Daniels Kuntz, *Colloquium of the Seven about Secrets of the Sublime.* (Princeton: Princeton University Press, 1975) xv.

[44] Ibid., xxxix.

conflict among his subjects. The sovereign's absolute nature, that is, permits him to withdraw permission at any time it seems to him expedient.[45]

In contrast, in Bodin's later work—the *Heptaplomeres*, which is "a dialogue between men of seven different religious faiths or philosophic persuasions"[46]—Forst says that Bodin sets out a "respect conception" of "mutual toleration" in which individuals respect each other as moral persons without endorsing their moral views.[47] But because Bodin never elevates the respect conception to the political level, he remains, Forst argues, "captive to the permission conception as what was politically possible and necessary at the time."[48]

On Heller's interpretation, the respect conception is already present in Bodin's political conception of the modern, legal state just because sovereignty is conceived legally. His view is that Bodin is the first modern thinker to conceive of sovereignty as what leading scholars in the English-speaking world writing at the same time as Heller described as "sovereignty in the legal sense."[49] As Heller interprets Bodin, sovereignty in this sense presupposes a relationship between state institutions and the legal subject such that the sovereign's positive or enacted law will have regard for the interests of those subject to the sovereign's power.

The difference, then, between Schmitt and Heller is as follows. Schmitt was determined to show that positivistic legal formalism would be ruptured by an extra-legal, political substance—the sovereign who made the distinction between friend and enemy and established the substantive homogeneity of the people. In contrast, Heller was determined to emphasize the juridical substance of legality and the legal nature of sovereignty that would permit a heterogeneous "people" to flourish on terms of freedom and social equality or "social homogeneity," a term he coined in a direct riposte to Schmitt's publication, just after *Sovereignty*, of his essay "The Concept of the Political."[50]

As Heller himself explains, Kelsen's theory of the modern, legal state was not only the leading theory of its time, but also was the logical and fully worked out culmination of the dominant strand in legal theory that wished to explain sovereignty as a matter of law. Further, despite the fact that he was writing *Sovereignty* at a time of relative stability in the Weimar Republic, so much so that the Social Democratic Party (SPD) in which he was an influential figure increased their share of the vote in the federal elections of 1928 at the expense of both the main nationalist party and the Nazis, he had a sense of impending doom, which he had conveyed already in

[45] Rainer Forst, *Toleration in Conflict: Past and Present* (Cambridge: Cambridge University Press, 2016), 143–52.

[46] Marion Leathers Kunz, "The Concept of Toleration in the *Colloquium Heptlamores* of Jean Bodin" in John Christian Laursen and Cary J. Nederman, eds, *Beyond the Persecuting Society: Religious Toleration Before Enlightenment* (Philadelphia: University of Pennsylvania Press, 1998) 125, 127.

[47] Forst, *Toleration in Conflict: Past and Present*, 151–2.

[48] Ibid.

[49] See C.H. McIlwain, "Sovereignty Again" (1926) 18 *Economica* 253; John Dickinson, "A Working Theory of Sovereignty I" (1927) 42 *Political Science Quarterly* 524 and "A Working Theory of Sovereignty II" (1928) 43 *Political Science Quarterly* 32.

[50] *Schmitt, "Der Begriff des Politischen"*.

1926 in "The Crisis of State Theory" and which informs both the Foreword and the last chapter of *Sovereignty*.

Heller took the crisis in state theory to reflect a wider social and political crisis, one to which the dominant Kelsenian strand had no helpful response. However, he was just as determined as Kelsen to explain the modern, legal state as a *Rechtsstaat*—to give an account of "sovereignty in the legal sense." That brought his theory so close at times to Kelsen's that Kelsen, in commenting on a public lecture Heller gave in 1927 before he had finished work on *Sovereignty*, expressed deep puzzlement at Heller's vehemence toward him. Indeed, he went further and suggested that Heller had silently appropriated most of the Pure Theory of law, a suggestion which Heller understood as a charge of plagiarism.[51] In return, Heller expressed equal astonishment and indignantly refused his "induction" into Kelsen's school.[52]

Put differently, in a manner closer to the spirit of Kelsen's enterprise than to Schmitt's, Heller wished to emphasize that the ultimate decider—the sovereign decision unit of the political order of liberal democracy—is entirely legally constituted. His intervention in the sovereignty debate can then be seen as seeking to rescue the importance of legality from Schmitt's critique of Kelsen, while retaining from Schmitt the thought that sovereignty cannot be understood except in terms of the actual exercises of power by some actual person or body of actual persons who have been authorized so to act. One might say that Heller seeks to elaborate a juridical conception of "the political," to use Schmitt's term, a conception that is peculiar to the modern, legal state but which does not seek to displace politics and which can respond appropriately to the paradox of sovereignty, which the next section sets out.

[51] Hermann Heller, "Der Begriff des Gesetzes in der Reichsverfassung" in *Veröffentlichungen der Vereinigung der Deutschen Staatsrechtslehrer*, volume 4 (Berlin: Walter de Gruyter & Co., 1928) 98, reproduced in Heller, *Gesammelte Schriften*, volume 2, 203. Kelsen's comments and Heller's response appear only in former at 168–80 and 210–4 respectively. The crucial paragraphs of Kelsen's comment are at 176:

> Heller's paper awakens two very ambivalent feelings in me. On the one hand, I am happy to be able to agree with him on all essential points. Had I myself given the paper, and I refer here only to its theoretical part, there would have been hardly any difference in the result. And so my astonishment is all the greater that Heller found it necessary to set up both me and my academic friends in general as opponents, as the representatives of a completely rotten "dominant theory", one which he openly has taken upon himself as a duty and service to eliminate.
>
> That Heller fails to acknowledge the theory of the [Kelsenian] School in the same degree as he actually utilizes it would not matter much to me. Any well-informed person can come to his own judgment on this matter. But I must energetically protest against Heller's attribution of opinions to me and my School when we hold the exact opposite.

[52] Heller's response is in *Veröffentlichungen der Vereinigung der Deutschen Staatsrechtslehrer*, volume 4 (Berlin: Walter de Gruyter & Co., 1928), at 202:

> The peculiarity of Kelsen's polemic requires a full answer. According to Kelsen, not only have I plagiarized him and his school and failed to recognize the sources of my thought, but I denied these sources and gave the appearance of attacking them. So the question remains open of whether I was so stupid as not to know better or so bad as not to want to know. I must utterly reject my induction into the Kelsenian School.

## The Paradox of Sovereignty

In engaging in this quest, Heller joins a long line of scholars who have tried to grapple with, even resolve, the paradox of sovereignty, which I presented earlier as one to do with the necessity of submission to an absolutist sovereign in order to have a tolerant civil society. But this is only one of the many ways in which this paradox manifests itself. In contemporary political philosophy, it is usually presented as a problem to do with individual freedom or "autonomy," following the influential argument by Robert Paul Wolff in *In Defence of Anarchism*.[53] Wolff asserted, following Kant, that the "autonomous man" is one who "gives laws to himself, or who is self-legislating." As such, "he is not subject to the will of another" and is "in the political sense of the word, *free*."[54] Since Wolff argued that submission to the authority of the state involves a forfeiture of autonomy, he concluded that the response to the "dilemma" between political authority and autonomy is to opt for autonomy.[55]

Two substantive points arise out of Wolff's terminology. First, the Kantian vocabulary of self-legislation is important. It tells us that the issue for an autonomous individual is whether the state has *de jure* or legitimate authority over him in that he should accept its laws as binding. It also indicates how the same problem can arise with states when the latter are conceived as autonomous or sovereign. It arises at the domestic level because it may seem that if one is bound only by one's own legislation, one is not bound at all, which is why Wolff gave his book its title.

Notice that this is not a denial of the existence of any constraints whatsoever, only of the constraints relevant to the kind of authority in issue. If it is moral authority, there may well be social, political, or prudential factors that limit the scope of an individual's legislative power, notably the coercive forces at the state's disposal when

[53] Robert Paul Wolff, *In Defense of Anarchism* (Berkeley: University of California Press, 1998, first pub. 1979).

[54] Ibid., 14, his emphasis.

[55] Ibid., 19. I do not think that there is any real difference between conceiving of the problem in terms of autonomy rather than freedom. For a contrary view, see Timothy Endicott, "Sovereignty" in Samantha Besson and John Tasioulas, eds, *The Philosophy of International Law* (Oxford: Oxford University Press, 2012) 245. Endicott argues that if one conceives of the problem in terms of autonomy rather than freedom, one can distinguish between those freedoms that are "necessary for a good life" of an individual and those that are not; 251. Similarly, state sovereignty "is potentially valuable, because it can serve the good of persons (within the state and without the state)"; 254. But his argument is all about potentiality—about whether sovereignty is "at least potentially compatible with the authority of international law"; 258. In this, he follows Joseph Raz's influential theory of authority (250–1). Raz sought to answer Wolff by proposing that authority is compatible with autonomy when the authority is better placed to determine what reasons apply to the subject of authority than the subject itself. (See Joseph Raz, "Authority, Law, and Morality" in Raz, *Ethics in the Public Domain: Essays in the Morality of Law and Politics* (Oxford: Oxford University Press: 1994) 194.)

On this view, international law has authority over states when and only when it reflects the reasons that already apply to states and is better at determining what those reasons are than the states themselves. (Moreover, these reasons will in turn have to be reasons that help the states to further the autonomy of the individuals subject to them better than the individuals could, if left to their own devices.) But, as both Heller and Schmitt would have retorted, this view does not address the question "who is to decide?" And with that question left unaddressed, we are stuck with the anarchical view of international relations, exactly Wolff's conclusion about the relationships between individuals. (For Raz's own provisional view, see Joseph Raz, "The Future of State Sovereignty" (November 18, 2017). Available at SSRN: https://ssrn.com/abstract=3073749 or http://dx.doi.org/10.2139/ssrn.3073749)

it comes to the enforcement of law as well as the force of convention and tradition in that individual's society. With the state, the denial is of the subjection of the state both to its own law and to international law. But still the state may be subject to the constraints set by social, political, or prudential factors, or even moral factors if one is some kind of moral objectivist or realist, or if one merely notes the existence of social or positive morality—what people take to be moral.

This last position is exactly the influential view set out by John Austin, the English nineteenth-century legal positivist, in his command theory of law. According to that theory, law is the commands of a legally unlimited sovereign, whom we identify by the fact that he is habitually obeyed by the bulk of those subject to his power but who obeys no one else, and who motivates the obedience of his subjects by attaching sanctions to each command that will in general make non-compliance too risky. At least in the domestic sphere, there is law on this theory in the sense of the law made by the sovereign for those subject to the sovereign's power. But in the international sphere, since there is no international sovereign, there is no law "properly so called," to use Austin's term. Austin denied for the same reason that there is constitutional law. What passes for both international law and constitutional law are, he said, rules of "positive morality" akin to the moral rules individuals in a particular society choose to obey. Such rules may be equipped with their own sanctions—the sanctions of disapproval by others. But since the sanctions are in a different register from the law's, they do not make such rules into law properly so called.[56]

Austin's position is consistent with Wolff's since it states that one's reason to obey the law does not require the autonomous individual to recognize the law as an authority, but only as a source of pain. Law is envisaged not as an authority but as a "gunman situation writ large," as H.L.A. Hart—the English-speaking world's leading legal positivist philosopher of the last century—put it.[57] But as Hart clearly saw, the attempt to understand the law as a matter of authority rather than sheer or unmediated coercive power risks a kind of absolutism about the law that he associated with Hobbes in which the commands of the sovereign are by definition legitimate; exactly the kind of absolutism that Hobbes is reputed to have inherited from Bodin.

On this view, Bodin and Hobbes, following him, opt for the inherent political authority of the state when faced with the dilemma between that authority and autonomy. Put in terms of the classical debate in political and legal theory, they think that if a state exists as a matter of fact, and so has *de facto* power, it will also have *de jure* or legitimate authority. And if that were right, there would be no paradox of sovereignty in Bodin, merely a dilemma, which brings me to the second substantive point that arises out of Wolff's terminology.

[56] John Austin, *Lectures on Jurisprudence or The Philosophy of Positive Law* 5th edn (London: John Murray, 1885, reproduced by Verlag Detlev Auvermann KG: Glashütten in Taunus, 1972) volume 1, 173, 183, 267,

[57] H.L.A. Hart, "Positivism and the Separation of Law and Morals" in Hart, *Essays in Jurisprudence and Philosophy* (Oxford: Clarendon Press, 1983), 49 at 59.

The distinction between dilemma and paradox matters because "paradox" often implies a statement that seems on the surface contradictory but may be shown to conceal some deeper truth that responds appropriately to the apparent contradiction. This distinction provides a useful marker between those who think there is a paradox, resolvable or not, and those who think there is merely a dilemma that faces one with a choice between power and law, as one can see not only in Weimar, but also in both the nineteenth-century discussion that laid the groundwork for the debate between Kelsen, Schmitt, and Heller and debates in the current era.

The main figure in the German debate prior to Weimar was Georg Jellinek, who developed a "two-sided" theory of state in an attempt to explain how a sovereign could be sovereign and yet bound by both constitutional and international law. Jellinek belonged to the school of "statutory positivism," which was not unlike Austin's command theory of law in that its legal theory was built on the idea of the primacy of statute law made by a legally unlimited and thus sovereign state. His predecessor in this tradition was Paul Laband who presented a legal theory that justified constitutional monarchism—the constitutional order of the late nineteenth-century Prussian state—at the same time as insisting on the exclusion of politics from legal science.[58]

Laband and other statutory positivists argued that the state ruled comprehensively through primary legislation, faithfully implemented by the administration, with judicial review for constitutionality of statutes prohibited, and review for the legality of official action under the law confined to seeing whether the officials had kept within the letter of the law. The legal order was thus understood as a "closed positive system of laws deriving from a sovereign source (the state)."[59] All rights were understood as the creatures of statute law. Individuals possessed no inherent rights against the state but only those rights that the state had seen fit to grant them in its legislation.

This apparently authoritarian theory is tempered by the fact that the public officials may exercise power against individuals only when authorized to do so by statute, and the enactment of statutes is the preserve of the legislature. And unlike Austin, Laband did not deny the existence of international law. Rather, he saw it as the product of treaties between states, enforceable as such by the states, and capable of becoming part of domestic law if the public law institutions of the state enacted international law provisions into domestic instruments.[60] However, he, like others in his school, had no way of explaining how as a juridical matter either domestic constitutional law or international law could be understood as legally binding on the sovereign. Both kinds of law were recognized as existing in fact, though how the "ought" of legal authority could be derived from the "is" of these facts was beyond

[58] See Peter C. Caldwell, *Popular Sovereignty and the Crisis of German Constitutional Law: The Theory and Practice of Weimar Constitutionalism* (Durham: Duke University Press, 1997), chapter 1, Kelly, *The State of the Political*, chapter 3, Koskenniemi, *The Gentle Civilizer of Nations*, chapter 3.

[59] Caldwell, *Popular Sovereignty and the Crisis of German Constitutional Law*, 34.

[60] Koskenniemi, *The Gentle Civilizer of Nations*, 185.

the reach of a legal theory of statutory positivism, as one might think Austin more frankly recognized when it came to the command theory of law.

But the frankness comes at a revealing cost—of denying that both international law and domestic constitutional law are law which makes the political project of subjecting political power to the rule of law futile. As I have already indicated in respect of Laband, his legal theory, despite his claims as to its scientific nature, was an attempt to develop an account of the *Rechtsstaat*—the rule of law state—which would explain the *juridical* nature of *constitutional* monarchy. That is, it would explain how political decision-making in such a system is not arbitrary because all decisions require prior legal authorization of a particular sort.

Exactly the same point can be made about both Austin and Jeremy Bentham, the founder of the English school of legal positivism, that is, the command theory of law, since their legal theory, while presented as scientific or value free, is hard to understand except as a part of their utilitarian project to reform the political and legal institutions of their society so as to maximize general happiness. There were differences between them, notably that Bentham, far from having doubts about whether international law is law, is credited with having coined the term "international law" and had, as the pioneering article on Bentham's vision of and for international law says, "grand plans for world peace: renouncing colonies, reducing navies and armies, settling international disputes in an international court."[61]

However, the recognition of constitutional law and international law as a matter of fact does not so much address the paradox of sovereignty as evade it, as is illustrated by Jellinek's two-sided theory. That theory responds to the paradox of sovereignty by taking the state to have two modes of being. It presents itself, on the one hand, as a matter of social facts about power, on the other, as a legal person. In its social side, there are constraints on the state's power—the constraints set by the needs the state must satisfy and by the other locations of social power in the society. In its legal side, on the other hand, the state may legislate as it pleases, but it is to be understood as legally constituted—as a system of legal norms. The authority of both constitutional law and international law is understood to come from the fact that the state has willed that it be subject to the limits to be found in the positive law of both—it has bound itself.

But the reasons for the state's acts of will are extra-legal, the subject matter of social and political theory. Therefore when the state wills in such a way that it no longer abides by these limits, the matter is not one on which law or legal science may speak. As a result, the two-sided theory consigned questions about the elements in the relationship to distinct fields of inquiry, on the one hand, social theory and political science, on the other, legal theory understood in a very particular way, as confined to the study not only of positive legal norms but also only those norms that are

[61] M.W. Janis, "Jeremy Bentham and the Fashioning of 'International Law'" (1984) 78 *The American Journal of International Law*, 405, 415. In my view, which I will not defend here, both the statutory positivists and the positivist command theorists adopted positivist theories of law on normative and political grounds in the way set out in Benedict Kingsbury, "Legal Positivism as Normative Politics: International Society, Balance of Power and Lassa Oppenheim's Positive International Law" (2002) 13 *European Journal of International Law* 401.

established by statute or, in the international realm, by agreements between states. At a political level, as a matter of legal theory, it assumed the legitimacy of the *de facto* state, but made actual legitimacy turn on considerations beyond legal theory.[62]

The challenge that Jellinek bequeathed to the public lawyers of Weimar was whether they could do better. Kelsen and Schmitt can be said to have continued to evade the challenge by turning the paradox into a dilemma and then choosing one of its two limbs. Kelsen did so by focusing exclusively on the legal side of Jellinek's theory, in his attempt to show that the authority of both constitutional law and international law is to be juridically explained as a matter of the normative structure of legal order, in which the basic norm provides the assumption that makes it unnecessary to resort to extra-legal political or social factors. Sovereignty, as we have seen, becomes a kind of property of legality, the title we bestow on a legal order rather than a norm-creating force with which legal theory must contend. Every state, Kelsen contends, is a *Rechtsstaat*, which is not to say that it is legitimate since, as he also says, law may have any content, and questions about the rightness or wrongness of that content fall outside the purview of legal theory. Schmitt, in turn, developed the political, social side, arguing that because legitimacy is located outside of law, and because law can be given any content, the sovereign is he who is able to make the decision that will attract the acclaim of "the people," that is, of that homogeneous group within the population who recognize themselves (and are recognized) as being on the friend side of the existential distinction between friend and enemy.

Notice that one can identify the problem of sovereignty as a paradox and regard the deeper truth to be that it cannot be resolved as a matter of theory, and so one should turn to practice. The question then arises whether one thinks it is resolvable in practice, as one might say pragmatically instead of theoretically, or will simply reproduce itself endlessly, leaving those who must make the decision with having to choose between two incommensurable options, a choice that will be determined by which better promotes the self-interest of the more powerful party.

Heller fully embraced a turn to practice, as is evidenced by his dedication of *Sovereignty* to Victor Bruns, the founding director of the Kaiser Wilhelm Institute for Comparative Public Law and International Law in Berlin, who encouraged a move away from the theoretical study of international law to the study of practice, and who gave Heller his first full-time academic position.[63]

However, Heller's position is rather ambiguous between the options just sketched, as one can see in his most elaborate attempt at a definition of sovereignty:

> [T]he sovereign is whoever has decided on the normal situation through a written or unwritten constitution and, because he intentionally maintains its validity, continues permanently to decide. And only the one who makes decisions on the normal constitutional situation can also make juristic decisions on the state of exception, sometimes "against the

62 See Caldwell, *Popular Sovereignty and the Crisis of German Constitutional Law*, 42–4.

63 For a discussion of Victor Bruns and the Institute for Comparative Public Law and International Law, see Felix Lange, "Between Systematization and Expertise for Foreign Policy: The Practice-Oriented Approach in Germany's International Legal Scholarship (1920–1980)" (2017) 28 *European Journal of International Law* 535.

law". Only he is reasonably entitled to make the final decision on whether his law must give way to the exigencies of the moment or not. If one were to assume two units of will that are independent of each other, of which one would make decisions on the state of exception and the other on the normal situation, one would be presuming two sovereigns in the same state.[64]

This definition is, of course, a direct response to Schmitt's "[s]overeign is he who decides on the exception." It is deliberately cumbersome to contrast the complexity Heller needed to convey with Schmitt's reduction of sovereignty to certain facts about power. It emphasizes that the sovereign is the ultimate decider, but in the legal sense, which one can glean only from the normal situation when the sovereign decides through the institutional mechanism of the constitutional order. But against Kelsen, and with Schmitt, Heller opposes reduction in the other direction.

More accurately, he opposed the elimination of the sovereign decision by its reduction to the totality of the norms of a legal order. And in opposing both reductions, he demonstrates his determination to preserve both sides of Jellinek's theory, but within an overall juridical structure. The question then becomes whether this complexity is sustainable and that has led to difficulties in understanding his position.

Consider, first, that in his fine book on Weimar legal theory, Peter C. Caldwell charts Heller's development from a kind of left-nationalist position in the first several years of the Weimar Republic to a position in the late 1920s which, whether he admitted this or not, advanced a theory of law that "corresponded better to that of left-liberals like Kelsen and Thoma than to the conservative theories of Schmitt and Smend that he had earlier sought to emulate."[65] The crucial transition in Heller's thought, suggests Caldwell, came in 1928 when, after a visit to Italy, Heller produced a critique of fascism, and consequently shifted his enemy "from Kelsenian liberalism to fascism."[66]

This claim, which is broadly correct, leaves Caldwell in two minds about what to make of Heller's *Sovereignty*. On the one hand, in sketching Heller's earlier position he describes the book as a defense of the "state's right to self-preservation" in a way that "justifies state actions against existing international or state law." Thus, "[f]rom the perspective of foreign affairs, Heller conceived of the state as a living, willing entity standing above law—hardly any differently, in other words, than did Carl Schmitt."[67] But, on the other hand, in discussing Heller's later position, Caldwell says that "at the heart of Heller's shift in focus was a new conception of the state, first elaborated in his 1927 work on sovereignty."[68]

[64] See 129 below.

[65] Caldwell, *Popular Sovereignty and the Crisis of German Constitutional Law*, 127–33. (This element of Heller's work survives into *Sovereignty*—see below 114.) Richard Thoma was, together with Gerhard Anschütz, one of the main public law scholars who devoted themselves in Weimar to a defence of the Weimar Constitution by means of a doctrinal interpretation of it in light of its liberal democratic commitments. See Michael Stolleis, *A History of Public Law in Germany: 1914–1945* (Oxford: Oxford University Press, 2004), 70–6.

[66] Caldwell, *Popular Sovereignty and the Crisis of German Constitutional Law*, 130.

[67] Ibid., 129. [68] Ibid., 131.

Second, Jens Meierhenrich has recently diagnosed Heller's position as legal positivist and "statist" in light of Heller's frequent claim that sovereignty transcends positive law because the sovereign can decide against the law;[69] and he suggests that Heller is intent on understanding the "is" rather than the "ought" of the state. In addition, Meierhenrich claims Heller along with Schmitt as one of the main proponents of what he describes as the "turn" in Weimar public law to "concreteness in philosophical thought," which involves a "war against abstraction" and a "concern with the situatedness of life"; though he does note that, in contrast to Schmitt, Heller's hope was to save democracy and the *Rechtsstaat* in making the turn.[70] But he also says that Heller established a "dialectical relationship" between the "normative sphere of law" and the "factual sphere of power."[71]

It is possible that Caldwell and Meierhenrich have identified contradictory positions in Heller rather than made contradictory claims about his position, namely, that he both regarded the sovereign as legally unlimited albeit constrained by factual or situational contingences, and that he was trying to articulate a new conception of the state that could respond to the state both as a normative entity—a *de jure* authority and as a wielder of power in fact. And even if one understands him as doing the latter, one has to keep in mind that Schmitt too responds to the state both as a normative entity and as a wielder of power. In Schmitt's theory, though, it is through the state wielding the power to make the distinction between friend and enemy that it becomes a normative entity—the source of all political legitimacy. Moreover, if Heller were doing the former, it may be that the world as it developed after the Second World War has developed to the point where his conception of state sovereignty is simply controverted by the facts, as I will now explain.

## From the Political to the Juridical?

Bardo Fassbender said in a 2003 collection on sovereignty that in his last work of 1934, Hermann Heller still referred to sovereignty as "a highest, exclusive, irresistible and independent power" of a state.[72] But, comments Fassbender, "[t]oday, such a power no longer exists, neither in a factual nor in a legal sense."[73] In his view, this original political meaning of sovereignty, which he recognizes as due originally to Bodin, has been replaced by the idea of "sovereign equality." With the founding of

[69] Jens Meierhenrich, *The Remnants of the Rechtsstaat: An Ethnography of Nazi Law* (Oxford: Oxford University Press, 2018), 87–8.

[70] Ibid., 87–8. [71] Ibid., 90.

[72] Fassbender, "Sovereignty and Constitutionalism in International Law," 124. Fassbender's reference is to Hermann Heller, *Staatslehre*, in *Gesammelte Schriften*, volume 3, 79, at 246 and 278. This book—Heller's attempt at a definitive statement of his theory of the state—was unfinished at the time of his death, and the manuscript was completed by his assistant Gerhart Niemeyer, who went on to a successful career as a political scientist in the USA. His first book was on international law—*Law Without Force: The Function of Politics in International Law* [1941] (New Brunswick: Transaction Publishers, 2001). It is dedicated to Heller and has a eulogy to him at xxvi, which concludes as follows: "Hermann Heller's life and death were a constant and forceful proclamation of the idea that to realize a genuinely rational order in the political side of human culture is not merely a pragmatic, but an ethical requirement."

[73] Fassbender, "Sovereignty and Constitutionalism in International Law," 124–5.

the United Nations in 1945, he claims, in a direct response to Heller's definition of sovereignty just quoted, that the "'sovereign state' of the past turned into a (primarily territorially defined) organization with a large number of legal obligations (arising with, without, and even against its will)—an organization which in the complex structure of the universal legal order is endowed with, comparatively, the highest degree of autonomy."[74] Fassbender dates the beginning of this development of this concept to the era of the League of Nations, even though the League itself did not establish sovereign equality.[75]

Fassbender's understanding of sovereign equality is the standard view in international law today, but he chooses to source it directly in an article by Kelsen in the 1944 *Yale Law Journal* and in particular from this passage:

> Therefore, the sovereignty of the States, as subjects of international law, is the legal authority of the States under the authority of international law. If sovereignty means "supreme" authority, the sovereignty of States as subjects of international law can mean, not an absolutely but only a relatively supreme authority. A State's legal authority may be said to be "supreme" insofar as it is not subjected to the legal authority of any other State; and the State is then sovereign when it is subjected only to international law, not to the national law of any other State. Consequently, the State's sovereignty under international law is its legal independence from other States.[76]

Kelsen goes on to argue that those who talk of sovereignty as "supreme power" either just mean "authority" by "power" or are making a causal claim about the reality of the international order, which cannot be true because the factual inequality of states means that there are states, for example, Lichtenstein, which have "no power at all." The only other alternative is an understanding of sovereignty as a "first cause, a *prima causa*, and, in this sense, only God as the Creator of the world is sovereign." This concept of sovereignty "is a metaphysical, not a scientific one, derived from a tendency to deify the State which inevitably leads to a political theory which is rather a theology than a science of the State."[77] That is, the only other alternative is Schmitt, though Kelsen does not deign to refer to him, but cites Bodin instead, adding that "it is characteristic of jurists to present as logically impossible that which is politically undesired because at variance with certain interests."[78]

As Fassbender, however, admits at the end of his essay, there is an "untamed side of sovereignty." The "political dimension" of sovereignty is an "ever present threat to the legal idea"—"which one can deplore or disapprove of" but which it would be a "mistake to ignore."[79] Here he quotes from Kelsen's book on sovereignty from the 1920s, written, he aptly says, during a time that Kelsen saw as a "transitional period" in international law, and whose character Kelsen described in the book as reflected in the "contradictions of an international legal theory which in an almost

[74] Ibid. [75] Ibid., 128.

[76] Hans Kelsen, "The Principle of Sovereign Equality of States as a Basis for International Organisation" (1944) 53 *Yale Law Journal* 207 at 208. See the extract in Fassbender, "Sovereignty and Constitutionalism in International Law," 129.

[77] Ibid. [78] Ibid., 212.

[79] Fassbender, "Sovereignty and Constitutionalism in International Law," 142.

tragic conflict aspires to the height of a universal legal community erected above the individual states but, at the same time, remains a captive of the sphere of the power of the sovereign state."[80]

The hope was that the international legal order established in light of the experience of the First World War would lead to the creation of such a universal legal community. For those who held that hope, it was premised largely on what one might call the legalist vision of an order in which all nations would agree to compulsory arbitration by an international court of all international legal disputes and in regard to disputes that could not be characterized as legal in nature to decision by a conciliation council of experts: that is, an impartial commission would be set up to try to define a settlement that is acceptable to the parties but not binding on them.[81] At the same time, substantive international law would be developed so as to provide a body of rules that could be drawn on by the international court. The effect would be not only that war would be outlawed, but also the conduct of politics by means of war would be by and large ended, since that same order would provide an effective system of sanctions against nations that failed to comply with the judgments of the court.[82] This legalist vision was espoused not only by theorists such as Kelsen, but also by experienced politicians such as the former US President Howard Taft and the Republican senator and general statesman Elihu Root.

This hope was, however, dashed, as the Covenant "abandoned the legalist paradigm almost entirely" by putting in place a legislative body rather than a court, composed of the Council, which had Great Power permanent members, and four rotating elected Lesser Power members, an assembly in which decisions were made by one member one vote, and secretary general as the administrative executive.[83] The legalist model was preserved only in that the Covenant envisaged the creation of the Permanent Court of International Justice to decide legal disputes between member states, but the Court had jurisdiction only if the states had agreed to opt it into its general jurisdiction or the jurisdiction arose out of a special agreement.[84]

[80] Ibid., quoting from the second edition of Kelsen, *Das Problem der Souveränität und die Theorie des Völkerrechts*, at 320, his translation.

[81] For discussion, see Lauterpacht, *The Function of Law in the International Community*, 268–77.

[82] See Stephen Wertheim, "The League of Nations: A Retreat from International Law?" (2012) 7 *Journal of Global History* 210; Hathaway and Shapiro, *The Internationalists;* Mark Mazower, *Governing the World: The History of an Idea, 1815 to the Present* (New York: Penguin, 2012), and the still very useful Alfred Zimmern, *The League of Nations and the Rule of Law: 1918–1935* (London: MacMillan, 1936).

[83] Mazower, *Governing the World*, 135–6;

[84] Article 36 of the **Statute of the Permanent Court of International Justice:**

> The jurisdiction of the Court comprises all cases which the parties refer to it and all matters specially provided for in treaties and conventions in force. The Members of the League of Nations and the States mentioned in the Annex to the Covenant may, either when signing or ratifying the Protocol to which the present Statute is adjoined, or at a later moment, declare that they recognize as compulsory ipso facto and without special agreement, in relation to any other Member or State accepting the same obligation, the jurisdiction of the Court in all or any of the classes of legal disputes concerning:
> (a) the interpretation of a treaty;
> (b) any question of international law;
> (c) the existence of any fact which, if established, would constitute a breach of an international obligation;

Moreover, the assembly had no lawmaking power and was subject to veto by any council member, and the only penalty for defiance by a member state of its commitments to the League was boycott and sanctions. The Council could recommend action against a member but had no resources for ensuring that action took place. Finally, despite the fact that US President Wilson had provided the main political impetus for the League, the USA did not become a member. The US Senate refused to ratify the Covenant in large part because it put in place a political body rather than the judicial system envisaged by the legalists. That effectively made the League the instrument of France and Britain, its two most powerful member states. In sum, the League failed to bring to a close the transitional period in which the legalist or internationalist hopes for an international legal order remained, as Fassbender put it, a "captive of the sphere of the power of the sovereign state."

Kelsen's 1944 article, as well as other of his writings of this time, were, then, built on a renewed hope that the Allied victory in the Second World War would end the transition by ushering in an international organization of nation states in which all disputes would be settled by an international court with compulsory jurisdiction,[85] a hope that still remains largely unrealized by the United Nations and the ensuing developments in international law and the institutions of the new international legal order, including the Permanent Court's successor in the International Court of Justice. Thus, Fassbender concludes by saying that more than fifty years after the founding of the United Nations the "contradictions have not disappeared." The power of the "political" "images of sovereignty was underestimated, a power, admittedly, perhaps greater than that of sovereignty's tamed version."[86]

I have drawn attention to the date of publication of this essay because at that time it was still possible for an international lawyer like Fassbender to make the argument that the world of international relations had been transformed by the development of both the institutions and the positive law of the international legal order, even as he recognized what he took to be the ever present potential for the untamed side of sovereignty to assert itself. And, in the 2000s, there has been a flurry of books on the institutions of the international order, including the international courts that have been developed to adjudicate its disputes, that support his claim about transformation.

For example, in a recent work on the role of international courts in the contemporary world, Karen J. Alter writes that there has been a "shift in the nature

(d) the nature or extent of the reparation to be made for the breach of an international obligation.

The declaration referred to above may be made unconditionally or on condition of reciprocity on the part of several or certain Members or States, or for a certain time. In the event of a dispute as to whether the Court has jurisdiction, the matter shall be settled by the decision of the Court.

85 Kelsen, "The Principle of Sovereign Equality of States as a Basis for International Organisation" at 214: "The only way to establish on the principle of 'sovereign equality' an international organization able to 'maintain international peace and security' more efficiently than the League of Nations did, is the establishment of an international community whose main organ is an international court endowed with compulsory jurisdiction."

86 Fassbender, "Sovereignty and Constitutionalism in International Law," 143.

of international law and in acceptable moral discourse ... away from a contractual conception of international law toward a non-Austinian rule of law conception where law exists beyond the confines of the nation-state and where law generates obligations for nation-states." [87] She and others argue that the shift away from the call for an international court with compulsory jurisdiction that so occupied Kelsen and others in the first fifty or so years of the last century should not be seen as a sign of the waning of international law. Rather, in place of one such court, one finds a multiplicity of international tribunals that decide on discrete regimes of international law and which cumulatively have transformed international law in the way Alter describes.[88]

But in a book published in this same period, Mark Mazower, the leading historian of twentieth-century international relations, delivers a rather different verdict:

> Jeremy Bentham envisaged international law two centuries ago as a way of spreading universal well-being, independent of nation or creed. Today, in contrast, the appeal to law has become a vocabulary of permissions, a means of asserting power and control that normalizes the debatable and justifies the exception.[89]

Mazower's reference to the exception is an altogether deliberate invocation of Schmitt,[90] and indicates the general theme of the book. He sets out the earlier vision of an international "empire of law"[91] articulated by figures such as Root, who appears in Heller's discussion of the drafting process of the Convention, and who as a leading American international lawyer, statesman, and winner of the Nobel Peace Prize in 1912, was, as I have indicated, one of the proponents of an international court that would reduce "clashes of interests and equity to matters of legal principle."[92] By the turn of the twenty-first century, according to Mazower, at the very time when in 2006 the American Society of International Lawyers at its centennial invoked the memory of its founder Root to "set America straight" in the dark days that followed the invasion of Iraq,[93] the "idea of a law binding upon all states and those governing them seems as far away as ever."[94] And this, note, is four years before the Trump era in international relations could be properly imagined!

In sum, we seem again to be in a "transitional period" in international law, the character of which is reflected in the "contradictions of an international legal theory which in an almost tragic conflict aspires to the height of a universal legal community erected above the individual states but, at the same time, remains a captive of the sphere of the power of the sovereign state." But it may appear that we are in such a period with one major difference.

[87] Karen J. Alter, *The New Terrain of International Law: Courts, Politics, Rights* (Princeton: Princeton University Press, 2014).

[88] See Mary Ellen O'Connell and Lenore VanderZee, "The History of International Adjudication" in Cesare P.R. Romano, Karen J. Alter, and Yuval Shany, eds, *The Oxford Handbook of International Adjudication* (Oxford: Oxford University Press, 2013) 40.

[89] Mazower, *Governing the World*, 404.

[90] As is evidenced by his references to Schmitt in the book, notably, ibid., 183–6.

[91] Ibid., chapter 3. [92] Ibid., 91–3, at 92. [93] Ibid., 92. [94] Ibid., 404–5.

In writing his book on sovereignty at the same time as the Great Powers were struggling to draft the Convention that would be the basis for the League of Nations and the international court that would adjudicate their disputes, Kelsen was able to hold onto the hope that the transition was a progressive one, as he could when, in 1944, he observed the seeds of a renewed attempt to craft an international legal order, this time with the benefit of the lessons learned from the failures of the order created by the League. But today with an acceleration of the trends that, according to Mazower, display the triumph of Schmitt in light of the perceived failure of post-Second World War experiment, the transition might seem to be going in precisely the wrong direction, at least from the perspective of those who seek to understand sovereignty in the legal sense.

Before we take the plunge into an abyss of pessimism, it is worth noting that when one looks at the literature on international law in the 1930s produced by those in Europe who wished to build the international legal order rather than destroy it, it is remarkable to encounter their sense of the importance of continuing with this task in a period when Nazism and fascism were on the ascendant. Consider these words of Georges Scelle in a book on international law published in 1934, at a time when, as he put it:

> The whole world is suffering from a kind of medieval anarchy made up of state tyrannies. The fiction of collective personality is reappearing in dogmas and in mystical doctrines with a virulence which is perhaps nothing but the death throes of political and legal structures in the process of transforming themselves to adapt to new needs.

Despite this bleak outlook, Scelle went on to say, referring directly to the persecution of the Jews and other political minorities in Germany which in October 1933 had been brought to the attention of the Assembly of the League of Nations:

> It may perhaps seem paradoxical to devote this first chapter to what the classic legal literature calls individual rights at a time when in many countries these rights are openly ignored or brutally violated by governments while other governments, and the League of Nations itself, which, it is submitted, have a duty to intervene and safeguard the law, do not appear willing to make the necessary effort to fulfil this legal duty. Their excuse can perhaps be found in their impotence. Without question, the law is in a period of regression. Is this a reason to refrain from setting forth the rules? Quite the contrary, it is important not to weaken their expression. Nothing could be more pernicious than to imagine that the violation of positive law can be confused with its evolution. Already in the history of humanity there have been several periods of regression followed by enlightened stages of progress. It is while waiting for the return of these enlightened stages that we are continuing with the academic study of legal phenomena.[95]

Scelle belonged to the French sociological school of law in which the main figure was the public law theorist Léon Duguit. This school understood law as the expression of a kind of social solidarity, though one that that was essentially universalistic in spirit,

[95] Quoted in Hubert Thierry "The European Tradition in International Law: Georges Scelle, The Thought of Georges Scelle" (1990) 1 *European Journal of International Law* 193, at 195–6.

that is, French as opposed to German.[96] As such, it was not only able to accommodate international law but led to a conclusion similar to Kelsen's about the subordination of sovereignty to law. Heller does not refer to Scelle. However, he does have quite a bit to say about Duguit, since he supposed that Duguit's legal theory suffers from the same flaws as Kelsen in its attempt to eradicate the state and sovereignty from its field of enquiry, albeit that the attempt is made on a sociological rather than a philosophical basis.[97] But, no less than Duguit's sociological school, Heller wanted a realistic social account of the state and sovereignty, just as no less than Kelsen he wanted a philosophical account of the same ideas in terms of legal norms, and so thought the academic task of articulating the content of the *Rechtsstaat* ideal of crucial importance, especially when that ideal was most imperiled.

The main issue for Heller's theory of sovereignty is whether his realism, or his turn to the concrete as I described earlier, overwhelmed the normative side of his legal theory. And, as the reader will see, there are moments in *Sovereignty* where it is hard to understand things otherwise. In the following section, "Deciding 'against Law'," I will discuss some of the examples that Heller supposes illustrate his claim that a mark of sovereignty is the ability of the sovereign to decide "against law," thus proving that "there is a state that is not identical to the legal order, and that is sovereign as a universal decision-making unit."

## Deciding "against Law"

Recall Lauterpacht's remark that Heller's *Sovereignty* "is a somewhat intolerant denial of international law as a system of law, and an affirmation of the absolute sovereignty of the state."[98] It may seem hard to resist Lauterpacht's claim given that Heller seems to endorse in his book the views of Erich Kaufmann, another public lawyer prominent in Weimar.

Kaufmann belonged to the organic school of law of Otto von Gierke. Since it was based on a romantic, Hegelian idea of law as German-ness, as reflecting a specifically German ethical community, it may seem ominous given the later reliance of Nazi lawyers on similar tropes about the "spirit" of German law.[99] Indeed, Kaufmann was an opponent of liberal democracy from the conservative right and held the view that international law is inferior to national law given that it cannot reflect the spirit of the nation. At most, it is the product of agreements between states, but it is binding

[96] See Koskenniemi, *The Gentle Civilizer of Nations*, chapter 4, "International Law as Sociology: French 'Solidarism', 1871–1950".

[97] He does engage quite deeply with the work of another member of this school, Nicolas Politis; for an account of Politis, see Koskenniemi, ibid., 305–9,

[98] Lauterpacht, *The Function of Law in the International Community*, 416–17.

[99] Though Gierke was a liberal, as was Hugo Preuss, often referred to as the "father" of the Weimar Constitution because of his role in its drafting, who followed the organic school and was deeply committed to the values of liberal democracy. See Peter C. Caldwell, "Hugo Preuss's Concept of the Volk: Critical Confusion or Sophisticated Conception?" (2013) 63 *University of Toronto Law Journal*, 347.

only so long as the states did not suppose that circumstances had changed such that the treaties no longer reflected the national interest.[100]

Kaufmann had a significant influence on both Schmitt and Heller, and in *Sovereignty* Heller quotes Kaufmann as saying that international law treaties only bind "as long as the situation of power and interests obtaining at the time they are concluded does not change so much that essential provisions of the treaty become incompatible with the right of self-preservation of the contracting states."[101] Put in legal terms, Kaufmann made the "*rebus sic stantibus*" proviso—that an agreement could not survive a serious change in the material circumstances under which the states had concluded the agreement—the fundamental principle of international law.[102] And, as Lauterpacht pointed out in 1933, in making that claim Kaufmann denied international law its authority.[103]

Heller says that the proviso "thus formulated must be unreservedly endorsed. It is to this extent merely an application to treaties under international law of the state right of self-preservation, and signifies nothing more than this right."[104] And earlier

[100] Kaufmann's position may also be more nuanced than his reputation suggests. Consider that Koskeniemmi, in his illuminating history of international law thought from 1870 to 1960, notes that some have seen Kaufmann as an "unwitting facilitator of fascism." But, he suggests, Kaufmann's work should be more charitably understood as an "effort to deal with the paradoxes and weaknesses that a purely rationalistic or a purely sociological scholarship entails – the mindless oscillation between voluntarism and naturalism that became the shared fate of variations of disenchanted-turn-of-the century jurisprudence after 1918." *The Gentle Civilizer of Nations*, 256. He also says that Kaufmann's "orientation towards the concrete and the substantive avoided the pitfalls of formalism and abstraction into which [the opposite camps of pacifists and nationalists] ... regularly fell"; 257. In offering his sympathetic gloss on Kaufmann, Koskenniemi may also be describing his own approach to international law, for he advances the endless reproduction thesis with ultimate determination by power politics throughout his influential body of work on international law theory, most notably in *From Apology to Utopia: The Structure of International Argument* (Cambridge: Cambridge University Press, 2005, Reissue with an Epilogue) chapter 4, "Sovereignty." I point out the incoherence of this approach in "Formalism, Realism, and the Politics of Indeterminacy" in Wouter Werner, Marieke De Hoon, and Alexis Galàn, eds, *The Law of International Lawyers: Reading Martti Koskenniemi* (Cambridge: Cambridge University Press, 2017) 39. In his response to the contributions, "Epilogue—To Enable and Enchant—on the Power of Law," ibid., 393, at 397, Koskenniemi accuses me of abstraction and of "having a two value tool kit": either it *is* law or then it is *not*. His emphasis. But what I show in my chapter is that he continually oscillates between these two alternatives, which means both that only facts about power can provide a provisional resting place and that, in the result, the rule of law is stripped of all content. It is this feature of his work that makes Koskenniemi, in his own words, a "closet Schmittean"; ibid.

[101] See below 177 quoting from Erich Kaufmann, Das *Wesen des Völkerrechts und die Clausula Rebus Sic Stantibus* (Tübingen: J.C.B. Mohr, 1911), 204. For discussion, see Stanley L. Paulson, "Some Issues in the Exchange between Kelsen and Kaufmann" in (2005) 48 *Scandinavian Studies in Law* 269. At 273, note 15, Paulson suggests that there are similarities between Kaufmann's (unsuccessful in his view) critique of Kelsen and Heller's. See also the section on Kaufmann in Jacobson and Schlink, eds, *Weimar: A Jurisprudence of Crisis*, 189.

[102] Here he took inspiration not only from Gierke, but also from Friedrich Julius Stahl, who had in the first half of the nineteenth century constructed a conservative positivist theory of law in a bid to justify the monarchy of his day. See Koskeniemmi, *The Gentle Civilizer of Nations*, 179–81.

[103] Lauterpacht, *The Function of Law in the International Community*, 420–3. Lauterpacht's trenchant criticism of Kaufmann's theory as well as of other theories of international law as mere coordination applies with equal force to the recent reinvention of such a theory in Jack L. Goldsmith and Eric A. Posner, *The Limits of International Law* (New York: Oxford University Press, 2005), a book oblivious to the existence of the history of the debate in which they engage.

[104] See below 177.

he emphasizes that the state's right to self-preservation as an international law person is greater than its right to preserve itself in the face of an internal threat that amounts to a state of emergency.[105] But he also qualifies his endorsement of Kaufmann in a way that introduces a tension into his account: "Of course, the state's absolute right of self-preservation does not mean its absolute implementation in every single case. Such a concept of sovereignty, which incidentally neither Bodin nor anyone else has advocated, would radically preclude any international law."[106] So the question is whether he is entitled to this qualification and what its content is.

Heller discusses two examples of treaties in which states sought to bind themselves without reservation to resolution of their disputes by some independent body. The first is the treaty between Italy and Switzerland of 1924, which followed a model of the time that required the parties to resort first to conciliation. If that failed, the dispute would go to the Permanent Court of International Justice, which would either issue a judgment or, if the Court did not consider the dispute to be of a juridical nature, the matter would go to binding arbitration *ex aequo et bono*, that is, on the basis of equity.[107]

This example interests Heller because of the apparent total commitment to binding judicial settlement. He finds in statements made by the Swiss Federal Council, the executive body of the parliament, as well as by the parliament itself, a commitment to sovereignty, because these statements highlight the treaty's basis in trust that the binding decisions would not violate sovereignty. In other words, he finds a reservation as to the right to assert sovereignty in cases where the preservation of the legal personality of the state is put at risk and so trust is lost.[108]

The second example Heller discusses is the Geneva Protocol, an attempt in 1924 to introduce compulsory arbitration in all matters to the members of the League, which was approved by forty-seven members. However, the attempt foundered when in 1925, after a change of government, Britain made it clear that it would not ratify the Protocol. Heller is less interested in the reasons that it failed than in highlighting the flaw in the treaty. The Protocol required basically that members of the League submit all disputes of a legal nature to the Permanent Court of International Justice, while all other disputes would go either to an agreed Committee of Arbitrators, or, if there was no agreement between the parties, to the Council of the League. If the Council could not resolve the matter either by conciliation or by making a unanimous decision, it was empowered to set up by majority decision a Committee of Arbitrators. A member state that failed to comply with a judicial or arbitral order would be subject to the sanctions mechanisms of Article 13 of the Covenant. Moreover, if a member state resorted to war in violation of its undertakings, it would be considered the aggressor.[109]

105 Ibid. 106 Ibid.

107 See below 178-9. For discussion, see Lauterpacht, *The Function of Law in the International Community*, 42–7.

108 Ibid. For Lauterpacht's disagreement with Heller on this point, see ibid., 185, note 3.

109 See below 179-80. See John F. Williams, "The Geneva Protocol of 1924 for the Pacific Settlement of International Disputes" (1924) 3 *Journal of the British Institute of International Affairs* 288 and James W. Garner, "The Geneva Protocol of 1924 for the Pacific Settlement of International Disputes" (1925) 19 *The American Journal of International Law* 123.

Two aspects of the Geneva Protocol interest Heller. First, it is, in his view, not really a juridical solution since ultimately settlement of political disputes would be by a political body, that is, the body appointed by the Greater Power-dominated Council. Second, and more important, is that Nicolas Politis, one of the main architects of the Protocol (and a member of the French sociological school), admitted at the time that the Protocol's arbitral jurisdiction did not permit review of international treaties or of territorial rights. But with such review excluded, Heller suggests, the gap was opened for the fact of sovereign power to assert itself.[110]

Heller makes an analogous argument in the domestic context in his sketch of an episode in 1925 in Austria when the government decided to stave off the collapse of the Central Bank by backing it with an amount that was almost a tenth of the entire revenue of the state without getting, as was constitutionally prescribed, prior legislative authorization. He quotes the Chancellor's defense of this measure as the required response to a dire state of emergency to make the point that emergency measures can be required even when the Constitution explicitly makes no provision for a state of emergency, a point in which Heller rather unkindly revels. For as he mentions, Kelsen was the one of the main drafters of the Constitution and "proudly" noted in his book on Austrian constitutional law the absence of such a provision.[111]

Heller's conclusion is that this is a

> case of an unconstitutional act of state, the validity of which is unquestionable, but for which the pure theory of law would not only have to condemn the government, but also to declare the act itself absolutely null and void. The magisterial representation of the people, as the executive, would have had to decide here whether the interest protected by observing one of the most important constitutional norms should be placed higher or lower than the interest that could only be protected by a violation of that constitutional norm. But only the representative unit of will, not the legal order itself, can balance interests and sometimes decide against the legal order.[112]

It may well then seem that if one puts this train of thought together with other claims in *Sovereignty* that Heller cannot in substance be prized apart from either Kaufmann or Schmitt; for example,

> the essence of sovereignty can be found in the possibility of finally and effectively deciding any issue involving the unity of social interaction in the territory, even sometimes in opposition to positive law, and of imposing this decision on everyone—not only members of the association, but absolutely all residents of the territory.[113]

Moreover, Heller neglects to mention that the Austrian government during the 1920s was headed by the clerical, conservative Christian-Social Party, who were also in charge of most Austrian provinces, but not of Vienna. Vienna was ruled by the Socialists, who also held over 40 per cent of parliamentary seats, but never

[110] See below 180. Heller was not alone in drawing this conclusion. See Zimmern, *The League of Nations and the Rule of Law: 1918–1935*, 348–9.

[111] Heller omits mention of the fact that Kelsen was also at this time on the bench of Austria's and the world's first Constitutional Court, an institutional innovation for which Kelsen was responsible.

[112] See below 133. [113] See below 128.

joined the government. The ruling party was corrupt and in the habit of borrowing money from provincial banks for speculation in the financial markets. It resorted to the emergency measure to save the Central Bank—the clearing bank for Austria's savings banks—before there could be a debate in Parliament, because it did not want a public discussion in Parliament of its practices. So there is a good case to be made that this measure was nothing better than the act of corrupt party politicians trying to cover up their miscarried investments undertaken illegally by using citizens' deposits at savings banks.[114]

Heller's treatment of the example is in part to be explained, in my view, as his giving way to the temptation of taking a cheap shot at Kelsen in revenge for Kelsen's claim in 1927 that Heller had attempted to cover his plagiarism of the Pure Theory with a cloak of invective. But his analysis of this example, when put together with his claim about state submission to compulsory arbitration, may seem to amount to a larger theoretical point. Even the constitution that Kelsen had himself designed to eliminate the possibility of a legally ungoverned state of emergency would be vulnerable to an assertion of sovereignty by the executive, just as a treaty that provided for the compulsory submission to arbitration of all disputes between states could not preclude a valid claim by a state on the basis of its right to preserve itself. Heller would then be embracing the same anti-legalist logic of Schmitt's argument, an impression that can only be reinforced when one notices that, in the discussion of federalism in *Sovereignty*, he insists that the federal state must be able to assert itself in times of crisis against the sub-state units.[115] In short, Heller's theory would amount to a leftwing version of Schmitt, as Michael Stolleis, the eminent historian of German legal thought, suggests when he says that "Heller's effort to set himself apart from Kelsen's Neo-Kantian positivism was almost pathological in its intensity, while upon closer inspection his opposition to Carl Schmitt is reduced to political—although in this realm fundamental—differences."[116]

However, it is important to see that Heller's position is much more nuanced than Schmitt's, even though his analysis of the Austrian situation is Schmittean. The key words in the passage just quoted are "magisterial representation of the people," which harken back to his criticism of Schmitt earlier in the book for substituting a notion of "organ sovereignty" for the legal idea of the sovereignty of the state. They also look forward to Heller's argument in 1932 in the *Preussenschlag*, the case in which the Prussian government contested the federal government's seizure of its state machinery.[117]

[114] See Nathan Marcus, *Austrian Reconstruction and the Collapse of Global Finance, 1921–1931* (Cambridge, Mass.: Harvard 2018) 275–6. (I rely also on personal correspondence with Professor Marcus, who generously provided me with some extra detail.) See also Charles A. Gulick, *Austria: From Hapsburg to Hitler* (Berkeley: University of California Press, 1948) volume I, 702–13.

[115] See below 135–37.

[116] Stolleis, *A History of Public Law in Germany: 1914–1945*, 176.

[117] For more detailed accounts of the case and the arguments see David Dyzenhaus *Legality and Legitimacy: Carl Schmitt, Hans Kelsen and Herman Heller in Weimar* (Oxford: Clarendon Press, 1997) and David Dyzenhaus, "Legal Theory in the Collapse of Weimar" (1997) 91 *American Political Science Review* 121. For an account of the precarious political situation in Prussia at the time, set in the context of the precarious situation in Germany as a whole, see Christopher Clark, *Iron Kingdom: The Rise and Downfall of Prussia 1600–1947* (London: Penguin Books, 2007), 640–54.

That intervention was part of a wider strategy by the government of rightwing aristocrats to get rid of the system of parliamentary government. It was supposed to work, first, by provoking civil strife in Prussia at the same time as hamstringing the Prussian government's ability to prevent such strife, second, by claiming that the ensuing "state of emergency" justified the takeover thus eliminating the main power base of the SPD, third, by crushing the communists at the same time as neutralizing Hitler by drawing him within the federal cabinet.

For the strategy to succeed, the *Staatsgerichtshof*—the Court charged with hearing disputes between the federal government and the *Länder*—had to uphold the validity of the federal government's claim to be justified by Article 48. This the Court substantially did, and so paved the way for the rest of the plan to unfold; though, as we know, it failed in one respect in that Hitler outmaneuvered the aristocrats and seized power in 1933. The *Preussenschlag* was thus a crucial moment in the breakdown of Germany's first experiment with democracy. Stolleis calls it a "milestone in the constitutional history of the downfall of the Republic"[118] and says that it "was a preview of the equally violent *Gleichschaltung* [political alignment] ... of the *Länder* by the National Socialists once they had come to power."[119]

Heller appeared in the matter on behalf of the SPD faction within the Prussian government, while Schmitt acted as the legal advisor to the chief architect of the measure, General von Schleicher, the Minister of Defence in the Federal Cabinet headed by Franz von Papen.

In his argument to the Court, Schmitt contested the Court's claim to have any jurisdiction over the matter.[120] He also argued that the legitimacy of a state institution stemmed from its independence from parliamentary politics, which rendered only the federal government capable of dealing with its enemies, who included those who wished to save parliamentary democracy. For on Schmitt's view, it was political parties in general that pose a threat to the sovereignty of the state. A decision to intervene to preserve parliamentary democracy would perpetuate the struggle between political parties that, according to Schmitt, could poison Germany. A government that enjoyed a parliamentary mandate was part of the problem since such a government is under the control of one or more political parties, which is why the President had to be considered to have an unlimited discretion.[121]

Heller's contention, in contrast, was that the idea of an unlimited jurisdiction is self-contradictory. The President's jurisdiction under Article 48 had to be limited by the very Constitution that granted that jurisdiction. Those limitations were the ones that accorded with the correct understanding at law of the presuppositions of the Constitution.[122] It was not political conflict *per se* that constituted an emergency,

[118] Stolleis, *A History of Public Law in Germany: 1914–1945*, 101. [119] Ibid., 102.

[120] The arguments made by the lawyers and the judgment of the Court are collected in *Preussen contra Reich vor dem Staatsgerichtshof: Stenogrammbericht der Verhandlungen vor dem Staatsgerichstshof in Leipzig vom 10. bis. 14 und vom 17. Oktober 1932*, (Glashütten im Taunus: Verlag Detlev Auvermann KG, 1976). For Schmitt's procedural argument, see 466–9.

[121] Ibid., 39–41.

[122] See also his argument in a paper published shortly afterwards, "Ist das Reich verfassungsmässig vorgegangen?" in Heller, *Gesammelte Schriften*, volume 2, 405.

but political conflict that threatened the maintenance of parliamentary democracy. A state of emergency is not simply a situation of political crisis: it is a constitutional-legal response to such a crisis. No matter the depth of political conflict, for a declaration of a state of emergency to be valid, that declaration must be aimed at the return to the normal, constitutional situation in whose service the relevant legal provisions stand. And that understanding of a state of emergency meant that both its definition and its resolution were framed by law.

His argument before the Court, then, amounted to more than a call to a return to the legal *status quo ante* of parliamentary democracy. He wanted the Court to understand that it had to play a role in restoring the institutional or organizational integrity of democracy. He was asking the Court to help keep alive the democratic pulse of the Weimar Constitution because this pulse should inform the judicial understanding of fidelity to law. In this context, he reasoned that the crucial question for the Court was whether the Prussian government had been willing and able to deal with the disturbance. And, he maintained, not only was it clearly willing and able, but it had, in view of the violence that followed the measure, proved itself better able to do so than the Commissioner appointed to govern Prussia. Heller warned the Court in the clearest terms of the consequences of a decision of the kind it eventually did give. If the Court were to uphold the validity of the Federal government's intervention, it would in effect uphold the contention that the participation of the SPD in government was itself a threat to public safety and order. The SPD's role in building democracy in Germany would come to an end and, he said, the consequences were obvious to all present.[123]

He noted that Arnold Brecht, the lawyer for the Prussian government, had invited the Court to speak clearly if it were to uphold the validity of the intervention. Heller repeated the invitation; for then, he said, speaking as a social democrat, it would be clear once and for all what the political situation of Germany was. But he said that, as a jurist and as a German, he wanted the Court to take account of the fact that the route one adopts to reach an end can be crucial and that one cannot build a legal order unless one genuinely binds oneself to the law.[124]

It is this analysis that is required by the idea of the "magisterial representation of the people," not the one involved in the cheap shot at Kelsen.[125] For had the issue in Austria been challenged in court, the question for the court would have been precisely whether the executive's step was justified in law. For, on the basis of the legal theory set out in *Sovereignty*, the *Rechtsstaat* is a very particular form of legal and normative order. What distinguishes the *Rechtsstaat* from absolutist forms of state is that it exhibits a division of powers between legislature, executive, and judiciary, which equips the bond between ruler and ruled with legal sanctions. And it is these

[123] *Preussen contra Reich vor dem Staatsgerichtsthof*, 77–8 and 379–80. [124] Ibid., 406–9.

[125] Kelsen published an analysis of the judgment in 1932, translated as "The Judgment of the *Staatsgerichtshof* of 25 October 1932" in Vinx, ed., *The Guardian of the Constitution*, 228. While critical of the judgment, his major criticism is of the Constitution for having failed to establish a Constitutional Court with clear jurisdiction to decide this kind of issue.

sanctions that operationalize what Heller called in later work the "polemical principle" of democracy or of the sovereignty of the people.[126]

That principle is that power in a democracy should go from bottom to top—all power resides in the people. The *Rechtsstaat* institutionalizes that principle by requiring that law be made by elected representatives, whose accountability to the people is legally ensured, and that same law must be implemented and interpreted by officials and judges who are similarly accountable to the law.

The principle is polemical in the sense that it is intended to provide a basis for a rule of law stance amidst political conflicts. Its polemical nature resides in two of its features. First, it opposes directly the autocratic principle which seeks, as far as possible, to unite all power in the hands of the ruler. Second, it points to the inevitable and sometimes very large gap in any *Rechtsstaat* between ideal and reality. The importance of its being seen as a polemical principle is that, once institutionalized, it requires a constant attempt to narrow the gap under the impulse of interpretations of the principle.

But given that the international legal order is neither a democracy nor exhibits such a separation of powers it does not amount, in Heller's view, to an order of rule in which a sovereign makes law to regulate the interactions of his subjects. Rather, it is a "contractual" legal order, in which law is made by formally legal sovereign states to regulate their interactions with each other. As he says in *Sovereignty*: "The emergence and demise of states is essentially not regulated by international law; they themselves regulate international law."[127] That view of international law usually either explicitly or implicitly denies it any authority, and we have seen that Lauterpacht's verdict in 1933 was that Heller's theory fell into the explicit denial camp. In the following two sections, "Sovereignty in International Law" and "Fundamental Principles of Law," I will suggest that Lauterpacht and Heller share much with each other and also with Kelsen. Their common ground is important because it indicates that there is a kind of logic to the legal idea of sovereignty to which all who wish to make sense of that idea are drawn. In addition, I will argue that the logic is political as well as legal, something Heller appreciated better than either Lauterpacht or Kelsen.

## Sovereignty in International Law

Heller begins *Sovereignty* with a reference to the *Wimbledon* case, decided by the Permanent Court of International Justice in 1923.[128] All he says about the case itself, perhaps because he assumes that his readers would be familiar with it, is that it "offered frequent opportunities to discuss the problem of sovereignty."[129] He chooses instead to focus on a claim made in argument to the Court by Professor

[126] Heller, *Staatslehre*, 360–1. See also the translation of extracts from this work as "The Nature and Structure of the State," David Dyzenhaus, trans. (1996) 18 *Cardozo Law Review* 1139, at 1182–3.

[127] See below 167.

[128] *S.S. Wimbledon*, [1923] *Publ. PCIJ*, Series A, no. 1, permanent link at http://www.worldcourts.com/pcij/eng/decisions/1923.08.17_wimbledon.htm.

[129] See below 167.

Jules Basdevant, France's legal representative and distinguished international lawyer, in which Basdevant poked fun at the argument of Germany's legal representative, saying: "I know that such a conception of sovereignty holds a considerable place in German jurisprudence, as it did formerly in French jurisprudence in consequence of the work of Jean Bodin."[130]

As Heller observes, Basdevant's point is that France, the country in which Bodin was born and formed his views, moved with other nations away from his "absolutist and imperialist mindset" to a position "compatible with the legal consciousness of our present day civilization" while Germany remained "mired" in Bodin's absolutism, as evidenced by her legal argument to the Court. Heller proceeds to argue that Basdevant along with others did not "know what Bodin was talking about" when he ascribed this view of sovereignty to Bodin.[131]

Heller does not comment on Basdevant's claim that an absolutist view of sovereignty, whether or not it was Bodin's, animated Germany's argument to the Court, nor on the fact that the Court rejected such an argument. And he returns to international law much later, as chapters 1—5 are devoted to rectifying the mistaken view of Bodin and unpacking the implications of the correct view for the modern conception of sovereignty mostly within the nation state, while chapters 6–9 are an in-depth discussion of the role of sovereignty in international law.

However, in opening *Sovereignty* with the *Wimbledon* case, Heller made the question of sovereignty in international law the book ends of his monograph; and in doing so he raised the question of the paradox of sovereignty in a way that brings to light the central tension of his argument, and indeed, of his public law theory as a whole. I will show here that, with the context of the case filled in, we can understand Heller's position better and in particular why his legal theory was not of the pragmatic kind that involves a total immersion in practice, but rather a theoretically informed pragmatism that allows for understanding the space in which decisions have to be made. Very useful is that the best account of the case I know is by Jan Klabbers, an international lawyer, who embraces the first kind of pragmatism.

Klabbers points out that *Wimbledon* was the "first contentious case decided by the first ever permanent international tribunal, the Permanent Court of International Justice."[132] At the time it was decided, he says, that "international law needed an authoritative decision to clinch its conception of sovereignty, and to bring it into line with the possibility of international law itself,"[133] thus facilitating the "development of international law as a more or less coherent system of rules binding upon states."[134] This was, in Klabber's view, the achievement of the decision, and he sees it as preparing the way for the more famous dictum in the *Lotus* case, decided by the same Court four years later in which it stated:

130 Acts and Documents Relating to Judgments and Advisory Opinions Given by the Court, [1923] *Publi. PCIJ*, Série C, no. 3, permanent link at https://www.icj-cij.org/en/pcij-series-c, 386–7.

131 See below 61.

132 Jan Klabbers, "Clinching the Concept of Sovereignty: Wimbledon Redux" (1998) 3 *Austrian Review of International & European Law* 345, at 347.

133 Ibid., 348.

134 Ibid.

International law governs relations between independent States. The rules of law binding upon states therefore emanate from their own free will as expressed in conventions or by usages generally accepted as expressing principles of law and established to regulate the relations between these co-existing independent communities or with a view to the achievement of common aims. Restrictions upon the independence of States cannot therefore be presumed.[135]

Klabbers argues that these two cases

together establish that in a horizontal order of sovereign equals international law is by no means impossible; indeed, it is precisely because states are sovereign that they can make international law. But the same conception of sovereignty entails that rules can only be made on the basis of consent; the rules of international law emanate from the freely expressed will of sovereign states.[136]

International law can thus be said to amount, he claims, to a "positivist system in that rules are created by the consent of the states themselves, and do not flow from elsewhere."[137] I believe that this conclusion and the premise from which it follows can be shown, through an analysis of the case, to be flawed in a way that establishes Heller's distance from Kaufmann, and even more important, his proximity to important elements of both Kelsen's and Lauterpacht's theories of international law.[138]

The dispute in the case arose over Article 380 of the Versailles Treaty which provided that the Kiel Canal—an internal waterway in Germany—"shall be maintained free and open to the vessels of commerce and of war of all nations at peace with Germany on terms of entire equality." In 1920 Poland and the USSR were at war. Germany was a party to the Treaty, though, as I have pointed out, a reluctant one. In 1920, she had issued two "Neutrality Orders" in connection with the war, which stated her stance of neutrality—that is, that she had adopted the legal status recognized by international law of non-participation in a conflict.[139] As a result, she prohibited the "export of arms, munitions . . . and other articles of war material in so far as these articles are consigned to the territories" of the warring countries.

As Eugen Schiffer, Germany's legal representative and Minister of Justice, pointed out, the war had spilled in dramatic ways across Germany's borders, with outbreaks

[135] *S.S. Lotus*, [1927] *Publ. PCIJ*, Series A, no. 10, 18, quoted in Jan Klabbers, *International Law* (Cambridge: Cambridge University Press, 2017, second edition), 25.

[136] Ibid., 27, [137] Ibid.

[138] For a more detailed discussion of the judgments, see Ole Spiermann, *International Legal Argument in the Permanent Court of Justice: The Rise of the International Judiciary* (Cambridge: Cambridge University Press, 2004) 175–86. Note that both Spiermann and Klabbers largely shares Koskenniemi's "critical" approach to international law which, in my view (see note 101 above), puts them in the same camp as Kaufmann. See also Clemens Feinäugle, "Wimbeldon, The" in the *Max Planck Encylopedia of Public International Law*, http://opil.ouplaw.com.myaccess.library.utoronto.ca/view/10.1093/law:epil/9780199231690/law-9780199231690-e234?rskey=pqgF4Q&result=1&prd=EPIL

[139] "Neutrality" is a kind of halfway station between an international legal order in which states have the right to go to war and one in which the use of force in international affairs is prohibited. Since the Charter of the United Nations prohibits the use of force, it may seem to make the doctrine of neutrality obsolete, but it in fact persists in international law. See Michael Bothe, "Neutrality, Concept and General Rules" in the *Max Planck Encylopedia of Public International Law*, http://opil.ouplaw.com.myaccess.library.utoronto.ca/view/10.1093/law:epil/9780199231690/law-9780199231690-e349?rskey=5Qq5jS&result=4&prd=EPIL

of violence and incursions by foreign troops so that Germany had had to intern 2,000 Poles and 65,000 Russians, lacked the means to deal with the situation because she had been disarmed by the Treaty of Versailles, and was receiving contradictory instructions from the Allied Powers.[140] Hence, she barred passage through the Canal to the S.S. Wimbledon, an English steamer chartered by a French company that was carrying munitions and artillery stores to the Polish naval base at Danzig.[141]

The majority of the Court—eight judges—held that the plain meaning of Article 380 required Germany not to bar passage because she was at peace with both Poland and the USSR. Two judges wrote a joint dissent, the Swiss international lawyer Max Huber and the Italian international lawyer Dionisio Anzilotti, both of whom figure in *Sovereignty*, particularly the latter.[142] The German-appointed, *ad hoc* judge and international lawyer Walter Schücking wrote a separate dissent.[143]

Huber and Anzilotti pointed out that a "purely grammatical" interpretation could not settle the issue.[144] In fact, the majority opinion implicitly recognized this claim as they went beyond their exercise of literal interpretation to say:

> The Court declines to see in the conclusion of any Treaty by which a State undertakes to perform or refrain from performing a particular act an abandonment of its sovereignty. No doubt any convention creating an obligation of this kind places a restriction upon the exercise of the sovereign rights of the State, in the sense that it requires them to be exercised in a certain way. But the right of entering into international engagements is an attribute of State sovereignty.[145]

The implication here is that Germany, in consenting to be bound by Article 380, gave up her sovereign right to assert her neutrality in a way that eviscerated one of her treaty obligations. But that line of reasoning is in tension with the one that followed immediately in which the majority reasoned from what they took to be the analogous jurisprudence on provisions in the treaties governing the Suez and Panama Canals that "the passage of a belligerent man-of-war does not compromise the neutrality of the sovereign state under whose jurisdiction the waters in question lie."[146] For if that were the main line of reasoning, neutrality would not be compromised and there would be no need for the majority to try to solve the paradox of sovereignty.

In my view, this second line of reasoning was forced on the majority by the reliance both by Schiffer[147] and by the joint dissent on the argument that these treaties showed that different explicit language in Article 380 was required if Germany was to be precluded from acting on her stance of neutrality. For Huber and Anzilotti

[140] Acts and Documents, 310–16. [141] Ibid., 310–16.

[142] For an account of Huber, see Koskenniemi, *The Gentle Civilizer of Nations*, 227–8. Heller was drawn to Anzilotti despite the latter's legal positivism because of Anzilotti's emphasis on state sovereignty as the foundation of international law. See Georg Nolte, "From Dionisio Anzilotti to Roberto Ago: The Classical International Law of State Responsibility and the Traditional Primacy of a Bilateral Conception of Inter-State Relations" (2002) 13 *European Journal of International Law* 1083.

[143] See Christian J. Tams, "Re-Introducing Walther Schücking" (2011) 22 *European Journal of International Law* 725.

[144] *S.S. Wimbledon*, 36. [145] Ibid., 25. [146] Ibid., 27.

[147] Acts and Documents, 344–50.

reasoned that the question posed by the case was whether the clauses of the Treaty relating to the Kiel Canal applied even when Germany had adopted a stance of neutrality or whether they "only contemplate normal circumstances, that is to say, a state of peace, without affecting the rights and duties of neutrality."[148] Since the latter was, in their view, the correct interpretation, they were thus invoking the *rebus sic stantibus* proviso of international law jurisprudence; a topic that we saw in the previous section exercises Heller in *Sovereignty*.

But as with the majority, this invocation depended on a particular conception of sovereignty, which they expressed in the following way: "The right of a State to adopt the course which it considers best suited to the exigencies of its security and to the maintenance of its integrity, is so essential a right that, in case of doubt, treaty stipulations cannot be interpreted as limiting it."[149] The Treaty would, they emphasized, have had explicitly to stipulate that the Canal was to remain open in a time of war between third parties if it were to have the effect of precluding Germany from barring passage.

In adopting this line of reasoning, the two dissenting judges were not, then, differing all that much from the majority since they accepted that, if Article 380 had been worded differently, Germany would have been bound to allow passage. Indeed, the passage just quoted nicely shows that international law's framing of sovereignty is in turn framed by sovereignty, such that the two are intertwined, which is exactly the aim of Heller's argument. Since the German judge used a technical argument about the nature of public servitudes to justify his conclusion that Germany could bar passage, ten of the eleven judges must be taken to have agreed that "the right of entering into international engagements is an attribute of State sovereignty" with the result that "a restriction upon the exercise of the sovereign rights of the State" is placed "in the sense that it requires them to be exercised in a certain way."

Hence, no judge accepted the argument put by Schiffer, at least as portrayed by Basdevant, as based on "the idea that [Germany] ... was in possession of full sovereignty, and that, by virtue of this sovereignty, she was right in limiting the obligations resulting to her from the Treaty of Versailles";[150] Schiffer, we should note, did argue, in what Klabbers calls an "ominous formulation,"[151] that "neutrality is one of the essential attributes of sovereignty" and thus in the nature of a "personal, imprescriptible and inalienable right."[152] However, it is unclear whether Basdevant's or Klabber's characterizations are entirely fair, given that Schiffer also claimed that he was not relying on the argument that Germany could invoke a defense of necessity.[153] Moreover, in Schiffer's closing remarks to the Court he claimed that his main argument did not depend on such a conception of sovereignty,[154] and in his opening statement he said that he had been ordered by his government "to assure the Court that Germany regards it with the most profound respect" and that Germany would "rejoice ... if the Court ... will more and more enlarge its activities for the purpose of solving all international conflicts."[155]

[148] *S.S. Wimbledon*, 36. [149] Ibid., 37. [150] Acts and Documents, 386.
[151] Klabbers, "Clinching the Concept of Sovereignty: Wimbledon Redux," 346.
[152] Acts and Documents, 342. [153] Ibid., 314. [154] Ibid., 303–4.
[155] Ibid., 309.

This opening statement does not read like an insincere abasement before the judges to prepare the way for an argument that in effect Germany could do as it pleased. Rather, it expresses the desire of Germany to be considered an equal member in the international law family of "civilized nations"—to quote from Article 38 of the Court's statute—to be part, that is, of a jural community. Similarly, the fact that the *ad hoc* German judge, as expected in international law matters, decided in favor of Germany, but was outvoted by the majority, does not show that the judicial reasoning was a charade, with judges seeking to get to the result that would reflect the balance of power as they wished it to be. Schücking was not only a dedicated international lawyer, but also one of the most fervent pacifists and legalists of his day. And that of the judges he delivered the most technical legal opinion evinces his undoubted commitment to resolving international disputes by peaceful legal means.[156]

I emphasize these points because they help to understand not only why Klabber's characterization of Germany's argument is controversial, but also why this gives us reason to doubt his conclusion that the upshot of *Wimbledon* and of the *Lotus* decision that followed it is a conception of sovereignty at home in a "positivist system [of international law] in that rules are created by the consent of the states themselves, and do not flow from elsewhere." For if these cases deliver a conception of sovereignty at home in an international law system in which the sole basis of legal rules is a positivistic doctrine of state consent, they reproduce the paradox of sovereignty by resurrecting the line of argument that runs from Laband to Jellinek, one which is supposed to somehow make coherent the ideas of the legally unlimited sovereign and the fact of international law, but cannot provide the juridical resources to do so.

As Lauterpacht pointed out in *The Function of Law in the International Community*, and we have seen that he thought the same was true of Heller, theories in which international law plays a mere coordinating function deny international law any authority because it can play that function only so long as a state deems it in its interests to coordinate in this fashion.[157] That this is the case is borne out by the fact that Klabbers does not in fact indicate a conception of sovereignty that was, as he suggests, "clinched" by the Court's decision. Rather, as he puts it, the Court reckoned with the "sovereignty dilemma" by rejecting the "standard textbook reconciliation" international law with state sovereignty through *rebus sic stantibus*, while embracing a pragmatic solution. It did so by concluding that in practice a sovereign may be found to have limited its sovereignty even if, at the level of abstract theory, this cannot be explained.[158] But this solution is of the pragmatic sort that leaves the one who decides with having to choose between the incommensurable options of legal authority and power, which leads to an oscillation between law and power that must ultimately be resolved by power.

[156] See Tams, "Re-Introducing Walther Schücking" and Koskenniemi, *The Gentle Civilizer of Nations*, 215–22.
[157] Lauterpacht, *The Function of Law in the International Community*, 415–28.
[158] Klabbers, "Clinching the Concept of Sovereignty: Wimbledon Redux," 362–4.

Moreover, in a short monograph of 1934, *The Development of International Law by the Permanent Court of International Justice*, Lauterpacht argued that in decisions such as *Wimbledon* and *Lotus*, one could conceive of the work of the Court "to a large extent . . . in terms of a restrictive interpretation of State sovereignty."[159] This claim may seem at odds with the lines we saw Klabbers quote from the *Lotus* decision. But Lauterpacht, in commenting on the same quotation, said that the "rigid positivist doctrine" that the Permanent Court seemed to be stating would be dismissed by "[m]any an international lawyer" as "obsolete and contrary to the very terms of Article 38 of the Statute."[160] He continued that the Court in fact "qualified considerably the principle that rules of international law emanate from the free will of States" in that it referred to that free will as expressed not only by conventions, but also by "usages generally accepted," and general acceptance, he pointed out, is acceptance "by the generality of States, not by every single State."[161]

Lauterpacht's argument is premised both on his view of the Court and his conception of law. He said of the Court that

> [for the] first time in modern history there has functioned an international institution of unprecedented authority able and competent to probe the legal value of some of the traditional pretensions. In the atmosphere of diplomatic negotiations and conferences these claims are high-sounding, uncompromising, clad in the garb of the dignity of States . . . An assertion by one sovereign State, provided that it is advanced in the plausible form of a legal phrase, is as good as that of another.

Prior to its establishment, he pointed out, "there was no agency to disprove them and to show by clear and final decisions that they were one-sided, arbitrary, and contrary to law."[162] The "critical attitude of the Court towards claims of State sovereignty" was not, he continued, "a case of judicial idealism in which the judges allow their sentiments to remain victorious at the expense of the law":

> The simple explanation of this striking phenomenon is that once a State has accepted the jurisdiction of the Court in a given case, the metaphysical majesty of sovereignty has largely

[159] Hersch Lauterpacht, *The Development of International Law by the Permanent Court of Justice* (London: Longmans, 1934), 89.

[160] Ibid., 102–3. Article 38:

> The Court shall apply:
> 1. International conventions, whether general or particular, establishing rules expressly recognized by the contesting States;
> 2. International custom, as evidence of a general practice accepted as law;
> 3. The general principles of law recognized by civilized nations;
> 4. Subject to the provisions of Article 59, judicial decisions and the teachings of the most highly qualified publicists of the various nations, as subsidiary means for the determination of rules of law. This provision shall not prejudice the power of the Court to decide a case *ex aequo et bono*, if the parties agree thereto.

[161] Lauterpacht, *The Development of International Law by the Permanent Court of Justice*, 103. In addition, Lauterpacht argued, ibid., that the principle that the Court articulated that "[r]estrictions upon the independence of States cannot . . . be presumed" does not amount to much since all it means is that if the Court, in using all the interpretative resources Article 38 enjoins it to use, cannot find a "reason for limiting a State's freedom of action, it will not presume such a limitation."

[162] Ibid., 104–5.

departed from it; it has become a plain party governed by the Statute and the rules of the court; a party who may put forward any pleas and arguments to which he attaches importance, but who can derive no hope from the mere fact that the argument has been advanced by a sovereign State. . . . Such submission means subjection to law with all its generality, comprehensiveness, and impatience of inconsistencies and evasion.[163]

These quotations may seem proof of the claim we saw Koskenniemi make at the beginning that Lauterpacht believed that "international lawyers, in particular international judges, should rule the world."[164] But Lauterpacht, here as elsewhere, is better understood not as holding this naïve view, but as trying to work out the implications of the experiment in creating a new international legal order that the League and the Permanent Court represented. He knew perfectly well that this was, as Koskenniemi says, a "political project" in competition with others, each imposing its own set of advantages and disadvantages on participants.[165]

Indeed, Lauterpacht began his book on the Permanent Court by pointing out that the Court had failed to achieve the end of being a "bulwark of peace" because it, "as indeed any other" court, is "dependent upon the state of political integration of the society whose law it administers."[166] And he recognized that international relations had unfolded in ways that failed to achieve the kind of integration desired by the founders of the League. However, the Court had, he said, been very successful in another respect. It "had consciously, and with few exceptions, consistently fulfilled its secondary function, namely, the developing of international law."[167] And in the closing lines of his work published the year before—*The Function of Law in the International Community*—he said that peace "is pre-eminently a legal postulate. Juridically it is a metaphor for the postulate of the unity of the legal system. Juridical logic inevitably leads to condemnation, as a matter of law, of anarchy and private force."[168] He thus bemoaned the fact that "modern international law" had "neglected to find a legal foundation for the so-called pacifism which it has relegated to the domain of morals and sociology" and thus the search for "higher legal principle." That search, he suggested in the very last line, can be "performed by means of the legitimate methods of juridical criticism and analysis."[169]

In making the distinction between the Court's failure in one respect because of the lack of political integration on which its primary function depended and its success in its secondary function of developing international law, Lauterpacht brought his theory very close to Heller's despite his rejection of what he took to be Heller's "intolerant denial of international law." Moreover, as one can see from Heller's critique of Kelsen in *Sovereignty*, Heller thought it just as important to explain the

[163] Ibid., 105.
[164] Koskenniemi, "Introduction" to Lauterpacht, *The Function of Law in the International Community*, xlvii.
[165] Ibid. See for example, Lauterpacht's paper "Sovereignty and Federation in International Law," which he did not publish, but which is dated around 1940, in Hersch Lauterpacht, *International Law, Collected Papers*, E. Lauterpacht, ed. (Cambridge: Cambridge University Press, 2009), volume 3, 5.
[166] Lauterpacht, *The Development of International Law by the Permanent Court of Justice*, 1.
[167] Ibid., 2.
[168] Lauterpacht, *The Function of Law in the International Community*, 446.
[169] Ibid.

assumption of the unity of legal order in terms of peace and as matter of "higher legal principle."

Both follow Kelsen in adopting the legal idea of sovereignty. But Heller, like Kelsen, wishes to set that idea within a general legal theory, while Lauterpacht is content to proceed from the assumption that the idea is sound and to devote his more theoretical work to demonstrating that it is not only consistent with international law, but also helps both to explain it and to advance the legalist project within it. Put differently, he supposes that the idea can be generated doctrinally, by elaborating a theory of international law practice and of judicial interpretation within that practice, in much the same way that Ronald Dworkin defended an "interpretive" theory of law with judges at its center in the second half of the century.[170] As I will now explain, Heller, in contrast to Lauterpacht, starts with a theory of the legal state and with that theory in place seeks to show how the state relates to international law.

## Fundamental Principles of Law

In *Sovereignty*, Heller places great emphasis on Section 3 of Article 38 of the Court's statute, which required it to decide in accordance with "the general principles of law recognized by civilized nations." He takes this Section to recognize the distinction he makes earlier in *Sovereignty* between "fundamental principles" of legal order and positive legal rules, and takes the job of the judges of the Court to be to concretize these fundamental principles into positive legal rules. This he describes as a creative act of legislation, but one which takes place within the "scope" of the fundamental principles, and which he thinks is qualitatively different from the equitable discretion that judges had in terms of Section 4.

In fact, there are only three points where Heller differs from Lauterpacht. First, Heller thinks that *non liquet*, or a judicial declaration that there is no law applicable to a dispute with the result that the judge has no jurisdiction, exists as an option in international law, though both think it does not exist in domestic law. Lauterpacht, in contrast, claimed in a lecture in 1937 that Article 38(3) was a "death blow" to legal positivism because it

> denies the fundamental tenet of positivism that custom and treaty are the only sources upon which the judge is entitled to draw [and] . . . in particular, the doctrine that there exist gaps in international law and that as a result international tribunals are at liberty, nay, are under an obligation, to pronounce a *non liquet* when the point at issue is not covered by either custom or treaty.

The Article, by "throwing open to the judge the unbounded field of the legal experience of mankind, in substance removes altogether the possibility of the absence of an applicable rule of law."[171]

[170] See Koskenniemi, *From Apology to Utopia*, 53–6, who attempts to debunk both.

[171] Hersch Lauterpacht, "Les principes généraux de droit comme source du droit des gens" (1937) IV *Recueil Des Cours* 97, 164. I will refer to the translated version, "The Place of International Law in Jurisprudence" in Lauterpacht, *Collected Papers*, volume 1, 93, 242–3.

This difference is more empirical than theoretical because it reflects for the most part Heller's lack of confidence that there existed as much of what Lauterpacht called "The Law behind the Cases,"[172] that is, the interpretative resources to decide any legal dispute that could conceivably come before the Court. He suggests that even if there was an international court in existence that was the equivalent of the Roman highest magistracy or *praetor*, there was simply not enough law in existence to make it possible for that Court to avoid a *non liquet* in all cases.[173]

Second, Heller wishes to source "general principles of law recognized by civilized nations" in state will because such general principles exist only through recognition, whereas Lauterpacht regarded Article 38 as "purely declaratory" because these principles had been recognized in arbitral practice and agreements prior to the statute and, moreover, such principles express "that social and legal necessity without which law, international and other, is inconceivable."[174]

This second difference is also not significant at the level of theory. Lauterpacht said that his claim about general principles did not do away with the role of the will of sovereign states and that Article 38 required the Court to take such will into account by making the first mandatory source of law—"International conventions, whether general or particular, establishing rules expressly recognized by the contesting States."[175] He did qualify this claim by saying that it is important that such will is always to be interpreted against a backdrop of principles of customary international law, recognized as a source of law in Article 38(2) as well as the general principles of law recognized by civilized nations.[176] But since Heller constantly affirms that state

[172] Lauterpacht, *The Development of International Law by the Permanent Court of Justice*, chapter 1.

[173] See below 148. The difference must also in part reflect Heller's civil law temperament. Lauterpacht, like both Kelsen and Heller, was a Jew whose early formation was in the Austro-Hungarian Empire, and had in fact been Kelsen's student in Vienna in the 1920s. But he moved to London in 1925 where he had quickly immersed himself in and embraced the common law tradition with its confidence that judges can find within the law legal solutions to all problems that might come before a court. See the biography by his son, also an eminent international lawyer, Sir Elihu Lauterpacht, *The Life of Hersch Lauterpacht* (Cambridge: Cambridge University Press, 2012). There is a recent resurgence of interest in Lauterpacht, as is demonstrated by the accounts of his influence in the last century in Koskenniemi, *The Gentle Civilizer of Nations*, chapter 5, Philippe Sands, *East West Street: On the Origins of Genocide and Crimes Against Humanity* (London: Weidenfeld & Nicolson, 2016); James Loeffler, *Rooted Cosmopolitans: Jews and Human Rights in the Twentieth Century* (New Haven: Yale University Press, 2018); and he emerges as the hero of Hathaway and Shapiro, *The Internationalists: How a Radical Plan to Outlaw War Remade the World*. For a polemical critique of Lauterpacht's claim that there is a "law behind the cases" see Schmitt, *The Turn to a Discriminating Concept of War* (1937) in Carl Schmitt, *Writings on War* (Cambridge: Polity Press, 2011) Timothy Nunan, ed. and intro., 48–53. Schmitt's argument is the precursor for the kind of critical theory of international law that emerged in the late twentieth century, as is E.H. Carr's classic *The Twenty Years Crisis* (1939) (Houndsmills: Palgrave, 2001). In chapter 2, at 38–9. Carr attempted to shred the project of Lauterpacht and other legalists—the "utopia of international theorists"—on the basis that it had no impact on reality. For an uncharacteristically polemical yet powerful response to this intemperate "realist" attack, see Lauterpacht, "Professor Carr on International Morality" in Lauterpacht, *Collected Works*, volume 2, 67. (Lauterpacht did not publish this paper. The editor, his son, suggests that it was written in 1941.) This response is worth reading today as if it were one to critical international law theory .

[174] Lauterpacht, "The Place of International Law in Jurisprudence," 242.

[175] Ibid., 243–4. [176] Ibid.

will is to be determined in a process of juristic construction, he and Lauterpacht are pretty much in agreement.

Third, Heller and Lauterpacht take opposite sides in the persistent debate in international law about how a state-like entity acquires international legal personality. The "declaratory theory" argues that recognition of an entity as a state merely confirms its legal status, while the "constitutive theory" argues that an entity that aspires to legal statehood requires the recognition of other states. The debate replays that over sovereignty in general. Legalists like Lauterpacht and Kelsen tend to argue that the legal idea of sovereignty requires the constitutive theory. In contrast, those who assert the primacy of a political conception of sovereignty will usually adopt the declaratory theory, and consequently the view that the decision by states to recognize an entity as a state is a political act. In *Sovereignty*, Heller proclaims his allegiance to the declaratory theory and in fact regards it as the "most important rationale and proof" of his conception of sovereignty.[177]

This difference is theoretical. But I will now show that the theoretical difference is more apparent than real despite the fact that the consensus today in international law is that the declaratory theory has prevailed. For the debate persists at least in that the elements that supported the constitutive side can no more be eliminated than the deciding dimension of sovereignty. In turn, that will explain why Heller's theory is not only less hostile to international law than Lauterpacht supposed, but also supplies an account of "the higher legal principle" which Lauterpacht thought international legal theory badly needed.

Heller's argument is that before a unit of "territorial decision-making power" comes into existence, there can be neither state law nor international law for it. Indeed, international law cannot come into existence before there are at least two such states capable of being regulated by it. However, he also says that no jurist can afford to ignore that the "concept of the capacity to act is insufficient" for the establishment of a state as the concept of sovereignty is required. He distinguishes between the recognition of a "fact situation as a state" and recognition of the same fact situation as an "international law person." In the former case, recognition is not constitutive, whereas in the latter it is not simply declarative. Put differently, the capacity of an entity to be the final legal authority within a territory is sufficient to establish that entity as a sovereign state, which does not mean that it has international law qualifications since these require both recognition by other states and a willingness by the state in question so to be recognized. It is this distinction that permits Heller to respond to the fact that there are sovereign states whose laws will be recognized by other states as having effects for other states, at the same time as these states are not recognized as capable of effects that are "normative in international law."[178]

[177] See below 163.

[178] See below 164-5. This distinction permits one to understand why marriages or contracts concluded in Taiwan will be recognized as valid by the courts of other countries while Taiwan since 1971 has not been recognized as having international law personality. See Oda Shigura, "Taiwan as Sovereign and Independent State - Status of Taiwan under International Law" (2011) 54 *Japanese Year Book of International Law* 386. (Shigura argues that this lack of recognition is most anomalous.)

In sum, what we can call internal sovereignty is a necessary condition for a state to acquire international law personality. But international law personality is not necessary for a state to be considered sovereign in this sense. This does leave Heller's theory unable to account for the example of states that are considered to have international legal personality, even though as a matter of fact they have ceased to exist. For example, when the USSR occupied and annexed the Baltic States of Lithuania, Latvia, and Estonia, the international community refused to recognize their annexation and considered their governments in exile to be the true representatives. Their statehood was considered to have been merely interrupted in 1940 and resumed properly with the dissolution of the USSR in 1991.

Heller would not regard this kind of example as a refutation of his theory. While he does not deal specifically with it in his discussion of the constitutive and declaratory theories, he cautions against letting exceptions drive one's theory, because one might end up constructing the international law person and hence "the anatomy of international law" "on the basis of a pathological object." As he says, "all juristic concepts are clear only at their center, but have an 'aureole' at the margins. Sovereignty forms the center of the concept of the international law person. To give it up because this concept, too, has an aureole would ... render the concept of the international law person completely incomprehensible."[179]

But there is also a substantive reason for Heller to regard this kind of international law personality as at best in the aureole, not the center, of the concept of sovereignty. The only candidate for bearer of sovereignty in the case of the Baltic states between 1940 and 1991 was a government in exile and to regard these governments in exile as sovereign would be to make the same mistake as Heller thought Schmitt made in claiming that the Reich President was in Weimar the true bearer of sovereign authority. It would, that is, confuse state sovereignty with organ sovereignty—the authority of one institution within the state apparatus with the apparatus as a whole.

Notice that the source of the confusion is the same. It stems from regarding the organ as the authentic voice of "the people," as representing "we, the people." Heller's objection to this claim is at once juridical and political. It is juridical because he follows Hobbes's precise "juristic" formulation in arguing that to say that "a people" "wills" something is to say that the state wills it, that is, the collection of institutions that make up the legal state. In expressing this will, the state performs the act of representation that follows from the assumption that each legal subject had agreed with every other legal subject that "on matters essential to the common peace," the unitary expression of state will must be accepted as the will "of all and each." Just in this formulation, Heller suggests, there is a democratic quality, even though to have democracy properly so called, there must be not only a people but also majority voting.[180]

It is political because it opposes the conception of the political advanced by Schmitt that seeks to reduce the essence of politics to an existential, extra-legal decision. It does so by elaborating a theory in which politics involves the renunciation of

[179] See below 167. [180] See below 107.

anarchic violence and a commitment to working out conflicts within the framework of the law. It is with the establishment of such a framework that sovereignty in the primary legal sense is achieved—that a legal state comes into existence. That such a state may not achieve recognition as an international legal person does not detract from its sovereignty in this sense.

In sum, Heller seeks to show explicitly, even as he chooses the side of the declaratory theory in the debate, why any realistic theory must account for both the declaratory and the constitutive aspects of the problem.[181] And while Lauterpacht took the constitutive side because he wished to emphasize that recognition is a juridical matter, that is, not merely political, he too acknowledged that "while recognition is constitutive in one sphere, it is declaratory in the other. It is declaratory in the meaning that its object is to ascertain the existence of the requirements of statehood and the consequent right of the new State to be treated henceforth as a normal subject of international law."[182] Moreover, while he regarded as a "grotesque spectacle" the prospect of a "community being a State in relation to some but not to other States" and said this prospect was a "grave reflection upon international law," he also fully conceded that this international law problem resulted from the lack of "political integration of international society."[183] Because, as we have already seen, he knew that precisely this lack made impracticable an international tribunal with compulsory jurisdiction, he had to resort to the vague idea that the constitutive theory was tempered by a duty on all states to the international community at large to grant recognition.[184]

That those who start off on one side of this debate seem to end up with a theory that imports the other side is often thought to lead to the conclusion sketched earlier: we should eschew theory and embrace a kind of pragmatism that regards practice as the only site where this issue, or for that matter the issue of the paradox of sovereignty that it reflects, can be resolved.[185] For it remains the case that whether or not an entity can exercise its statehood depends on its recognition by other states, and that it remains open to each state to decide whether or not to treat an entity as a state in their relations with it. Furthermore, recognition patterns are treated as playing an evidentiary role, which introduces an element of circularity. As a result, there are many examples of inconsistent practice that illustrate (a) the political dimensions of recognition (both when states decide, for political reasons, decide

[181] See James Crawford, *The Creation of States in International Law* (Oxford: Clarendon Press, 2006), chapter 1.

[182] Hersch Lauterpacht, *Recognition in International Law* (Cambridge: Cambridge University Press, 1947), 75.

[183] Ibid., 78. The section is entitled "The Problem of Recognition and the Political Integration of International Society," at 77.

[184] Ibid., 74–5.

[185] Crawford, *The Creation of States in International Law*, 19–28, Koskenniemi, *From Apology to Utopia*, chapter 4, Kalmo, "A Matter of Fact?" in Kalmo and Skinner, eds, *Sovereignty in Fragments*, 114. As these three note, Kelsen switched sides completely, from the declaratory to the constitutive. Kalmo argues that H.L.A. Hart's conception of sovereignty is helpful here but does not note that that conception issues in the Schmittean conclusion that, in difficult cases, "all that succeeds is success." See Hart, *The Concept of Law* (Oxford: Clarendon Press, 1994, second edition), 153.

to withhold recognition of entities that meet the criteria—e.g. Taiwan—or to recognize entities that do *not* meet the criteria—e.g. Kosovo) and (b) the frequently invoked rationale for the declaratory theory, that is, that recognition is a political decision for each state to make, and that the declaratory theory allows for that by liberating the existence of the entity in question from the recognition by others.[186] As I will now show, Heller's pragmatism makes room for a kind of pragmatic decision-making that responds to such circularity without reducing the content of law to whatever happens to have been decided.

His theory accomplishes this task in that it poses the question whether states should withhold recognition of international law personality when the entity that desires it has failed to establish itself as a *Rechtsstaat*, in the same way that states, in exercising their discretion whether or not to recognize another state, may take into account the latter's democratic nature, as well as its commitment to human rights.[187] Now this theory appears only in embryonic form in *Sovereignty* and Heller never fully elaborated it, as he died in 1933 while still working on his *Staatslehre* or "theory of state."

The main elements of the theory emerge in *Sovereignty* mainly through Heller's account in his first two chapters of Bodin. Above all, Heller emphasizes the legal nature of Bodin's conception of sovereignty. Sovereignty is legislative power—the power to make binding, final decisions about law for all those within a territory.[188] He also emphasizes that while for Bodin the sovereign is legally unlimited, this is only in the sense that he is free from positive law—*legibus solutus*. No sovereign is, however, legally unlimited in another sense, for all are subject "to the laws of God, of nature, and of nations."[189] The job of sovereignty is to make decisions that will give concrete expression to these laws informed by the social, political, and economic context in which the state institutions operate. It is such laws that Heller calls, in a phrase he regards as appropriate in a secular age, "fundamental legal principles."

[186] This confusion has led to an interesting situation in a Canadian case—*Parent v Singapore Airlines Limited and the Civil Aeronautics Association* (2003) 133 *International Law Reports* 264 (Quebec Superior Court)—in which the Court concluded that Taiwan met the traditional criteria for recognizing statehood at international law and so, under international law, was a state. As a result, Taiwan was entitled to state immunity despite the fact that the Canadian government continues to adhere to the "one China policy" and has not recognized Taiwan. For discussion, see Campbell McLachlan, *Foreign Relations Law* (Cambridge: Cambridge University Press, 2014), chapter 10, at 401–2. In my view, Heller would not have regarded Taiwan as sovereign in any sense if it is correct, as I have been told by Taiwanese constitutional scholars, that if Taiwan were to put in place a constituent assembly to draft a new constitution, China would immediately invade. As a result, Taiwan is stuck with the 1947 Constitution that the retreating nationalist forces brought with them.

[187] For an argument that this should be the case, see Criddle and Fox-Decent, *Fiduciaries of Humanity*, 63–76, where they set out an "earned-sovereignty paradigm."

[188] For a contemporary account of these features of Bodin's thought, see Daniel Lee, "Unmaking Law: Jean Bodin on Law, Equity, and Legal Change" (2018) 39 *History of Political Thought* 269. Compare Martin Loughlin, "Why Sovereignty?" in Rawlings, Leyland, and Young, *Sovereignty and the Law*, 34, who offers a Bodinian account of sovereignty that is remarkably similar to Heller's, except for the fact that he claims that "there can be no fetter on the law-making authority of the State, whether deriving from divine law or natural law"; ibid.

[189] See below 63.

The idea of sovereign subjection to law has, Heller says, been preserved in the secular era. But, he argues, in its dominant form, as exemplified in Kelsen's Pure Theory, this is done through eliminating the fundamental principles involved in the second sense of subjection and substituting for them the first sense, that is, positive law. In making the sovereign subject to positive law alone, he argues, more than the fundamental principles are eliminated. For a sovereign who is utterly subject to positive law becomes identical with positive law. In other words, sovereignty itself is eliminated and in this way the dream is achieved of the *Rechtsstaat*—of the elimination of arbitrariness from political life through putting in place the impersonal rule of law.

That achievement is at most theoretical. In practice, the moment cannot be eliminated when some person or institution must make a concrete, final decision, so sovereignty will constantly assert itself. Indeed, Heller details many instances where Kelsen and others who would eliminate sovereignty recognize the futility of this task; and, as I have already mentioned, he takes Schmitt's signal but only service to legal theory to be his argument that the deciding sovereign must be brought back into the center of legal theory. It is Schmitt's only service, because for the sovereign properly to re-enter legal theory, he must come accompanied by the fundamental legal principles that it is his job to concretize and that make sense of the idea that sovereign power is ultimate legal power.

In *Sovereignty*, Heller does not provide much detail about such principles. He asserts a distinction between ethical and logical fundamental principles and in his discussion of international law puts both the principle of equality of states and the principle that states must keep their agreements—*pacta sunt servanda*—on the logical side of the distinction. He also argues that the ethical principles take their color from the context in which they are concretized.[190] In his *Staatslehre* and in other later work he is more forthcoming, with the major change being that the principle of equality is said to be both an ethical and a logical fundamental principle. In the paragraphs that follow I will supplement the account in *Sovereignty* of Heller's theory of state with material from these later works.[191]

In *Sovereignty*, and again in *Theory of State*, Heller regards as crucially important to legal order the juristic assumption that a legal order is autonomous, that is, a closed or gap-free system of norms. It is this assumption that makes it possible for law to be studied dogmatically, as a discrete phenomenon with its own peculiar structure rather than as, say, the mere effects of social and other forces. What makes the assumption crucially important is that it is constitutive of legal order. It makes it possible to order a society along legal lines; in particular it makes possible constitutional legal order, an order that binds the powerful to the rule of law. In these respects, Heller's position is very close to Kelsen's, but note also to Lauterpacht's when we recall his claim that "juridically" peace "is a metaphor for the postulate of the unity

[190] See below 150.

[191] These paragraphs are adapted from Dyzenhaus *Legality and Legitimacy*, chapter 4. The extracts from Heller's *Staatslehre* on which the paragraphs are based are to be found in Hermann Heller, "The Nature and Structure of the State," 1139.

of the legal system." All three saw law as a gap-free and contradiction-free system of norms and gave priority in the legal order to a basic or constitutional norm.

On the one hand, Heller points out that legal order brings immense advantages to the powerful because of the certainty imparted by a framework of legal rules applied and enforced by state institutions. It permits the powerful to transform a fairly tenuous hold on power in a very fluid situation into a firm hold in a relatively stable situation. This aspect of the *Rechtsstaat* Heller calls the law-formative character of power: legal order secures and even increases the resources of the powerful. On the other hand, he always emphasizes that increased and more stable power comes at a price: the powerful perforce find themselves constrained by the legal order. This aspect of the *Rechtsstaat* Heller calls the power-formative aspect of law. What connects these two aspects, establishing a dialectical relationship between law and power, is ethics; more precisely the ethical fundamental principles of law. The function of the juristic assumption is to serve legal order conceived as a dialectical unity of law, power, and ethics. In this way, Heller seeks to bring together in one juridical framework both sides of Jellinek's two-sided theory of the state.[192]

The assumption does this service by enabling an interpretation of the law, in particular of the law of the constitution, which strips the law of its quality of temporality in order to help ensure its historical continuity. The law is necessarily temporal, in a state of flux because it is but part of an ever-changing, overarching political and social order. The role of law in that overarching order is to give the order some relative stability and that requires the jurist to ignore the flux for the purposes of stability-enhancing interpretation.

Heller thus rejects Kelsen's view that the demand that law should be seen as gapless is a logical, *a priori* one set by a scientific understanding of law. The result of this view is that law is thought of as a logical system of norms. For Heller, by contrast, law as it exists is always full of gaps. The juristic assumption that law is an autonomous system is not made for the sake of science or logic but as a moral duty of the jurist. The jurist must interpret the law as if it were free of gaps to facilitate the endeavor of the *Rechtsstaat* in achieving an aim that in reality can never be achieved. That aim is of ensuring that the whole of the state organization will function in compliance with norms. Now, this duty would not amount to much if the only legal norms that counted were the norms of positive law. But, as we have seen, for Heller law includes the fundamental principles of law, especially those he terms ethical.

His view in his *Staatslehre* seems to be that the logical principles are essential to the form of law, while the ethical principles give law both its value and its substance. The logical are, he says already in *Sovereignty*, the "constitutive principles of the form of pure law."[193] They are universal conditions of legal knowledge, in that they will play a role wherever there is law, in the same way as grammar is to be found wherever there is speech. For example, the principle of equality before the law, whether of states in the international order, or of individuals in the state order, is in one sense a logical fundamental principle of law, since in order for there to be law to govern both

[192] See, for example, Heller, *Staatslehre*, 179–81.

[193] See below 88.

you and me, we have to accord each other formal reciprocal recognition as bearers of rights and duties. But to give content to the idea of equality one has to positivize an understanding of substantive ethical fundamental principles of law.

Thus, while logical fundamental principles are formal, in the sense that all law, to be law, must observe the requirement of legality, it is the ethical fundamental principles that the positive law must seek to express. The substantive *Rechtsstaat*, the substance of the rule of law, is derived from these ethical fundamental principles, by contrast with the formal *Rechtsstaat*, which will be in place wherever there is the form of law. In his view, it is their very lack of determinate content that permits ethical fundamental principles of law to stabilize a constitution. The ethical aims of legal order are then expressed in the ethical fundamental principles of law. They are supra-positive in the sense of being beyond positive law. But they are not supra-cultural: they are principles that formulate the values embedded in our cultural practices, which the *Rechtsstaat* institutionalizes.

In Heller's vision, the ethical fundamental principles of law are presupposed by positive law in a dynamic way, which makes the principles accessible to reason. The principles are given content in the positive law by the process of democratic reason and reason is the criterion by which that content is elaborated and evaluated. Moments of authoritative interpretation are necessary debate stoppers where an exercise of political power is what ends the debate. But each interpretation is authoritative only within the institutional structure of the *Rechtsstaat*.

What then are these principles? On Heller's view, this question is wrongly posed if it is meant to elicit a list of timeless ethical or moral principles. The principles cannot be determined in the way the question seems to require because their determination depends on the cultural practices of the inhabitants of a particular state. The principles are those values that the culture regards as constitutional values—as the legal foundation of social cooperation. As such, they make up the stock of values that is the "substantive constitution in the narrow sense." If there is a written constitution, it will, in so far as it is possible, try to formulate the values of the substantive constitution in one document—a "formal constitution." And this document may try to rank the values by putting some on a list of basic rights out of the reach of simple parliamentary majorities.[194]

For Heller, the distinction between the formal constitution and the substantive constitution is not a hard and fast one, just as he thinks that the general distinction between form and content in law is not hard and fast. But his thesis about form and content was quite different from Kelsen's view that law simply provides the form into which the powerful may pour any ideology they choose.

While Heller does not think that there is a list of timeless ethical or moral fundamental principles of law, he also does not think that just any ideology can be injected into the law of a democratic *Rechtsstaat*. His position seems altogether contemporary in that it aims to undermine the dichotomy between moral absolutism and an "anything goes" kind of relativism. While he did not live to present this aim in detail,

[194] Heller, "The Nature and Structure of the State," 1212–3.

he clearly saw the *Rechtsstaat* as the institutional expression of this position, particularly when its political institutions are democratic.

The *Rechtsstaat* is an organization or institutional structure which seeks to realize the polemical principle of democracy. It aims to make the exercise of political power accountable to the people by requiring justification of exercises of such power to them. Heller is clear that the organs of state might have to act in an emergency to uphold law, in the sense of ethical fundamental principles of law, in the face of positive law. We have also seen that he is clear that legal interpretation is to be guided by more than the value of certainty, where the interpretative assumption is the dogmatic one that the legal order is a gap-free and contradiction-free system of positive laws. It must be guided by the judicial and general juristic sense of the ethical fundamental principles of law that those norms must aspire to concretize. Even Kelsen, as Heller notes, sometimes concedes that the assumption of unity brings the Pure Theory of Law close to natural law. And he expresses much interest in the natural law direction in which Alfred Verdross—an international lawyer and prominent member of Kelsen's circle in Vienna—was pushing a Kelsenian theory of international law, though he did not think that Verdross had pushed far enough.

Verdross did in fact go further in the 1930s and is considered to be primarily responsible for developing the idea of *jus cogens*—that there are norms of international law that are peremptory neither because states have consented to be bound by them, nor simply because they have been established over time as customary.[195] Rather, they are binding because they must be considered fundamental to the international legal order, that is, they are the equivalent of Heller's fundamental principles of law.

It is significant that, in developing this idea, Verdross also came round to articulating a position very close to Heller's claim about the state's right of self-preservation, as he in this way brought to the surface the logic of the legal idea of sovereignty, in particular that recognition of the role of fundamental legal principles must be accompanied by recognition of the right of the legal subject to preserve itself, whether human individual or state. In an influential article of 1937, he argued that the ability

[195] On *jus cogens*, see Dinah Shelton, "Normative Hierarchy in International Law" (2006) 100 *American Journal of International Law* 291. On Verdross, see David Dyzenhaus, "A Monistic Approach to the Internationalization of Constitutional Law" in Iulia Motoc, Paulo Pinto de Albuquerque, and Krzysztof Wojtyczek, eds, *New Developments in Constitutional Law: Essays in Honour of Andràs Sajó* (The Hague: Eleven International Publishing, 2018) 97, which relies on the following sources: Bruno Simma, "The Contribution of Alfred Verdross to the Theory of International Law" (1995) 6 *European Journal of International Law* 33; Jochen von Bernstoff, *The Public International Law Theory of Hans Kelsen: Believing in Universal Law* (Cambridge: Cambridge University Press, 2010, Thomas Dunlap, trans.); Aoife O'Donoghue, "Alfred Verdross and the Contemporary Constitutionalization Debate" (2012) 32 *Oxford Journal of Legal Studies* 799; and Thomas Kleinlein, "Alfred Verdross as a Founding Father of International Constitutionalism?" (2012) 4 *Goettingen Journal of International Law* 385. I will not deal here with the vexed question of the relationship between general principles of international law, *jus cogens* norms, customary international law, obligations *erga omnes*, and so on. See Shelton, "Normative Hierarchy in International Law"; Wolfgang Friedmann, "The Uses of 'General Principles' in the Development of International Law" (1963) 57 *American Journal of Intentional Law* 279; Alfred Verdross, "*Jus Dispositivum* and *Jus Cogens* in International Law" (1966) 60 *American Journal of Intentional Law* 55; and M. Cherif Bassiouni, "A Functional Approach to 'General Principles of International Law'" (1990) 11 *Michigan Journal of International Law* 768.

to make a treaty presupposes the prior existence of formal legal norms that make it possible for two or more states to make a binding treaty. "That is the reason why the *possibility* of norms of general international law, norms determining the limits of the freedom of the parties to conclude treaties, cannot be denied *a priori*."[196]

In addition, there are two kinds of substantive norms. First, there are "different, single, compulsory norms of customary international law," for example, the norm that states not disturb each other in the use of the high seas, which has the effect that two states may not conclude a treaty that tended to violate the norm. Second, there is the "general principle prohibiting states from concluding treaties *contra bonos mores*":

> This prohibition, common to the juridical orders of all civilized states, is the consequence of the fact that every juridical order regulates the rational and moral coexistence of the members of a community. No juridical order can, therefore, admit treaties between juridical subjects, which are obviously in contradiction to the ethics of a certain community.[197]

Verdross also insisted that a compulsory norm "cannot be derogated either by customary or by treaty law . . . A treaty norm, violative of a compulsory general principle of law, is, therefore, void."[198] He recognized that this claim presents "difficulties" because the ethics of the international community are less developed than those of national communities and because it includes "different juridical systems, built upon different moral conceptions." But the "courts of civilized nations give an unequivocal answer": treaties may not "*restrict the liberty of one contracting party in an excessive or unworthy manner or which endanger its most important rights*."[199]

> In order to know what international treaties are immoral, we must ask what are the moral tasks states have to accomplish in the international community. In doing so, we must restrict ourselves to find those principles which correspond to the universal ethics of the international community. We must, so to speak, try to find the *ethical minimum* recognized by all the states of the international community, and must leave aside those particular tasks of the state represented only by particular régimes.[200]

These tasks amount to "maintenance of law and order within the states, defense against external attacks, care for the bodily and spiritual welfare of citizens at home, protection of citizens abroad."[201] It follows that a treaty would be void if, for example, it bound a state "to reduce its police or its organization of courts in such a way that it is no longer able to protect at all or in an adequate manner, the life, the liberty, the honor or the property of men on its territory."[202]

An implication of Verdross's position is that if a validly enacted norm of international law violates a fundamental legal principle, it loses its authority over the subjects over whom it claims authority because it undermines their status as free and equal members of a jural community. Fundamental legal principles thus set a

[196] Alfred Verdross, "Forbidden Treaties in International Law: Comments on Professor Garner's Report on the 'The Law of Treaties'" (1937) 31 *American Journal of Intentional Law* 571, at 572, his emphasis.

[197] Ibid. [198] Ibid., 573. [199] Ibid., 574, his emphasis.

[200] Ibid., his emphasis. [201] Ibid., emphasis removed. [202] Ibid.

limit to the positive law. With this condition in place, one can appreciate why the insistence on the right to self-preservation accompanies it, that is, a violation of the fundamental principles entails a subversion of legal personality.

It still is not, however, clear how that limit is to be set. Verdross, following Kelsen, acknowledged the possibility that in any domestic legal order norms might come to be enacted that violate norms of international law and yet there exists no procedure for invalidating the former. But they thought this was no more of a problem than the fact that, within such an order, norms might come to be enacted that violate norms of that order's constitutional law and yet there exists no procedure for invalidating the former.[203]

To say that it is no more of a problem is not to say that it is unproblematic; and both Kelsen and Verdross argued that legality requires that a procedure be institutionalized, in the domestic case through the establishment of a constitutional court, in the international case, by the establishment of a court of universal jurisdiction.[204] They also acknowledged that, in the absence of such an institution, the persistence of the violating norm might have the result that with time it replaced the norm it had violated. The difference between Kelsen and Verdoss, or at least Verdross as he moved closer to a natural law position, is that Verdross must be committed to holding that, when the norm violated is a fundamental legal principle, the tension between it and the violating norm cannot be eradicated even when there is no legal procedure available that can issue in a final decision on the matter.

What this goes to show, as suggested, is the complexity that results when one recognizes that sovereignty is both a matter of fundamental legal principles and of having institutions in place that can make an effective, binding decision. That complexity is exactly what Heller sought to elaborate in *Sovereignty*. He shared with Kelsen and Lauterpacht a commitment to elaborating the legal idea of sovereignty. But he differed from both in that he did not think that international society would ever achieve the stage of political integration that would permit the establishment of a court with effective, universal jurisdiction. If, against his prediction, that stage were to be reached, he makes it clear in *Sovereignty* that international law would be at an end, because there would exist a world state.

In addition, even if such a court were established, Heller did not have enough confidence, as we have seen, in the development of substantive international law to suppose that the legal resources sufficed for the court to avoid *non liquet*. But these qualifications on the thought of other legalists did not, in his view, commit him in any way to the denial of the authority of international law, as charged by Lauterpacht. Rather, he would have argued for the "relative normativity" of international law, to

[203] Alfred Verdross, *Die Einheit des rechtlichen Weltbildes auf Grundlage der Völkerrechtsverfassung* (JCB Mohr (Paul Siebeck): Tübingen, 1923), 159–69.

[204] See, for example, Alfred Verdross, "Reichsrecht und internationales Recht" (1919) 7/8 *Deutsche Juristenzeitung* 291. I refer to this paper as reproduced in Hans Klecatsky, René Marcic, Herbert Schambeck, eds., *Die Wiener rechtstheoretische Schule: Hans Kelsen, Adolf Merkl, Alfred Verdross* (Vienna: Europa Verlag, 1968), volume 2, 2059, at 2062.

adopt the title of a well-known article from the 1980s,[205] and would not have been surprised, I think, to discover that in place of such an international *praetor*, one finds the multiplicity of international tribunals that decide on discrete regimes of international law to which authors today draw our attention.

As I have also indicated, Heller differed from Kelsen and shared with Lauterpacht the quest to find the higher legal principles at the base of legal order, but differed from both in that he regarded the quest as part of a deeply political project. Rather than trying, as did Kelsen, to debunk Schmitt by showing the flaws in his reasoning from the perspective of a value free legal science, Heller opposed Schmitt by elaborating the politics of a commitment to legality. Heller had already argued in 1926 that a counterrevolution against the idea of rational legality would have to reach back beyond the absolutist period to seek a justification on the basis of a personalized deity. But this harkening back, he says, would be a revolution against both Bodin and Hobbes, since Hobbes, with others of his time, had replaced the idea of a personal god with the idea of human nature or reason. Such a reaction is against the Enlightenment and it can justify no stopping point for whatever forces it unleashes and whose driving vision it endows, whatever its content, with the romance of an aesthetics that is in awe of any absolute power.[206] And it is in this thought, says Heller in 1928, that one can find the true kernel of Schmitt's claim that the specific political distinction is the distinction between friend and enemy. Schmitt, in making the friend/enemy distinction the fundamental distinction of politics, sought to do away with the internal politics of a state.[207] Ultimately, though, as Heller argues in the last chapter of *Sovereignty*, it is not courts or other legal institutions that will save us, but the individual legal conscience, the topic of the following section.

## The Individual Legal Conscience

At the end of *Sovereignty*, Heller returns to the paradox of sovereignty in order to evaluate its implications for the individual legal subject, the citizen. He emphasizes that the modern condition is one in which we have to make decisions in a deeply uncertain, secularized world, where ethical certainty exists only in highly personal religious spheres. The only other source of certainty is that which law offers through providing a regular, predictable framework for common life. To have that certainty, we must subject ourselves to the state, to the sovereign organization that is both constituted by law and that makes law possible, because it is law that makes a common life possible. In subjecting ourselves, we should keep in mind that all the organization does is positivize ethical prescriptions. It cannot pronounce on them finally and so it is not the ultimate ethical authority and might even act in such a way that

[205] Prosper Weil, "Towards Relative Normativity in International Law" (1983) 77 *American Journal of International Law* 413.

[206] Hermann Heller, "Die politischen Ideenkreise der Gegenwart" in *Gesammelte Schriften*, volume, 1 267, at 287–9.

[207] Heller, "Political Democracy and Social Homogeneity," 258–60.

it violates the very ethical presuppositions of its own existence. This would also amount to a violation of legality, since such prescriptions are also legal.

In many respects, these sentiments resonate with those to be found in the work of other Weimar-era social democrats or left-liberals, often Jewish, who were committed to the success of Germany's first experiment in democratic constitutionalism. Most notably in the context of this discussion of sovereignty, the sentiments resonate with themes in Kelsen's work, in particular his account of the way in which a principle of legality plays a role in sustaining a commitment to democracy in an age in which citizens have to negotiate the "torment of heteronomy."[208] This is the tension that arises out of the fact that the individual who rightly knows that he is sovereign when it comes to judging the good has to find reasons to submit to the sovereign decisions of the collectivity, even when these decisions conflict with the individual's strongly held views about what is right.

The stance recommended by such thinkers asked the citizen to recognize both the primacy he should give to his own judgments and that in a secular era those judgments have to be viewed as relative to the individual, with the consequence that the collective understanding of the common good must trump the individual's. Such an ethical stance will lead both to a valuation of positive law, in particular to rule by the statutes enacted by a democratic parliament that are general in form and that apply for the most part prospectively, so that legal subjects may guide their conduct by the law.

However, what distinguishes Heller from Kelsen is that Heller provides an argument barred to Kelsen by the value-freedom of the Pure Theory, one that seeks to show that the positive legal form is substantively valuable. The point of the democratic institutional structure of the *Rechtsstaat* is to make it possible for the values of social and political order to be positivized in a way that makes the powerful accountable to the subjects of their laws. Morality, in the sense of the values that the collectivity can legitimately require we live by, is just the set of values that are concretized through the positive law.

The subjects of the law become its authors, first, through the fact that it is their representatives that enact legislation; hence the enhanced legal force of statutes. But their authorship does not end there since authorship continues through an appropriate process of concretization of the legislation. What makes that process appropriate is that the interpreters of the law must regard themselves as participating in a process of legislation which instantiates fundamental ethical principles of law. Most abstractly, these are the principles that promise both freedom and equality to all citizens. The ultimate check on delivery of such promises can be nothing other than the individual legal conscience—the individual citizen's sense of whether the law is living up to its promise. However, before that limit case is reached, the case in which the individual feels compelled to deny the state's claim to be an authority over

[208] See Hans Kelsen, Nadia Urbinati, and Carlo Invernizzi Accetti, eds., *The Essence and Value of Democracy* (Plymouth: Rowman and Littlfield, 2013, Brian Graf, trans.) [1929], 27. For discussion, see Lars Vinx, *Hans Kelsen's Pure Theory of Law: Legality and Legitimacy* (Oxford: Oxford University Press, 2007), chapter 4.

him, legal officials, including judges, have to understand that they are under a duty to concretize the law in ways that respects law's promise.

I mentioned at the beginning that Wolfgang Schluchter, writing in 1968, concluded a book on Heller by saying that contemporary political and social theory should not decline Heller's legacy. If one surveys contemporary philosophy of law and legal theory in the English-speaking world today, Schluchter's observations have, in my opinion, even greater force in these times. On the one hand, in philosophy of law, the dominance of legal positivism in many quarters means that we once again are faced with the "ghostly unreality of a theory of state without a state and a theory of law without law," as legal positivist philosophers deliberately construct a theory that has as little contact with legal practice and problems as possible. On the other hand, in legal theory that does attend to problems and practice, in particular in constitutional and international law theory, there is not only a turn to Schmittean accounts in an allegedly scientific, diagnostic mode,[209] or in a mode of giving ultimate value to an existentially conceived politics of authenticity,[210] or as a way of debunking international law by showing how it is an elaborate disguise for national self-interest,[211] but also a turn to Schmitt himself as the direct source of inspiration.

Recall Scelle's observation in 1934:

> The whole world is suffering from a kind of medieval anarchy made up of state tyrannies. The fiction of collective personality is reappearing in dogmas and in mystical doctrines with a virulence which is perhaps nothing but the death throes of political and legal structures in the process of transforming themselves to adapt to new needs.[212]

This description may well seem to apply to the world we live in, which would explain the "crisis in state theory" exemplified in the return of Schmitt. Perhaps all we can hope for is, as Scelle suggests, that what might appear to be a transition away from the legalist vision to a pre-Enlightenment era is in fact the final death throes of those tendencies in our political culture that still yearn for the certainties of a pre-Enlightenment era. It would then be high time to return to the work of those in the interwar years who, with Kelsen, Heller, and Lauterpacht, set out the legalist vision that has remained a work in progress even during more auspicious times.

But, as I have argued in this Introduction, it is important in particular to return to Heller's *Sovereignty*. For he made clearer than perhaps anyone else writing at that time the politics of the legal idea of sovereignty and so why the preservation and maintenance of that idea is both valuable and requires constant political effort. There is no trace, however, in his work of a naïve Western universalism that results in an imperial projection of power under the guise of morality. As his reference to the experience of colonial peoples reveals, he was all too aware of the kinds of abuse that can be perpetrated in the name of fundamental principles.[213] He was also completely aware that the idea of law and legal order he was defending is, as an

[209] See Martin Loughlin, *Foundations of Public Law* (Oxford: Oxford University Press, 2010).

[210] See Paul Kahn, *Political Theology: Four New Chapters on the Concept of Sovereignty* (New York: Columbia University Press, 2012).

[211] See Goldsmith and Posner, *The Limits of International Law*.

[212] Text to note 96, above.

[213] See below 151.

historian of the ancient world recently put it, an "invention . . . in the West."[214] And he would have agreed fully with the conclusion of that work—that "the formalism of its law remains for now the destiny of the West; its civil soul; its only fully utterable public discourse" and that this idea "continues to speak to us: about the possibility of a historically determined relationship between form and power as the sole element upon which we can (thus far) rely for an order of the world that is at the same time both realistic and open to hope."[215]

## A Brief Biographical Note

Heller was born in 1891 in Teschen, part of the Austro-Hungarian empire.[216] His family were Jewish and his father was a lawyer. He studied law in Vienna, Innsbruck, and Graz. In 1914, he volunteered for the Austrian army and at the end of the war returned to his studies, first in Leipzig, then in Kiel, where in 1920 he was awarded his habilitation, the European senior doctorate required for entry into the academic profession. His supervisor was Gustav Radbruch, one of Germany most influential philosophers of law. Heller was immediately caught up in the birth pangs of the Weimar Republic. Already a member of the SPD, he and Radbruch participated in the armed resistance to the *Kapp putsch*, which sought to overthrow the new order.

Heller's bid to secure an academic position was thwarted by anti-Semitism and he occupied himself for several years with worker education and promoting the social democratic movement. In 1926, he was appointed to an academic position in Berlin at the Kaiser Wilhelm Institute for Comparative Public Law and International Law. In 1928, the Prussian government appointed him to the rank of *Extraordinarius* (professor without a chair) in the Berlin Law Faculty despite the Law Faculty's resistance, and in 1932 he was appointed as *Ordinarius*, a professor with a chair, in the Frankfurt Law Faculty.

Heller was not the first choice of the Faculty. Rather, they wanted a respected practitioner, but he declined the offer. Among those who were then considered were Schmitt and Heller. It appears that the Faculty were strongly divided between them on political grounds while, it appears, united in a common appreciation of their scholarly merit. In the end, with the support of the Dean, Heller got the offer.[217]

Heller's appointment lasted at most nine months. In early 1933, the National Socialists had seized power and begun their policy of *Gleichschaltung*—the political alignment along ideological lines of German society. This alignment was not

[214] See Aldo Schiavone, *The Invention of Law in the West* (Cambridge, Mass.: Harvard University Press, 2012).

[215] Ibid., 460.

[216] See Christoph Müller, "Hermann Heller (1891-1933): Vom liberalen sum sozialen Rechtsstaat" in Helmut Heinrichs, Harald Franzki, Klaus Schmalz, and Michael Stolleis, eds, *Deutsche Juristen Jüdischer Herkunft* (Munich: CH Beck, 1993) 768–80.

[217] Notkar Hammerstein, *Die Johann Wolfgang Goethe-Universität Frankfurt am Main: Von der Stiftungsuniversität zur staatlichen Hochschule* (Neuwied: Alfred Metzner, 1989), volume 1, 142–3. For a more detailed account, see David Dyzenhaus, "Hermann Heller and the 'Jewish Element' in German Public Law Theory" in Epple *et al.*, eds, "*Politisierung der Wissenschaft*", 209.

confined to the political sphere. The universities were also politically aligned by various laws, beginning with The Law for the Restoration of the Professional Civil Service of 1933.

In early 1933, when Hitler seized power, Heller was on a lecture tour of England. He was warned by friends against a return to Germany where he might face detention and a trial on a charge of political crimes. He had been invited to be a guest professor in Madrid, and so he asked for leave from the University for the summer semester of 1933 and the winter semester of 1933/34,[218] but was formally dismissed from his position on September 11, 1933. He died on November 5 of that year of a heart condition, a relic of wartime service.

Heller thus spent very little time as a professor at Frankfurt. Moreover, much of his energy during that time must have been focused on politics in Berlin because of his involvement in the *Preußenschlag*. But, despite the fact that in the nine months of his effective tenure of his appointment Heller was hardly a presence in the Law Faculty, it is clear that he felt that on the whole he was supported by his new colleagues in Frankfurt, especially by the Dean. For on October 5, 1933, exactly a month before his death, and having just learned from the newspaper that he had been finally dismissed from the Faculty, he sent a warm letter of thanks to the Dean for his support and asked him to convey the thanks to those among his colleagues from the Law Faculty who had not turned against him.[219]

Germany in general and Frankfurt University in particular had, however, changed radically between Heller's appointment and his letter to the Dean. Stolleis comments that the "racial and political dismissals under the Nazi state fell so heavily upon Frankfurt that the closure of the university seemed imminent,"[220] which was not surprising given that politically "the majority of the faculty was 'social liberal' in its thinking, democratic, and republican ... in keeping with the traditions of the old trading city and an intellectual climate that was shaped by its Jewish bourgeoisie."[221] Such changes, let alone the horrors to come, were perhaps unimaginable in early 1932 even to politically attuned and realistic sorts, as I think is attested by the Law Faculty's discussions around Heller's recruitment.

[218] Hammerstein, *Die Johann Wolfgang Goethe-Universität Frankfurt am Main*, 226.

[219] Reproduced in Inge Staff, "Hermann Heller (1891–1933)" in Bernard Diestelkamp and Michael Stolleis, eds, *Juristen an der Universität Frankfurt am Main* (Baden-Baden: Nomos,) 187, 199.

> My dear Dean,
> I have learned from the newspaper of my definitive dismissal from my post as a university teacher. Despite everything, it is important to me that I do not take my leave of the Frankfurt Faculty without a word. Insofar as the convictions of individual members of the Faculty have during the last months or weeks changed, I ask that they will not take my parting words to have any bearing on them. But in regard to those colleagues who have, despite the intervening events, maintained a benevolent memory of me, I ask that you convey to them my heartfelt thanks and good wishes. My indestructible belief in the intellect that alone elevates us above the animal kingdom and that constitutes our dignity as humans, gives me the certainty that I would be connected in the future to these colleagues, if the external circumstances of such a relationship are not permitted.
>
> In this sense, I am sincerely thankful for all the humane accommodation that you, my most esteemed Dean, as well as the Faculty, have shown me.
>
> Yours sincerely,
> Hermann Heller.

[220] Stolleis, *A History of Public Law in Germany: 1914–1945*, 275.

[221] Ibid.

On July 17, 1933, Heller wrote a postcard to Schmitt from Madrid congratulating him on his appointment as Prussian State Councilor: "Hermann Heller sends his congratulations on the more than deserved honour bestowed on you by Minister Göring."[222] In light of the rivalry between him and Schmitt, both academic and political, he must have intended its lapidary tone to indicate not only that he was unsurprised by the fact that Schmitt had climbed so quickly and enthusiastically aboard the Nazi train, but also that Schmitt had prepared the way for the train to leave the station. Perhaps Heller meant in addition to convey that whatever Schmitt's particular reservations about Hitler, that is, his preference for a dictatorship of the aristocratic right to the plebeian National Socialists, there was no great surprise in either his immediate attempts to curry favor with the National Socialists after their victory or in the success of these attempts.

On January 20, 1934, Karl Mannheim, the sociologist who had also been purged from Frankfurt University in 1933, wrote from London to Albert Einstein in the USA to inform him that Heller—"the legal scholar whose high esteem you share"—had died: "the first significant victim of the emigration experience."[223] Heller had been discussing with Einstein establishing a German university in Belgium where the academic refugees would teach, in this way preserving the culture of the liberal German academy, in particular, the German-Jewish influence within that culture.

[222] Mehring, *Carl Schmitt*, 264.

[223] Letter dated January 20, 1934, sent from the London School of Economics and Political Science, Einstein Archive, Jerusalem.

# Foreword to the Original German Edition

I commit this work to the public in full awareness of the great gamble it involves. It does not and cannot pretend to be exhaustive; it should be taken as an initial breaking of ground to prepare to rebuild the theory of the state on foundations that have been shaken. On the question of methodology, aside from a few remarks strewn throughout the text, I will say only one thing here. If we permit the theory of the state to place not the state, but some law, be it causal or normative, at its center, instead of taking as its starting point the meaning or nature of that concrete political unity in multiplicity that we call the state, we must ultimately end in more or less the same place as the contemporary theory of state law that lacks both state and law, and which banishes the lawmaker from its scope as something unjuristic, while recognizing the criminal as an organ of state. This last flowering of natural science conceptualization must be recognized as a symptom of a dominant method that functionalizes all individuality and is unable to allow either the concrete form of the state and the human personality, or that of the law, a logical-systematic meaning. This method must be destroyed at its roots, and state law theory restored to its original literal sense as an understanding of the essential juristic structure of the state and its institutions.

# I

# The Crisis of the Dogma of Sovereignty in the History of Ideas

The unsettling of all the intellectual and societal bases of the present day has also called into question the theory of sovereignty that dominated constitutional theory for three centuries. At the so-called Wimbledon Trial, held in August 1923 before the Permanent Court of International Justice, which offered frequent opportunities to discuss the problem of sovereignty, Basdevant, the well-known international law theorist and the legal representative of France, observed: "I know that such a conception of sovereignty holds a considerable place in German jurisprudence, as it did formerly in French jurisprudence in consequence of the work of Jean Bodin."[1]

Basdevant's words were obviously meant as an ironic critique of the theory of sovereignty prevailing in Germany, a theory that, in the opinion of many foreign and numerous German jurists, remains mired in Bodin's absolutist and imperialist mindset, and is incompatible with the legal consciousness of our present day civilization.

Before we justify or atone for Bodin's theory of sovereignty, let us first agree on what it is. It appears to me that many of those who talk about Bodin do not really know what Bodin was talking about. If we compare the judgments about Bodin that have been passed on from generation to generation with quotations from his work that have similarly been passed on, we must conclude that this great theorist of the state is one of the most often quoted but least read of authors. It is said that he taught that supreme power was unlimited,[2] but also that, as a partisan of French absolutism, he had no sense of our modern concept of state sovereignty.[3] The image of Bodin sketched in the mind of an ingenious German state theorist is typical.

[1] Société des Nations (ed.), *Publications de la Cour permanente de la justice international*, Série C (Actes et documents relatifs aux arrêts et aux avis consultatifs de la Cour), No. 3, Leiden, no date, vol. 1, p. 369. See Ernst Wolfast, *Der Wimbledonprozeß vor dem Völkerbundsgerichtshof*, Basel 1926 (Internationalrechtliche Abhandlungen, vol. 1), p. 60 f.

[2] Among many others, see Georg Meyer, *Lehrbuch des Deutschen Staatsrechts*, 7th edn, edited by Gerhard Anschütz, vol. 1, Freiburg 1914, p. 22; but see also Hermann Rehm, *Geschichte der Staatsrechtswissenschaft*, Freiburg 1896 (Handbuch des öffentlichlichen Rechts der Gegenwart, introductory volume, Department 1), p. 223, although to him in particular (ibid. p. 228) "a closer look" reveals strict limits to Bodin's concept of sovereignty.

[3] Georg Jellinek, *Allgemeine Staatslehre* (1900), 3rd edn (ed. Walter Jellinek), Berlin 1914, p. 457 ff.; Rehm, op. cit., p. 224; Meyer/Anschütz, op. cit., vol. 1, p. 22; Fritz Stier-Somlo, *Deutsches Reichs- und Landesstaatsrecht*, vol. 1, Berlin 1924 (Grundrisse der Rechtswissenschaft, vol. 18), p. 57.

According to him, Bodin wrote a book about majesty, "the sovereign majesty who was none other than the king of France, the unlimited monarch subject to no law, but who is rather the creator of all right and wrong and master of all laws; one who can only be bound by his own word, because he gave it, but who can absolve himself when he breaks this word; the all-powerful one, for whom mankind can only be subjects or enemies."[4]

What does this characterization have to do with the historical Bodin, and what do his teachings mean to us today? We know that his concept of sovereignty was the result of a war fought by the French state under the leadership of the king and the University of Paris against the king's subjection to the Catholic Church and the empire, as well as against the subordination of state power to the feudal barons;[5] even before Bodin, the "initially relative, comparative concept of royal sovereignty" had changed to "an absolute one."[6] The state, represented in the king, which had heretofore only been "superior" in its relationship to the Church, empire, and barons, now became "supreme" [*supremus*]. Bodin was the first to claim sovereignty as a defining criterion of the state.[7]

"For supreme power loves unity," taught Aeneas Silvius, a precursor of Bodin, who in Kaiser Friedrich III's day was still defending the sovereignty of imperial world domination.[8] More than a hundred years later, we find in Bodin the same fundamental idea of the unity of a political power that is externally independent and rules internally without resistance. Living in the midst of religious civil wars, which posed a mortal threat to him, he indeed saw only the French king as the possible political person of unified supreme power in his country. Yet Bodin, the Huguenot, was as little a partisan monarchist as Hobbes, whose thinking has been distorted with similar frequency and who wrote in a similar political situation. Neither ever refrained from conceiving the theoretically conceivable sovereign persons as either "prince" [*princeps*] or "people" [*populus*].[9]

In regard to the nature of sovereignty in Bodin's sense of the term, it is an observation of great theoretical consequence that Bodin considered all of his seven rights of sovereignty to be contained within the legislative power: "Under this same sovereignty of power for the giving and abrogation of the law are comprised all the other rights and marks of sovereignty: so that to speak properly a man may say that there is only one mark of sovereign power considering that all other rights thereof

[4] Albrecht Mendelssohn Bartholdy, 'Souveränitäten', in *Die neue Rundschau*, volume 34 of the *Freien Bühne* (1923), p. 98.

[5] Jellinek, op. cit., p. 440 ff.; Rehm, op. cit., p. 188 f.; 204 ff.

[6] Jellinek, op. cit., p. 449.

[7] Jean Bodin, *De republica libri sex*, latine ab autore redditi, Lyon 1586, book I, cap. 8 (p. 78): "For so here it is appropriate to define what sovereign majesty is, which neither lawyer nor political philosopher has yet defined." [84]

[8] On him, see Rehm, op. cit., p. 196 ff. (Aeneas Sylvius Piccolomini [Pius II.], *De ortu et auctoritate imperii Romani* (1446), chap. 22).

[9] Jean Bodin, op. cit., book 1, chap. 8 (p. 80): "The prince or the people in whom sovereignty resides." Book I, chap. 10 (p. 150) [86]: "law is the right command of him or them, which have sovereign power above others, without exception of person." Book 1, chap. 8 (p. 92) [156]: "But in a popular estate nothing can be greater than the whole body of people"; especially book 1, chap. 10 (p. 151f.) [99]; book 11, chap. 1 (p. 176). Thomas Hobbes, *Elementa philosophica de cive*, Amsterdam 1647, chap. VI, 1 annotation (p 90 ff.); chap. XII, 8 (p. 199 f.).

are contained in this, *viz.* to have power to give laws unto all and every one of the subjects, and to receive none from them."[10] Soon after, Bodin even noted explicitly that he only listed the additional rights of sovereignty "But forasmuch as the word *Law*, is too general a mark ..."[11]

One would thoroughly misunderstand Bodin's theory if one claimed that he accepted the sovereignty of state power as a given and provided no scientific justification for it.[12] On the contrary, Bodin's justification itself is the most brilliant part of his theory of the state and has the most relevance for the present: after all, he recognized the problem of sovereignty as the most fundamental of all problems of normative science because it concerned the relationship between norms and individuality. However, to understand the nature of Bodin's concept of sovereignty and the infamous "freedom from law" [*legibus solutio*] of the sovereign, it is necessary to know that Bodin distinguished strongly between "statutory law" [*lex*] and "fundamental legal principles" [*ius*]: "But there is much difference between fundamental legal principles and statutory law: for fundamental legal principles still without command respects nothing but that which is good and upright; but a law imports a commandment. For the law is nothing else than the commandment of a sovereign, using of his sovereign power."[13] Bodin's sovereignty is by no means limitless.

"For if we should say that he only has absolute power who is subject to no law; there should be no sovereign power in the world, seeing that all the princes of the earth are subject to the laws of God, of nature, and of nations"; "for all princes and peoples of the world are subject to the laws of God and of nature."[14] The subjects of a sovereign who violates these legal principles were allowed to refuse him obedience.[15] But the positive legal principles "of such as concern the state itself: which I both would and wish, if possibly it might be, that they should still be most firm and immutable." But, he adds, "not because the state ought to serve the laws, seeing that they are made for the maintenance of the state, and of the society of men: neither that any man wishes the safety and preservation of the laws, but for the state's sake."[16]

This is Bodin's undying achievement. He was the first to view the connection between the individuality of the state and the geographic and climatic conditions of life,[17] and to take into account its geopolitically, anthropologically, and historically unique situation; nevertheless, he subjected the state's individuality to the highest legal principles. However, positive law could never place absolute limits on the sovereign: "For it is appropriate that the sovereign prince should have the laws in his power, to change and amend them, according as the case shall require, even as the master pilot ought to have the helm always in his hand, at discretion to turn it, as

[10] Bodin, op. cit., book I, chap. 10 (p. 155) [162–3]; see book I, chap. 10 (p. 150): "there are those who distinguish law from privilege", etc.

[11] Ibid., book 1, chap. 10 (p. 155) [163].

[12] See Jellinek, op. cit., p. 597.

[13] Bodin, op. cit., book 1, chap. 8 (p. 101f.) [108]: Bodin's concept of 'positive law' is ambiguous. See Rehm, op. cit., p. 223, note 6.

[14] Bodin, op. cit., book 1, chap. 8 (pp. 84, 86) [84, 92].

[15] Ibid., book III, chap. 4 (p.293 ff.).

[16] Ibid., book IV, chap. 3 (p. 426) [471].

[17] Ibid., book V, chap. 1 (p. 491 ff.).

the weather or the occasion requires."[18] Precisely because Bodin still recognized the highest legal principles, he also understood the relativity of all earthly things, and steered clear of the immanent utopia of a positivized "natural order" [*ordre naturel*]. A sovereign is one whose orders can bind all others; human legislation, however, requires constant adaptation "as the infinite variety of places, times, and persons shall require."[19] This adaptation can only, however, be undertaken by the sovereign himself, "for it is appropriate that he who is a sovereign not to be in any sort subject to the command of another."[20] Therefore, Bodin had to reverse the slogan of the monarchomachs, "law makes the ruler" [*lex facit regem*],[21] such that "ruler" [*rex*] is understood as the sovereign and *lex* as positive law. Thus, the only sovereign person is one "who next unto God acknowledges none greater than himself."[22]

What sovereignty meant to Bodin's personal life, and at the same time to the history of European humanity, becomes clear in its ultimate form in Bodin's final and perhaps most significant work, *Heptaplomeres*.[23] In this religious dialogue, his disgust at theological bickering and revulsion at the horrible bloodshed of the wars of religion are palpable. At the end, he calls upon Tertullian's authority to show that compelling a profession of religion is contrary to religion.[24] As a result, Bodin concluded, the seven disputants, belonging to seven different faiths, "maintained piety and integrity in admirable harmony through common study and coexistence, but held no disputation about religion thereafter, although each one professed *his* religion with the greatest sanctity of conversion."[25] Thus began the secularization of the sovereign state, whose tolerance allowed each to be blessed in his own "fashion" [*façon*], and which, for that reason, had to make its system independent of church and theology; it had to become the supreme earthly sovereign power.

As a result of ways of thinking that also originated in Bodin's century, in the nineteenth century the concept of sovereignty began a process of degeneration; to briefly summarize the causes and the result of this degeneration today, it is without a person, and therefore without a home. The history of this process is the history of the depersonalization of an entire world view, which began with the inherent legal thinking of the Renaissance; its legal history branch is the history of the depersonalized *Rechtsstaat*.

The modern *Rechtsstaat* was born of the belief, characteristic of the entire modern era, in the existence and cognizability of a natural order of the world that determines our lives with a steadfast legality over and above any personal arbitrariness. According

18 Ibid., book 1, chap. 8 (p. 92) [98].

19 Ibid., book 1, chap. 8 (p. 94) [100]. In the French edition (*Les six livres de la république* [1576], 2d ed., Paris 1577, p. 106): "to break or change the law in accordance with the demands of the case, the times, and of persons."

20 Bodin, *De Republica*, book 1, chap. 8 (p. 85) [91].

21 Rudolf Treumann, *Die Monarchomachen, Leipzig 1895* (Staats- und völkerrechtliche Abhandlungen, vol. 1, part 1), p. 77 and note 4.

22 Bodin, op. cit., lib 1, chap. 8 (p. 80) [86].

23 Published for the first time from the distributed manuscript by G. E. Guhrauer, *Das Heptaplomeres des Jean Bodin*, Berlin 1841. See Wilhelm Dilthey, *Weltanschauung und Analyse des Menschen seit Renaissance und Reformation*, in *Gesammelte Schriften*, vol. 2 (G. Misch, ed.), Leipzig 1914, p. 146 f.

24 Bodin in Guhrauer, *Heptaplomeres*, p. 158.

25 Ibid., p. 159.

to deistic natural law, God has revealed this "natural order" positively once and for all; now, however, the objectivity of law and legal right cannot be shaken even by divine subjectivity. At the start of the sixteenth century, Gabriel Biel was already saying, "If (what is impossible) there were no God, that is to say, divine reason, or if that divine reason were in error, still, if someone were to act contrary to right reason, whether angelic, human, or some other, he would commit a sin."[26] In contrast to medieval man, modern man finds it more dignified to subordinate himself to the inexorable power of impersonal law, rather than to personal rule. The ideal of factuality and of objectivity appears to us to be a structural principle of legal right; we believe ourselves to be free when we are subject to a law, which mocks any arbitrary acts and any reaction from our side. All of natural law, in the form renewed by the Renaissance, is marked by the effort to escape the legal significance of any individual authority through the postulate of a universal "natural order." Hugo Grotius had already proposed a universal axiom of legal theory located in the nature of the human condition and independent of individual caprice: "The law of nature, again, is unchangeable—even in the sense that it cannot be changed by God. Measureless as is the power of God, nevertheless it can be said that there are certain things over which that power does not extend; for things of which this is said are spoken only, having no sense corresponding with reality and being mutually contradictory. Just as even God, then, cannot cause that two times two should not make four, so He cannot cause that which is intrinsically evil be not evil."[27]

As long as this "natural order," imbued with the secularized substance of the Christian heritage, possessed substantive legal postulates with generally binding force; as long as something like freedom and equality were the just objectives of the struggle of the culturally representative classes; as long as that was the case, no one doubted that justice required the decisions of an actual will in order to be achieved. Until the beginning of the nineteenth century, the natural law of the Enlightenment was also aware that the natural order inherent in society cannot dispense with the historical reality of individual authorities. The great problem for the politics of practical natural law was therefore the question of how the individual will of the ruler, whether autocratic or democratic, could be made objective—how sovereignty could be deprived of its arbitrariness. The problem of making the will of the ruler objective is the problem of the *Rechtsstaat*: A legal norm should without exception have priority over any individual entity! In the classical thought of the *Rechtsstaat*, the root of which was none other than the theory of popular sovereignty, the "general will" [*volonté générale*]—the people as a unity of will—forms the basis for the communal values that are constantly realized anew through law. Of "the sovereign formed only by the particulars that compose it," Rousseau said that "simply because it is, is always what it should be."[28] Montesquieu's theory of separation of powers is nothing less

[26] In Dilthey, op. cit., p. 279 note 1 (Gabriel Biel, *Collectorium Sententiarum*, Tübingen 1501, book 11, *distinctio* XXXV, *quaestio unica, art.* 1).

[27] Hugo Grotius, *De jure belli ac pacis* (1625), book 1, chap. 1, § 10, v.

[28] Jean-Jacques Rousseau, *Du contrat social, ou principes du droit politique* (1762), book 1, chap. 7. See Immanuel Kant, *Die Metaphysik der Sitten* (1797), in *Gesammelte Schriften* (Kgl. Preußische Akademie, ed.), vol. 6, Berlin 1907, § 52 (p. 340); § 45 (p. 313); § 46 (p. 313): the state in the idea of the "pure

than a technique to place undiluted power in the legislation of this value-bearing and lawmaking "general will."[29]

The task of this thinking about the separation of powers, democratization, corporations and institutions was to make it conceivable that the will of state representatives could be purged of subjectivity, and that the will of the state as an objective norm could be independent of individual arbitrariness. In the era of natural law, there was no doubt that the "general will" was a "sufficient condition" [*conditio per quam*] of positive norms, and that the objectivity of positive laws was based in the universality of the subjective will of the state. Even for Hegel, the people as a unity of will was still an acceptable sovereign person.[30]

This changed in one fell swoop when the basis for political ideas lost its binding force. In Germany, this situation arose around the middle of the previous century, following the Revolution of 1848. Once the bourgeoisie believed neither in a binding political task nor in itself, legitimized the monarchy only in relative fashion,[31] and denied natural law's substantive ideas of freedom and equality, little was left of the classical bourgeois theory of the *Rechtsstaat* but bourgeois security—the formal, positivist legality intended merely to provide a bulwark against the onslaught of proletarian demands. At the same time, however, this deeply unsettled the concept of a "general will," whose existence and power is unimaginable, in the long run, without a universally binding political idea that can be attributed to all and which unites individual wills. Legitimacy would be displaced by the surrogate of formalist legality,[32] and the substantive *Rechtsstaat* by what Max Weber called rational forms of government, characterized by the belief that only impersonal obedience is owed, always and everywhere, within an objectively existing authority, that every 'ruler' is in turn subject to an impersonal, rationally-determined order, and that every obedient person thus obeys only 'the law.' It is immediately obvious what difficulties this legal theory encounters in understanding the concept of sovereignty, and how close it gets to understanding the will of the state exclusively as ideal objectivity; independence and supremacy are ascribed only to norms, no longer to a will. On this path, the concept of sovereignty must inevitably become depersonalized if it is followed consistently.

And indeed, in the mid-nineteenth century, Joseph Held[33] already noted that one of the oddest phenomena of the modern state was the extraordinary significance

republic," that is, the "unity of a large number of human beings under law," in which the "united will" of the people itself possesses and exercises legislative power. Georg Wilhelm Friedrich Hegel, *Vorlesungen über die Philosophie der Geschichte*, in *Werke*, vol. 9 (ed. E. Gans), 3rd edn (ed. Karl Hegel), Berlin 1848, p. 92: "The people are moral, virtuous, powerful, in that they create whatever they want."

[29] See Hermann Heller, *Der Begriff des Gesetzes in der Reichsverfassung, Gesammelte Schriften*, vol. 1, p. 203.

[30] See p. 93 f.

[31] See Hermann Heller, *Die politischen Ideenkreise der Gegenwart*, see *Gesammelte Schriften*, vol. 1, p. 302 ff.

[32] Gerhard Anschütz, *Die Verfassung des Deutschen Reichs*, 4th edn, Berlin 1926, p. 5: legitimacy is not one of "the essential elements of state and law."

[33] Joseph Held, *Staat und Gesellschaft vom Standpunkte der Geschichte der Menschheit*, part 3, Leipzig 1865, p. 253 f.

ascribed in our era to legislative and judicial activity, and in that connection, the concept of "a purely legal, only constitutional obedience." He said that the most fruitful products of this characteristic of our era should be considered, among other things: "The theories of the *Rechtsstaat*, of the sovereignty of law" and "the overwhelming significance of legal formalism." When Hugo Preuß addressed his 1888 polemic to the concept of sovereignty, he was absolutely correct to claim that eliminating the concept from the doctrine of the law of the state was "merely a small step in the direction long since taken by our discipline."[34]

With the complete depersonalization and evacuation of the idea of the *Rechtsstaat*, the degradation of the concept of sovereignty has reached its conclusion today in the writings of Krabbe and Kelsen. This is the end of the history of an imminent utopia that is expressed, from a theological perspective, as the development from theism to deism to the immanence of an idea accomplished in this life, but from a legal perspective, is a regime ruled by law that is not mediated by individuals. The last remnants of the moral pathos of the Enlightenment's universalist natural law, the mainstay of the old universalist rule-of-law liberalism, live on in Krabbe the Dutchman's doctrine of 'legal sovereignty.' This depersonalized sovereignty of law, according to Krabbe, is based on the idea of "an impersonal power particular to legal norms because they are legal norms," while state sovereignty is based in the concept "that power [is rooted] in a personal right of command."[35] The development of the *Rechtsstaat* ultimately culminates in the unconditional victory of law, "to the exclusion of any original power of authority."[36] Thus triumphs the grand idea "that *intellectual power* has replaced *personal power*. We no longer live under the rule of persons, be they natural or constructed (legal) persons, but under the rule of norms, intellectual forces . . . These forces rule, in the strictest sense of the word."[37]

Behind Krabbe's sovereignty of law we still find the liberal idea of the *Rechtsstaat*, though in quite faded form, and thus a material remnant of sovereign state will; it is this lack of formalism, these substantive remnants, with which Kelsen reproached him.[38] Kelsen, along with his small but active legion, became a voice in the dispute with the dogma of sovereignty, to which prevailing doctrine was able to cling at the

[34] Hugo Preuß, *Gemeinde, Staat, Reich als Gebietskörperschaften. Versuch einer deutschen Staatskonstruktion auf der Grundlage der Genossenschaftstheorie*, Berlin 1889, p. 135.

[35] Hugo Krabbe, *Die Lehre von der Rechtssouveränität*, Groningen 1906 (echoed in Krabbe, *Staatsidee* (see note 36), chap. 3); on this, see Antonius Alexis Hendrikus Struycken, *Recht en gezag. Eene critische beschouwing van Kraabe's Moderne Staatsidee*, Arnhem 1916.

[36] Hugo Krabbe, *Die modern Staats-Idee*, 2nd edn, The Hague 1919, p. 8.

[37] Ibid., p. 9

[38] Hans Kelsen, *Das Problem der Souveränität und die Theorie des Völkerrechts. Beitrag zu einer reinen Rechtslehre*, Tübingen 1920, p, 24 ff. If this study makes particular reference to Kelsen's doctrine, this is not because Kelsen's conceptual board game, as arbitrary as it is astute, has otherwise been ignored with helpless silence, as the Czech jurist Franz Weyr claims more boldly than correctly, "Hans Kelsens 'Allgemeine Staatslehre,'" in *Juristenzeitung für das Gebiet der Tschechoslowakischen Republik*, Brünn and Prague, 7 (1926), p. 74; nor is it because Kelsen has written the most extensive monograph on the problem, but solely because he represents the tendency of the dominant doctrine inaugurated by Laband with particular consistency, though also particular lack of success. A precursor of Kelsen's was Karl Kormann, "Grundzüge eines allgemeinen Teils des öffentlichen Rechts," in *Annalen des Deutschen Reichs*, 44 (1911), p. 857, who believed that the concept of sovereignty was unnecessary for modern legal dogma. See Hermann Heller, *Die Krisis der Staatslehre* (see p. 5 ff.).

cost of generating contradictions. We shall see to what extent Kelsen is nothing less than the logical executor of the testament of the dominant doctrine.

The concept of sovereignty's homelessness in the system of the 'pure theory of law' arises necessarily from this doctrine's depersonalization. Never has the depersonalization of the legal worldview been more radically accomplished, nor the basic problem of any science of norms, the problem of norms and individuality, more radically denied. To Kelsen, each person is merely the fictional personification of a normative order—the state and the legal order are thus identical. For one who has gained insight into this "personification mechanism,"[39] it is self-evident that a will can have no legal authority, and no one but 'the' legal order can be sovereign. This indeterminate legal order, indicated, however, by a definite article, is even in the pure theory of law naturally a vestige of Enlightenment natural law. Kelsenian natural law, which he liked to call upon at times,[40] was only preserved in his work, however, due to the logical cohesion of its intellectual elements. In accordance with these presuppositions, it lacks any soul, any content; it is without belief or passion. After all, Kelsen wished to be nothing but a positivist, who—in excluding any ethical, political, or social content—sees every state as a *Rechtsstaat* and law as form that can have any content whatsoever. Nevertheless, in those places where his speculations are not simply built on anarchist foundations, he cannot for a moment deny their origins in a commitment to liberal democracy. Occasionally, even in Kelsen, the impersonal "natural order" appears as a legal ideal to be achieved; "in overcoming the doctrine of the sovereignty of individual states," he prophecies, "the existence of an objective international order of peoples, or more correctly world legal order, above the individual states, independent of any "acknowledgment," a "world state" [*civitas maxima*], will assert itself."[41] But the 'pure' theory of law becomes particularly fascinating in its struggle against the dogma of sovereignty when it joins with Marxist natural law and teaches that human beings, called upon to "produce" and "implement" the law and enforce coercion "in pursuit of their own interests" vis-à-vis others, will become an autonomous site of power, a state ruling over its subjects. But this "undoubted ... fact" does not interest the formal-liberal democrats and lies "beyond any legal comprehension."[42]

The meaning of this critical concept in the system of the pure theory of law cannot be clearly determined. In this case, as always, Kelsen's alleged freedom from contradiction does not stand up to closer inspection. On the third page of his monograph on sovereignty, it is described as a "necessary concept" whose "correct and ineliminable core"[43] the author will establish; but on the last page, he says that the idea of sovereignty must be "radically suppressed";[44] elsewhere, he explains that it is "high time that this concept, after playing a questionable role in the history of legal science for centuries, should finally disappear from the dictionary of international law."[45]

[39] Kelsen, op. cit., p. 289.

[40] Ibid., p. 214, 252; but see op. cit., p. 306 f., note 1, where natural law is branded an "arbitrary claim" or "political postulate" from the point of view of positive law insights.

[41] Ibid., p. 320. [42] Ibid., p. 260. [43] Ibid., p. 3 f., note 2.

[44] Ibid., p. 320.

[45] Hans Kelsen, "Souveränität," in Karl Strupp (ed.), *Wörterbuch des Völkerrechts und der Diplomatie*, vol. 2, Berlin 1925, p. 559.

In a work that appeared shortly thereafter, the suppression of the complex of ideas about state and sovereignty seems not yet to have succeeded; for here sovereignty proves to be "just as much a cardinal problem of the theory of state and of law."[46] It also happens that the "only true sovereignty, that is, that of the universal order of international law" is mentioned,[47] although it is not clear whether this, too, must be suppressed or perhaps may be sovereign because it not yet a unit of power. Then suddenly the "*sovereignty of the state* [is] ... identical with the *positivity of law*,"[48] but is also a symbol of the "unity of the legal system and *purity of legal knowledge*."[49] An "embarrassment of riches" [*embarras de richesse*] of meanings for this word, which leaves little to wish for in variety! One may be permitted to suggest that Kelsen's own idea of sovereignty is not yet developed at all, to say nothing of the sovereignty problem it creates.

The attacks on the concept of sovereignty initiated by Hugo Preuß came from a fundamentally different direction. Here we go from Romanticism to Germanistic corporatist theory and end in modern syndicalism. Despite the differences in time period and personality, Preuß's natural law, democratic view did not differ from that of the early Romantics. The similarities lay, however, mainly in their federative tendencies, their opposition to the centralized, 'unorganic' state, and their enthusiasm for a corporative structure of the common life of the polity. According to Preuß, starting at the beginning of the nineteenth century the previously firm, unified concept of sovereignty began to "pull itself apart and fade."[50] The concept had merely been the main principle of the absolutist state, but now, he maintained, the fundamental principle of the modern *Rechsstaat* was developing from German law; it was summoned to suppress and replace the Romance-language concept and the Romance word "sovereignty."[51] When we see his 'organic' concept of the state struggling against the sovereign will of the all-powerful state,[52] which "absorbs any signs of life," we are reminded of the organic doctrine of the early Romantics and their common opposition to Frederick the Great's mechanical, un-German 'machine.' "No state has been administered as a factory, as Prussia, since the death of Friedrich Wilhelm the First," said Novalis,[53] whom we know was, like the young Friedrich Schlegel, no stranger to enthusiasm for 'Republicanism.'[54] Pacifist universalism and naturalistically-coloured organology—antipathy towards the centralism that absorbs every affiliated district and community—returned in Schelling's various systems.[55] The young Hegel's antipathy towards the Frederickian state arose from a common Romantic source; it was, said Hegel, "a basic preconception that

[46] Hans Kelsen, *Allgemeine Staatslehre*, Berlin 1925 (Enzyklopädie der Rechts- und Staatswissenschaft 23), p. 103.

[47] Kelsen, *Problem der Souveränität*, p. 189.

[48] Ibid., p. 86.

[49] Kelsen, *Staatslehre*, p. 106; Kelsen, *Problem der Souveränität*, p. 189.

[50] Preuß, *Gemeinde, Staat, Reich* (see note 34), p. 126.

[51] Ibid., p. 136.

[52] Ibid., p. 133.

[53] Novalis, *Glauben und Liebe* (1798), in *Schriften* (J. Minor, ed.), vol. 2, Jena 1923, p. 157.

[54] Ibid., p. 150; 160; 269 f. On Schlegel see Wilhelm Metzger, *Gesellschaft, Recht und Staat in der Ethik des deutschen Idealismus* (E. Bergmann, ed.), Heidelberg, 1917, p. 224 f.

[55] See Metzger, op. cit., p. 237 f.

a state is a machine with one single spring that communicated its movement to the—incidentally endless—gears."[56] Later, once the formation of the higher state authorities had been completed, he believed it was time to integrate the "*subordinate* guild spheres and communities" back into the state. "A vital connection is only in a structured whole, whose parts form specific, subordinate spheres."[57]

The historical thread leads from Beseler's Germanic corporate theory and its brilliant development by Gierke, through Preuß. While Krabbe and Kelsen negated sovereignty, because they both negated diversity and individuality, for Preuß the reverse was true: sovereignty negated the element of plurality in unity.[58] By contrasting his organic view of the world and the state with a mechanistic view, Gierke's student expressly invoked Schelling.[59] "Today, international law and the law of more narrowly political associations, that is, the law of political self-administration, are the allied opponents and conquerors of the concept of sovereignty."[60] "While the precise and purely conceived notion of sovereignty contrasts the state, in its absolute isolation as the only entity of its kind, with all other phenomena of legal existence, it views the organic theory of the person as a link in the great chain of organisms and persons,"[61] as "a consubstantial link in the chain of the human polity."[62] Thus to Preuß, the concept of sovereignty became a "root of all evils" [*radix malorum*]; its elimination from the doctrine of the law of the state was the primary condition whose fulfillment alone would make possible the progress of the modern theory of the state.[63]

The anti-étatist trend of revolutionary syndicalism, widespread among the French and Italians in recent decades, which has also enjoyed a small following in Germany since the World War, had no connection to the above-mentioned works and had a different social basis, but it was remarkably similar in its federative, anti-centralist aspirations.[64] Of course, anyone wishing to build the political world on non-centralized workers' syndicates would necessarily hold a hostile view of the dogma of sovereignty, which was not particularly relevant to syndicalism in any case.

[56] (G. W. F. Hegel, *Die Verfassung Deutschlands* (1801-2), in *Sämtliche Werke* (ed. G. Lasson), vol. 7, 2nd edn, Leipzig 1923 (Meiners philosophische Bibliothek, 144), p. 28). See Hermann Heller, *Hegel und der nationale Machtstaatsgedanke in Deutschland, in Gesammelte Schriften*, vol. 1, p. 119.

[57] (G. W. F. Hegel, *Verhandlungen in der Versammlung der Landstände des Königreichs Württemburg im Jahre 1815 und 1816*, in *Sämtliche Werke*, ibid., vol. 7, p. 176 f.) see Heller, ibid., p. 129. See Hegel, *Grundlinien der Philosophie des Rechts, oder Naturrecht und Staatswissenschaft im Grundrisse*, in *Werke*, vol. 8 (ed. E. Gans), Berlin 1833, § 290 (p. 383), that "the actual strength of the states lie in the municipalities."

[58] Preuß, *Gemeinde, Staat, Reich*, p. 212. [59] Ibid., p. 138, 140. [60] Ibid., p. 118.

[61] Ibid., p. 174.

[62] Ibid., p. 208. See also pp. 122, 223 and the polemic against Laband, p. 165.

[63] Ibid., pp. 98, 92. However, Preuß's portrayal also suffers from serious contradictions. While he generally opposes the sovereignty concept as such, even in Gierke (e.g. p. 176), he then does find the sovereignty concept, as formulated by Gierke, Brie, et al, compatible with the *Rechtsstaat* and international law (p. 104).

[64] Literature in Ernst Drahn, "Syndicalism," in *Handwörterbuch der Sozialwissenschaften*, 4th edn, vol. 7 (1926), p. 1192; one should not judge revolutionary syndicalism, as does Werner Sombart (*Sozialismus und soziale Bewegung*, 6th edn, Jena 1906, 1, chap. V) only according to the familiar literati who are often not acquainted with the movement. See Christian Cornélissen, "Über den internationalen Syndikalismus," in *Archiv für Sozialwissenschaften und Sozialpolitik*, 30 (1910), especially p. 162 f.

The most passionate attacks on the dogma of sovereignty arose from the ideas of French syndicalism. It was Léon Duguit, with his lively, contradictory spirit, who undertook to develop a "realistic" theory of the state without the state.[65] If we do not place too much weight on the methodological contrasts, it is hardly surprising that the results of Duguit's naturalist sociologism largely coincide with Kelsen's pure theory of law. Both saw it as one of their main tasks to free legal scholarship from metaphysics, and both referred to the scientific formation of concepts, in contrast to the 'mythological' thinking of the jurists.[66] From this perspective, even to Duguit, a state will or state personality seemed like an unscientific fiction. He found it paradoxical to "suppose that public power does not exist" but was "profoundly convinced" of its non-existence. State authority is nothing but "a scholastic and empty form."[67] He enthusiastically agreed with the syndicalist Berth that "Yes, the state is dead!" but was careful, as the author of a theory of the state, to add: "or rather is in the process of dying,"[68] or "on the point of death. Happily; because if the collectivist doctrine triumphs, it would replace the state with a monstrous power . . .; it would amount to the crushing of the individual and the return of barbarism."[69] It is interesting that Duguit's anarchic individualism recognized a passive and an active "right of resistance" inhering in each person to "laws contrary to legal right,"[70] and how, on the other hand, he was able to radically depersonalize the legal world. The concept of subjective right was, according to Duguit, "a notion of metaphysical order, which should have no place in the positive organization of modern societies."[71] Here, too, the "natural order" played a fateful role; in accordance with Duguit's sociologism, he was interested not in a "law" [*loi*] that accorded with one or another principle, but in one that forced people "until they conformed to the conditions of real life of a given society, determined by the observation and the rational analysis of its evolution and its structure."[72] This "social norm" became a "legal rule" through "the conscience of the mass of individuals" and their "feeling of justice."[73] But the state has nothing to do with making law; "law is not the creation of the state since it exists beyond the state[;] . . . the idea of law is completely independent of the idea of the state as it imposes itself on individuals."[74] It is almost unnecessary to note that this also means that "the belief in the existence of a sovereign state power corresponds to nothing real, so that it is in the process of disappearing;"[75] we may say of the prevailing theory of sovereignty, "however logical it might be, it has no atom of positive reality, that it

[65] A good summary of Léon Duguit's doctrine is found in his *Le droit social, le droit individual et la transformation de l'état*, 3rd edn, Paris 1922; in addition, his *Souveraineté et liberté*, Paris 1922, and his comprehensive *Traité de droit constitutionnel*, 5 vols, 2nd edn, Paris 1921–1925. See Adolf Menzel, "Eine 'realistische' Staatstheorie," in *Österreichische Zeitschrift für öffentliches Recht*, 1 (1914), p. 114 ff.

[66] Duguit, *Traité*, vol. 1, p. 10 f.; Duguit, *Droit social*, p. 27 f.

[67] Duguit, *Droit social*, p. 22. [68] Ibid., p. 40. [69] Ibid., p. 156.

[70] Duguit, *Traité*, vol. 3, p. 659 ff., 735 ff.; this right of resistance however remains only theoretically 'incontestable," ibid., p. 746.

[71] Duguit, *Droit social*, p. 4; Duguit, *Traité*, vol. 1, p. 6, 164.

[72] Duguit, *Droit social*, p. 62; Duguit, *Traité*, vol. 1, p. 18.

[73] Ibid., *Traité*, vol. 1, p. 36, 45. [74] Duguit, *Traité*, vol. 1, p. 33.

[75] Duguit, *Droit social*, p. 1 f.

is a construction of a metaphysical formalism, curiously and logically put together, but altogether alien to concrete reality and today is on the path to collapse."[76]

Marxist and anarcho-socialist literature is particularly instructive on the problems with the concept of sovereignty. However, Marxism, with its one-sided interest in economics, never managed an independent discussion of the problem, despite the fact that it is close enough to the dictatorship of the proletariat.[77] But it is hard to imagine a more radical rejection of state sovereignty than that which follows from the Marxist system. Here the crucial element is not, as a superficial observation might lead one to believe, the emphasis on class struggle. This may call into question the sovereignty of the contemporary state; but where there is struggle there must also be sovereignty. Sovereignty is fundamentally contested, however, by the ideal of an impersonal, authority-free "natural order," which Marxism shares with bourgeois, rule-of-law liberalism. Engels repeatedly formulated an idea of Saint-Simon's as follows: "The government of persons is replaced by the administration of things and the direction of the processes of production."[78]

From the beginnings of modern natural law theory, the idealistic idea of a "natural order," which ultimately leads to the concept of a universal law of right, has run parallel to a positivistically inverted ideal of a causal-law natural order which necessarily abhors the sovereignty of state individuality. In Marxism, the principles of legal right are merely the mirror image of the laws of economics; and the sovereignty of the latter, their impersonal force, their scientifically ascertainable necessity, should replace any kind of individual or personal authority, which amounts to nothing more than economic exploitation. It is clear that this scientific predictability of social existence, undisturbed by any irrational personal powers, is the legacy of the bourgeois ideal of security. Here, too, the problem of the tension between norms and individuality is finally resolved—in this case, in a collective direction, in which individuality is erased. The human being has finally "become a species being in his individual relationships";[79] there is no longer "a requirement of the case, of the times and of persons" [*exigence des cas, des temps et des personnes*]. We encounter the same concept of an impersonal, objective "natural order" among almost all anarcho-socialists, who describe this order in words that often recall Biel and Grotius. "Only the law may rule over human beings," said Proudhon, but "[t]he legislative power belongs only to reason, methodically recognized and demonstrated.... Justice and legality are two

[76] Duguit, *Souveraineté*, p. 77; Duguit, *Traité*, vol. 2 (1923), p. 93 ff.

[77] We will address below Antoine Menger's interesting doctrine of sovereignty, far removed from Marxism, *Neue Staatslehre*, 3rd edn, Jena 1906, p. 164 ff. What is distinctive about Menger as well (op cit., p. 161), is the attack on the concept of the state personality, which makes it possible for the purposes of the most prominent interest groups to seem to be the purposes of all.

[78] Friedrich Engels, *Herrn Eugen Dühring's Umwälzung der Wissenschaft* (1878), 10th edn, Berlin 1919, p. 302 (see Henri Claude de Saint-Simon, "In the present state of enlightenment, the nation needs only to governed, that is to say, administered in the best possible fashion," *Du système industriel* (1821), in *Oeuvres de Saint-Simon*, vol. 5, Paris 1869 (*Oeuvres de Saint-Simon et d'Enfantin*, vol. 21), p. 151).

[79] Karl Marx, *Zur Judenfrage* (1843), in Franz Mehring (ed.), *Aus dem literarischen Nachlaß von Karl Marx, Friedrich Engels und Ferdinand Lasalle*, vol. 1, 2nd edn, Stuttgart 1913, p. 424.

things as independent of our approval as is mathematical truth."[80] Bakunin, too, wanted to recognize only "natural, economic, and social laws, not authoritatively imposed but inherent in things, in relations, in situations ..." Those who today call themselves "free citizens" are, in contrast, always forced to "obey the representatives of law—human beings."[81]

In the English language, a noteworthy attempt to engage with the problem of sovereignty was undertaken by Harold J. Laski, a socialist associated with Marxism.[82] However, his sometimes ingenious, generally quite contradictory views, an odd mix of English liberalism and pragmatism with Gierke's corporatist theory and syndicalist anti-étatism, could hardly count as Marxist on any single point. Because he completely misunderstood the dogma of sovereignty, his polemics have the nature of tilting at windmills.[83] Laski's emphatic assertion that "my allegiance is divided between the different groups to which I belong"[84] was never contested, while the sentence he so vehemently fought, "what the State wills has therefore moral preeminence,"[85] had not been claimed by anyone. Symptomatic of dogmatic history, however, is his repeated assertion that "the real rulers of a society are undiscoverable ... The will of the State, in fact, is the will of government as that will is accepted by the citizens over whom it rules."[86] The lack of a sovereign person is the reason Laski rejects the theory of state sovereignty. But he cannot find a person because he sees nothing in the representation problem but "the problem of enabling me to have contact with those men" ("whose actions reveal a purpose sufficiently akin to my own to enlist my support.")[87]

Attacks on the prevailing theory of internal state sovereignty have remained relatively small in number. These attacks do not clearly indicate what crucial theoretical difficulties the sovereignty problem raises for the prevailing doctrine.

Attacks on external state sovereignty have been far more numerous and vehement, especially since the World War. Again and again we encounter the view that Bodin's absolutist concept of sovereignty is 'outdated' and no longer appropriate

80 Pierre-Joseph Proudhon, *Qu'est-ce que la propriété? Ou recherches sur le principe du droit et du gouvernement*. Premier mémoire, 1st edn, Paris 1840, p. 23, 235. Like a shot, this absolutely objective lawfulness was followed suddenly by the nation as the legislating person: "Only the nation has the right to say, 'be it known and decreed'" (ibid., p. 236).

81 Michael Bakunin, "Philosophische Betrachtungen über das Gottesphantom," in *Gesammelte Werke*, vol. 1, Berlin 1921, p. 215. See the defense of anarchism by the neo-Kantian Marxist Max Adler, *Die Staatsauffassung des Marxismus. Ein Beitrag zur Unterscheidung von soziologischer und juristischer Methode*, Vienna 1922 (Marx-Studien, vol. 4, part II), p. 205 ff., and Hermann Heller, "Sozialismus und Nation," in *Gesammelte Schriften*, vol. 1, p. 478 ff.

82 Harold J. Laski, *Studies in the Problem of Sovereignty*, New Haven 1917; Laski, *The Foundations of Sovereignty and Other Essays*, New York 1921; Laski, *A Grammar of Politics*, London 1925 (reprinted 1926), p. 44 ff.

83 The American Westel Woodbury Willoughby, *Fundamental Concepts of Public Law*, New York 1924, p. 44, noted on this: "He [Laski] persistently adds to the jurist's conception of sovereignty qualities which the jurist expressly excludes, and that it is upon the basis of this false definition that he denies to sovereignty that omnipotence which jurists ascribe to it."

84 Laski, *Studies*, p. 15 85 Ibid., p. 8.

86 Laski, *Grammar*, p. 56. But a few sentences later he says, "The community over which they preside must be given the chance to decide that it prefers a different body of men as governors. There is, that is to say, no permanent right to power." See Laski, *Foundations*, p. 28 f.; Laski, *Studies*, pp. 7, 17.

87 Laski, *Grammar*, p. 265.

for the international legal situation. Let us ask here, too, what status the historical Bodin ascribed to the sovereign person of international law. According to Bodin, far from facing no external limits, the sovereign was bound not only by "divine fundamental legal principles" [*ius divinum*] and "natural" [*naturale*], but by the "laws of all peoples, based as these are in natural and divine law."[88] The law of private property shared the inviolability of "the law of peoples" [*ius gentium*],[89] while contract law enjoyed the sanctity of natural law.[90] Not even the danger of the demise of the state could free it from contractual obligations: "Seeing then that faith is the only foundation and support of justice whereon not only states but all human society is grounded."[91] Nevertheless, in Chapter 4 of the third book, one of the most important but least cited sections of his *Republic*, Bodin not only comes to the conclusion that the magistrate must carry out the "prince's commands" [*iussa principis*], "if not contrary to the laws of God and nature ... although it seems to differ from the laws of other nations,"[92] but also rejects the magistrate's right to disobey or resign his office because of laws "that seem to him contrary to the laws of nature, albeit that they indeed be not contrary thereunto."[93] We will give Bodin's very important reasons in detail: "For the equity and reason which we call natural is not always so clear and manifest, but that it finds impugners. Yes, oftentimes the greatest lawyers and philosophers are therein entangled, and of quite contrary opinions, and the laws of peoples are therein sometimes so repugnant, that some of them appoint reward, and some others punishment for the selfsame fact."[94]

The existence and justification for Bodin's sovereign person was beyond question. A common will of the state, as the sovereign person, seems to have become problematic in today's world, in both its existentiality and its ethical and political justification. The reasons are the same in international law as they are in constitutional law for the degeneration of the dogma of sovereignty. Surrogates for universalist natural law—pacifist and economic security ideologies—are what deny the sovereignty of today's nation states and in part promote, in part proclaim it as an attribute of a world organization or of international law.

A radical group among the opponents of the theory of sovereignty would prefer to completely eradicate it from international law; the polemics of another, more moderate group address only the absolute nature of the concept in international law.

In Germany, aside from Kelsen, only a few authors, apparently under his influence, have called for the complete elimination of sovereignty from international law.[95]

[88] Bodin, *De Republica* (see note 7), book 1, chap. 8 (p. 84).

[89] Ibid., book I, chap. 8 (p. 103). [90] Ibid., book I, chap. 8 (p. 87; see 100).

[91] Ibid., book V, chap. 6 (p. 594); but excluded from the sanctity of contract were "immoral contracts" [*pacta turpia*] (ibid.).

[92] Ibid., book III, chap. 4 (p. 289) [313]. [93] Ibid., book III, chap. 4 (p. 290) [314–15].

[94] Ibid [315]. See the immediately subsequent explanation of why the decision of the "multitude" [*multitude*] and not the "wise" [*sapientes*] is to be followed.

[95] See Josef Laurenz Kunz, "Völkerrechtsreform," in Karl Strupp (ed.), *Wörterbuch des Völkerrechts und der Diplomatie*, vol. 3, Berlin 1929, p. 297. Sovereignty as an "impediment" to international law, the most important thing the "struggle against that dogma." Further, with the usual consistency, see Karl Strupp, *Grundzüge des positive Völkerrecht*, 2nd edn, Bonn 1922, p. 44: The entire concept of sovereignty had to disappear from international law; on p. 61, however, the state is called externally "omnipotent."

Far more cautious are the constant, ever growing number of voices that merely advocate limiting the prevailing concept of sovereignty.[96] A good overview of the foreign literature striving for the theoretical reduction of sovereignty—also the best writing on this topic—has been provided in French-language pieces published by the American James W. Garner[97] and Politis of Greece.[98] The former opposes any theory of sovereignty that ascribes to the state "unlimited juridical powers in regard to other states and their nationals, powers which are not subject to any control, other than those that the state imposes on itself, and which confer the right to rule its own conduct and internal politics as a sovereign and without regard for other states; to make itself the sole judge of its international obligations, to choose the form of its government and to change it at will."[99] The old, absolutist theory of sovereignty does not fit today's international situation: "in place of 'an anarchy of sovereignties' we have a society of independent states, united by legal right and connected by an intense solidarity of interests. From the economic point of view, the world appears in large measure as a unity."[100] Garner does not contradict those who claim that the world, even before the League of Nations, had the character "of a federation endowed with corporative juridical personality."[101] He sees in the prevailing dogma of sovereignty "the principal obstacle to a world organization," "an obstacle to the maintenance of peace and to the progress of the common interests of states."[102]

In this context, the theory of "world sovereignty," suggested by Wilson's secretary of state Robert Lansing, should be noted as characteristic to the highest degree. However, this practical politician was uninterested in legal sovereignty; he called it "an agreeable phrase to the present generation."[103] In his opinion, however, it

Elsewhere (Karl Strupp, *Theorie und Praxis des Völkerrechts*, Berlin 1925, p. 8), he considers the concept of sovereignty in international law to be "absolutely unnecessary and merely confusing." See also Hans Wilhelm Thieme, *Die Fortbildung der internationalen Schiedsgerichtsbarkeit seit dem Weltkrieg*, Leipzig 1927 (Frankfurter Abhandlungen zum Kriegsverhütungsrecht, vol. 1), p. 33 f. Before Kelsen, however, Otfried Nippold, in *Die Fortbildung des Verfahrens in völkerrechtlichen Streitigkeiten*, Leipzig 1907, p. 59, had already claimed that sovereignty was "not a particularly international law principle." An overview of foreign literature that wishes to thoroughly banish sovereignty dogma from the juristic literature is found in Francis William Coker, "Pluralist Theories and the Attack upon State Sovereignty," in Ch. E. Merriam and H. E. Barnes (eds), *A History of Political Theories. Recent Times*, New York 1924, III chapter.

[96] Quite convolutedly, Siegfried Marck, *Substanz- und Funktionsbegriff in der Rechtsphilosophie*, Tübingen 1925, p. 133: "Sovereignty in the absolute sense of the absolutely unconditional validity of an order, the autonomy of a system can only belong to law, never to the state as an association." Most recently, Richard Thoma, "Staat," in *Handwörterbuch der Staatswissenschaften*, 4th edn, vol. 7 (1926), p. 755: the state could, "if in humanity law is to have any validity at all not be set in place as absolutely sovereign" (see ibid., p. 750 f.). Alfred Verdroß, *Die Einheit des rechtlichen Weltbildes auf Grundlage der Völkerrechtsverfassung*, Tübingen 1923; Louis Le Fur, "Le droit naturel ou objectif s'étend-il aux rapports internationaux?," in *Revue de droit international et de legislation compare*, 52 (1925), pp. 59–79.

[97] James W. Garner, "Des Limitations à la souveraineté nationale dans les relations extérieures," in *Revue de droit international et de législation compare*, 52 (1925), pp. 36–58.

[98] Nicolas-Socrate Politis, "Le problème des limitations de la souveraineté et la théorie de l'abus des droits dans les rapports internationaux," in *Recueil des Cours*, 6 (1925 I), p. 5 ff.

[99] Garner, op. cit., p. 37 f. [100] Ibid., p. 52. [101] Ibid., p. 53.

[102] Ibid., pp. 55, 54.

[103] Robert Lansing, *Notes on Sovereignty from the Standpoint of the State and of the World*, Washington 1921, p. 83.

was possible "to conceive of the human race as one body"; "from the very nature of things" it should follow "that in this unorganized mass of humanity there must be a certain body of individuals possessing a physical might sufficient to compel obedience by every member of the human race throughout the world. Such superior physical might constitutes sovereignty, and, since its only limit is the earth, it may properly be termed World Sovereignty."[104]

Lansing does immediately argue that this "physical force" possesses no "definitive manifestation"; however, he assures himself that "the existing of such supreme force is self-proving." He thus concludes that the "dominant body of individuals possess the World Sovereignty and is itself the World Sovereign."[105] As a matter of politics, we can certainly understand this American's views in 1921.

Most recently, N. Politis provides a particularly detailed contribution to the struggle against the dogma of sovereignty. His arguments, his basic concepts of state and law, are representative of the international intellectual trend characterized in this section. Politis believes that "along with all other legal rules, those of international law are the products of economic needs and are gradually established in the juridical conscience of peoples".[106] He sees the state as "a pure abstraction" behind which "vain fiction" there is only "one lone real personality: that of the individual." Consequently, and quite typically, Politis concludes: "If the state is a pure abstraction, the international community as it has been composed until the present, as a meeting of states, is an even greater abstraction." After all, in reality it had "the same human structure as internal political communities. It is altogether simply composed of individuals grouped into national societies."[107] Politis also tells us that the modern state tends to be "no more than a power which commands in order to become a federation of public services that administer."[108] On this basis, Politis develops his attack—extremely radical theoretically, but politically quite cautious—against the dogma of sovereignty. Essentially, he believes it has already been overcome, "virtually abolished." "Attacked by the ceaselessly changing necessities of life, reduced to shreds, ruined to the point of no longer deserving a place in the domain of memories, it continues to dazzle our vision and to put a stop to thought."[109] But, "what assures the final triumph of this new conception of international law is the irremediable ruin to which is doomed the other fundamental principle of the classical doctrine: that of sovereignty."[110] Based on a wealth of literature, the author finds that "a general anathema is raised against it, which condemns it irremediably."[111] This condemnation is provisionally addressed only to the absolute version of the concept of sovereignty. But it is not enough to revise the concept and cleanse it of exaggerations; Politis also thinks it necessary, for theoretical and practical reasons, to "eliminate it completely and definitively from juridical language including similar expressions and no longer to speak of sovereignty."[112] Referring explicitly to Kelsen, Krabbe, and so on, he would reserve sovereignty "to law and for later for the

[104] Ibid., p. 57. [105] Ibid. [106] Politis, op. cit., 109; see p. 111.
[107] Ibid., p. 6. [108] Ibid. [109] Ibid, p. 10.
[110] Ibid. See ibid., p. 111: "The dogma of sovereignty has perished. It answers to nothing real."
[111] Ibid., p. 17. [112] Ibid., p. 19.

international community."[113] Politis has no doubt "a good part of the imperfections of our science are due to the persistence in use of the idea of sovereignty."[114] It poses an unavoidable dilemma for science: "Either the state is sovereign, in which case it could not be subject to imperative rules; or it is subject and so is not sovereign."[115] To the theory that international law was grounded in the will of states, he responds: "States, being only a fiction, have no element of will."[116] In practice, however, sovereignty has caused much worse harm. It has allowed "the provision of the appearance of justification to all the arbitrary pretensions of governments. It gave them the pretexts for their intransigence, their ambition, their imperialism. It impelled them to wars and to conquests."[117]

After these preliminaries, we might assume that Politis is about to finally carry out the exorcism. But it soon becomes apparent that his statements are meant to apply only to the politics of law. Pacifist observations, as the author notes, are in danger of being futile precisely "because they encounter a formidable obstacle in the actual state of international law dominated by the idea of sovereignty."[118] Taking account of this situation, Politis acknowledges that in matters of the "reserved domain" [*domaine reservé*], "each country can demand an absolute power."[119] And now, one is a bit surprised "by the terrible and fateful antinomy offered by international law," as well as by the finding that international law "ignores precisely and excludes from its forecasts the most urgent and most anguished problems of the present time." Still more: "It abandons them to the free discretion of states, to the mercy of particular interests, to the struggle of economic antagonisms. Instead of preventing and moderating conflicts, by its silence it provokes and worsens them."[120]

We can accordingly accept that sovereignty has not by any means been overcome by a positive law perspective. We need not consider the question of whether the name change suggested by Politis from "sovereignty" to "liberty" is more than a question of terminology, or whether it also has a civic educational significance.[121] Politis himself states that his important application of the "theory of abuse of right" to international law does not affect the dogma of sovereignty, and we may believe him when he says that this theory is well-suited to "eliminate progressively the dangerous character [of sovereignty]."[122]

With Politis, we come to the end of our ponderous literature review. At least we gather from him that the dogma of sovereignty in constitutional law and international law has, on the one hand, become highly problematic in the international literature, but on the other hand, no authors, whatever they might suggest or promise, have dared to eliminate the concept of sovereignty completely. Often, they simply try to call it something else, or to locate it elsewhere by declaring the government sovereign or constructing a legal or world sovereignty. But all—not

113 Ibid., p. 18 114 Ibid., p. 19. 115 Ibid., p. 14. 116 Ibid., p. 30.
117 Ibid., p. 20.
118 Ibid., p. 11. See p. 111: "actual international law, still dominated by the idea of sovereignty."
119 Ibid., p. 43 120 Ibid., p. 56; see p. 112. 121 Ibid., p. 21.
122 Ibid., p. 109.

only those mentioned here—agree that Bodin's concept of "absolute" sovereignty has been overcome.

The reader may have noted that all the attacks on the dogma of sovereignty cited here are based in a more or less shared, if often unclear, overall concept of state and law, the roots of which go back to the natural law view of an impersonal "natural order." The theoretical crisis of the sovereignty dogma is therefore mainly, though not solely, a crisis of the sovereign person, the state. The systematic development of the sovereignty concept to be undertaken in the following pages will therefore be compelled, first of all, to highlight the basic concepts of state and law, in order to show, with their help, the theoretical necessity or superfluity of the sovereignty concept in its prevailing form, or in a revised version.

# II
## Rule and Order

Every legal problem, without exception, is rooted downwards in sociology and upwards in the sphere of political ethics; all legal problems are not only accessible to both causal and normative approaches, but in fact require both.

The sociological problem of sovereignty, and thus the fundamental sociological problem of public law, is the relationship between rule and order. No one has yet denied that the problem of rule belongs in sociology; and no public law scholar, despite lawyers' aversion to sociological questions, has been able to skirt the concept of rule. More controversial is the possibility of dealing with the concept of social order ontologically and, even more so, the legal fruitfulness of such an interpretation. One of the tasks of this chapter will be to show that a public law theory could not manage without establishing independently the causal structure of its subject, the legal order. The problem of sovereignty is so muddled not least because jurisprudence has become entangled in the net of its terms, with no regard for causation.

"Obedience constitutes rule" [*Oboedientia facit imperantem*] is one of Spinoza's great, clear sociological insights.[123] To rule means to enjoy obedience, regardless of whether those who obey agree inwardly with the orders, and, in particular, regardless of whether the interests of the obedient are promoted. It is obvious that rule can lead to the autonomy of the ruled; that compliance can rest on promotion of interests and can appear as spontaneous, active enthusiasm. But rule remains a relationship between two wills, the motivation of one will by another; the idea of rule over things, always mediated by a ruling will, is thus eliminated once and for all. In a practicable sense that differs from the too-general concept of power, rule means: ensuring compliance using one's own means; if necessary, compelling obedience using one's own means. In this sense, the employer rules over the worker, but the latter does not rule over the former when he sues him for his wages.[124] We will deal later with the fact that this ideal-typical concept of rule—obedience to orders without regard for consent, as well as enforceability using one's own means—does not occur in its pure form in actual society. Incidentally, the concept of rule invariably shares this fate with any concept that comes into being through logical isolation and idealization.

[123] Echoes are found in numerous places; see, e.g., "it is the will to obey that makes one a subject," [obtemperantia subditum facit] Benedict de Spinoza, *Tractatus theologico-politicus* (1670), in *Opera* (ed. J. v. Vloten and J. P. N. Land), vol. 1, Den Haag 1882, p. 565.

[124] On this, see Max Weber, *Wirtschaft und Gesellschaft*, 2nd edn, Munich 1925, vol. 2, p. 604. Max Wenzel, *Der Begriff des Gesetzes. Zugleich eine Untersuchung zum Begriff des Staates und Problem des Völkerrechts*, Berlin 1920 (Juristische Grundprobleme, 1st treatise), p. 219 ff.

The concept of social order is ambiguous;[125] it can mean a type of human behavior or an order of norms. In the first case, as experience shows, social order denotes that, within a social group, certain people will behave in certain ways under certain circumstances. A social order thus consists of nothing more than the empirical chance of consistent behavior, the fact that we can expect certain behavior; order is predictability.[126] Predictability is to a certain degree the requirement of all human culture, since human coexistence can only be organized coexistence: "We only gain power over life in society to the extent that we understand and use regularity and structure."[127] It is undeniable that the behavior of those who seem psychologically alien remains ultimately unpredictable and an eternal mystery; if, however, a misunderstood idealism takes from this fact a rejection of any observation of causality in society, it is condemned to sterility, and furthermore forgets that, in most cases, even scientific regularity must work with unknown intermediate elements.

The necessary manifestation of rule is social order; every type of rule presents itself from below as an order.

A mistake often made by lawyers is to reverse this sentence when it comes to the legal order. Austin and his analytic school in England thus arrived at this proposition: "right is what is commanded" [*jus est quod jussum est*].[128] Not every more or less consciously created social order is a system of rule; it can arise as much by promise as by command. Thus, among consciously created orders, we distinguish between orders of rule and contractual orders.

Every consciously created order emerges and persists through a meeting of wills. This unification of two or more wills is necessary both for each individual norm and for a comprehensive order of norms. For every order is possible only according to one single specific principle; that is, any ordering rule must determine, implicitly or explicitly, that a particular person in a particular situation must behave in a particular way. Only this type of individualized rule is capable of carrying out the ordering function. It is very significant that many, indeed most, consciously created rules implicate a range of determinations that are not expressed explicitly because they are assumed to be obvious in these legal contexts—yet without which they would, for example in a foreign legal context, lack sufficient individuation.

There are very important differences arising out of sociological necessity between the structures of an order of rule and a contractual order. For an order of rule, an essential characteristic is the existence of a 'ruler,' that is, a permanent, universal, and effective decision-making unit. It does not matter whether this entity of unitary command comes about through a single will or through many wills united in some way into a decision-making unit.

[125] See below, p. 110 f.

[126] Weber, *Wirtschaft und Gesellschaft*, p. 1 ff.; Weber, "Über einige Kategorien der verstehenden Soziologie" (1913), in *Gesammelte Aufsätze zur Wissenschaftslehre*, Tübingen 1922, p. 432 ff; Hermann Jahrreiss, *Das Problem der rechtlichen Liquidation des Weltkriegs für Deutschland*, Leipzig 1924 (Leipziger rechtswissenschaftliche Studien, vol. 8), p. 13 f., 44 f.

[127] Wilhelm Dilthey, "Das Wesen der Philosophie," in Paul Hinneberg (ed.), *Die Kultur der Gegenwart*, part I, sec. VI (Systematische Philosophie), 3rd edn, Leipzig 1921, p. 3.

[128] See John Austin, *Lectures on Jurisprudence*, 2 vols, 5th edn, London 1911, vol. 1, p. 86 ff.

The decision-making unit of command is an absolutely necessary conceptual element of an order of rule, if only because obedience is impossible without an unambiguous understanding of the command on the part of those who submit.[129] There can be varying degrees of certainty of command, but it has absolute minimum and maximum limits. The minimum level of certainty that makes behaving in accordance with orders possible in the first place is determined by the ultimate effect sought by the command. Whether sufficient individuation is present depends, among other things, on the intensity of the community of agreement among the individuals involved in the power relationship, and can only be specified in each concrete case. 'March!' is not a command if it does not at least also specify the goal of the march, whether expressly through words or gestures or tacitly through known conventions. A further clarification of the command can be added to the individuation. This will prove necessary in any more comprehensive power relationship. The hierarchy of organs of power therefore reflects a hierarchy of clarification of command that cannot be enforced from the top down, because it is not foreseeable. Thus, for example, a command individuated by establishing the goal of the march can be clarified by providing the speed of the march, its route, rest periods, and so on for the smaller and smallest groups, depending on conditions, "according to the demands of the case, of the times and of persons."

It follows from the above that the certainty of command also has maximum limits. No command is ever able to fully determine the will to which it is addressed. It can determine a specific direction for it.[130] It cannot achieve more precision because it wants the order to succeed. It must necessarily presume a minimum of personal initiative in the execution of orders, because no body of commands can tap into the temporal, locational, and especially personal circumstances that must be considered at the time of execution. In this regard, there is only conscious obedience and no absolutely complete concretization of the command.

Rule thus means specific orders and binding decisions. But decision-making—and upon this depends nothing less than everything—is, to the extent we are considering human beings, exclusively a function of human, personal judgment. In this fact lies the final reason that an impersonal "natural order" is forever incapable of taking on the decision-making function. Whether one views this "order" as a law of is or ought, it must always be decided on as a matter of choice, even if the choice is not free, by human beings, that is, by people who differ spatially and temporally, socially and individually. Growing awareness of the law-governed existence may certainly influence human decision-making to an increasing degree, but it will never replace it. The fact that it is night does not decide whether it ought to be light or dark; for humans prefer overcoming the natural darkness of night through the artificial

[129] On the negation of state acts due to vagueness, see Karl Kormann, *System der rechtsgeschäftlichen Staatsakte. Verwaltungs- und prozeßrechtliche Untersuchungen zum allgemeinen Teil des öffentlichen Rechts*, Berlin 1910 (Manuldruck 1925), p. 280, and the sources mentioned there; e.g., Friedrich Oetker, *Konkursrechtliche Grundbegriffe*, vol. 1, Stuttgart 1891, p. 50; the "non-individualized judgment" is one of the "absolutely void facts."

[130] See below, p. 124 f.

light of electricity. The either–or that every decision signifies can only be attributed to human beings.

But even if one envisions humanity as a unified organization of rule, the legislation and application of laws remains bound to individual decisions. What is true of ideas in general is particularly true of the idea of law: it just appears in an unfamiliar form! Even the most objective human decision therefore remains a subjective decision, and wherever the issue is not only unity of purpose but also ordering social behavior the unmediated rule of an idea is not possible. Even if the motive of obedience is strengthened by the obligating power of an idea, along with habit, interest, and inclination, the unity of wills that individuates the spirit of the idea remains indispensable.

These insights, in themselves simple, have been obscured today by ideas that are all closely related to the formalized, impersonal legal worldview of the present time. In the political sphere, the sociological background of these types of ideas becomes clear if one recalls that, in the bourgeois *Rechtsstaat*, the dependence of representatives on the people is achieved by elevating the laws that flow from the "general will" above any state action.[131] A formal democracy that has lost the substantive idea of the *Rechtsstaat*—whose representative classes no longer believe in its right to represent them and whose class contradictions make a "general will" unlikely—has an understandable interest in countering the idea of class dominance by propagating the ideology of a completely objective rule of law. As in the religious idea "all are equal before God, here it appears, in light of a similar idea, that law . . . is a power that is so far above the individual that its variety vanishes into nothing."[132] The universalist expansion of this idea of an impersonal legal order is supported in turn by the growing economic interconnections among states, pacifist ideas, and institutions of the League of Nations. And this formalist ideology is believed precisely because there is no faith in a material idea of law that would require individual decision-making units in order to become law.

In face of such obfuscation, we must cling to the fact that, as in every order of rule, so also in democracies, there must be a 'ruler,' an effective decision-making unit. For in every system of government, the minimum number of command decisions, the basic form of rule which must be replicated in every concretization, is determined only by the ruler. The existence of rule is conditioned by the fact that the concretization to be achieved by the institutions has consistent limits in the commands individuated by the ruler. The unity of rule is a unity of the will of the ruler. The commands of all institutions of rule are signaled in the basic structure determined by individual units of command; their commands are not new and original, but are somehow derivative commands. Therefore, concretization ultimately can only be understood through individuation. This structure of rule is found everywhere, including in places where the content of commands emerges democratically through the harmonization of the wills of the subjects. No doubt the determination of the

[131] On the following, see Hermann Heller, *Der Begriff des Gesetzes in der Reichsverfassung*.
[132] Gerhard Anschütz, *Die Verfassungsurkunde für den Preußischen Staat vom 31. Januar 1850*, vol. I, Berlin 1912, p. 108.

community by the ruler corresponds with sociological necessity to a determination of the ruler by the community. All such difficulties have their basis in the fact that the community, in its opinions, is necessarily ambiguous and changeable and as such, as "public opinion," does not represent a decision-making unit that could make clear rules. We will return to this problem of sovereign persons later in greater detail. Here we will confine ourselves to the assertion that, because there is no rule without individuated commands, there is also no rule without a ruler—that is, without a decision-making unit that is always formed by individual historical processes of will.

Ruling means gaining obedience, effectively commanding. It is also of great juristic importance that the decisiveness of command is required for it to be effective and enforceable. The consistent effectiveness of commands is essential to the entirety of rule, but not to the individual commands. No authority is ever followed by everyone at every moment; but it vanishes the moment it can no longer reckon with acknowledgment to a sociological relevant degree, that is, for its achievement as a whole. "Obedience constitutes the ruler." Therefore, physical force is essential for rule only as a substitute or addition to "obedience." Force is indispensable only to replace acts of submission by individuals. But the decisiveness of the command remains primary—for the point of rule is not to force, but to force to some end.

For the sake of both decisiveness and effectiveness, the order of rule requires an actual ruler, an historically located individual unit of will and effect within a multiplicity of wills.

Contrasting with the system of rule is the second class of consciously created orders, the contractual systems, characterized by the lack of an effective, universal decision-making unit. Of course, there are also contracts within and based on an order of rule. Much of what will later be said about contractual systems is also true of these contracts within such an order. But the pure type of contractual order emerges outside an order of rule. This does not mean that the duality or multiplicity of wills here would otherwise be disorderly—if only because every consciously created order is only the rational part of the social content that is constructed upon innumerable social orders that are not consciously created. But a contract forms a consciously created harmonization of wills that is most certainly capable of individuating rules. Without such an intentional decision-making unit, neither an order of rule nor a contractual order is possible. Nevertheless, the sociological and legal distinction between the two systems is immense. It is the inclination of natural law to blur this distinction. In contrast, Bodin emphasized it frequently, and polemically: "Wherein we see many to be deceived, which makes a confusion of laws, and of a prince's contracts, which they call also laws; as well as he which calls a prince's contracts pactionary laws [etc.]."[133] Precisely in order to emphasize the diference between the sovereign's bonds and its stronger contractual obligations, Bodin said, "We must not then confound the laws and the contracts of sovereign princes, for that the law depends of the will and pleasure of him that has sovereignty, who may bind all his subjects, but cannot bind himself."[134]

[133] Bodin, *De Republica* (see note 7), book I, chap. 8 (p. 86 f.) [92].
[134] Ibid., book I, chap. 8 (p. 87) [93].

The lack of insight into the varieties of orders of rule and of contractual orders has caused most of the misunderstandings of the sovereignty problem. The differences are found in the decisiveness and effectiveness of each order. Any social order is historically unique; a contractual order, individuated at the moment of its emergence by an agreement of wills, says only that in the best case certain behavior can be expected by certain people in certain situations. But this rule lacks a decision-making unit that constantly adjusts its implementation and development to changing people and powers. Even if we presume that the given multiplicity of wills presupposes the best imaginable will for respecting the rules—the best possible will for agreement on ends and means—the existence of rules that may originally have seemed clear appears to be constantly threatened by a proviso of the type "as long as these conditions persist" [*clausula rebus sic stantibus*] because of the ambiguity of every expression and the possibility of misunderstanding every sign, especially when fundamental values differ, and people, times, and circumstances change. In contrast, the order of rule in its ideal-type form—that is, thoroughly organized and rationalized—may not refuse to make any decisions; it must be capable of deciding on the limits of the parties' wills in every conflict at any time—that is, universally and constantly.

Legal positivism, which ascribes to individuality neither a logical nor a legal function, completely ignores this distinction between contractual systems and systems of rule, emphasizing quite one-sidedly only the second, though also significant, difference in the effectiveness of each system. "So I wish, so I desire, let my will stand for reason" [*Sic volo, sic jubeo, stat pro ratione voluntas*] is not by any means only the maxim of tyrants; it also clearly describes each individual decision-making unit's conception of ordering technique. Everyone knows that ultimately there is no logical resolution of controversial questions of values. If an established order applies to these questions, their calculability nevertheless requires a specific calculation method that cannot be calculated. Even in a community of beings that agreed on all their values, individuated rules would be necessary that, regardless of content, would fulfill their ordering task through their mere existence. "Even the 'divine hosts' would not be able to join a drill routine."[135] A contractual order lacks this constant decisiveness. But at the same time, this means that its effectiveness is different from that of an order of rule. Even if a party to the contract is subject to a praetor, and even if he can express that "thus" [*sic*] in every case—he would lack his own means of carrying out his own maxim against opponents. Certainly, we should not neglect to mention all the unconsciously established social orders that, often enough, succeed in ensuring that purely contractual orders are adhered to more precisely as orders of rule—for example, because the interests of the parties compel this. Nevertheless, it should have become clear that orders of rule are 'orders' to a far greater degree, since the regularity of behavior in them can, as a rule, be calculated far better than in contractual orders. It depends not only, and not primarily, on whether the ruler physically forces the regularity of behavior; what matters is that, as

[135] Gustav Radbruch, *Grundzüge der Rechtsphilosophie*, Leipzig 1914, p. 172.

a unit of will among a multiplicity of wills, he constantly and universally determines its regularity.

The observations in this chapter, which will be explained in later chapters, are considered ideal-types of orders of rule and contract. The fact that social reality offers fluid transitions between the two types is exactly what makes the construction of such ordering schemas scientifically necessary.

We call sovereign those decision-making units that are subject to no effective universal decision-making units. The extent to which today's states count as sovereign will be discussed soon. In any case, their sovereignty must be considered as an historical category. The Middle Ages had nothing resembling the modern state—a monist association of territorial authority that brings order and subordinates every decisive entity on its territory into a central decision-making unit. In the modern era, intercourse has grown immensely and is continually increasing. It thus requires growing predictability of social relationships, which can only be achieved, in turn, through systematic order by way of a decision-making unit equipped with increasing scope. It is hardly probable, though not impossible, that Europe will in future replace state sovereignty with feudal capitalism, for example, which would once again dissolve political rule into a bundle of private law use rights.

Regarding the state's external manifestation, given the manifold erroneous misconceptions, we must not shy away from the banal observation that the earth today, and for the foreseeable future, constitutes no uniform governing order, no individualized order of rule. If any organized coexistence is to be possible on it at all, it is today only possible, essentially, in the form of a contractual order. Contracts outside of orders of rule have only made complete sense when they are concluded between thoroughly independent persons who are capable of consistently living up to their agreements—that is, they do not need the unpredictable approval of a third party. But the behavior of a person of sovereign rule—that is, a foreign, effective, and universal decision-making unit—is unpredictable. If we disregard the meeting of contracting parties in uninhabited parts of the world, we know these subjects of rule only as states. Only they count as independent, because—and as long as—they are capable of making binding promises authoritatively to their members without the intervention of third parties. This order of rule is thus a prerequisite for that contractual order.

This brings us directly to consideration of the problem of sovereignty, the legal resolution of which has numerous prerequisites. First, several brief methodological remarks are essential.

So far, we have spoken of will and agreements of will that individuate social orders. There seems to be no bridge leading from these entirely real wills to the law of today's prevailing legal science. After all, it has—not merely through its logical conclusion in Kelsen—been as thoroughly caught in a concept of 'ought,' in contrast to 'want,' as a spider in its own web. Here the scientific concept of 'will' plays a role which, given that it is exclusively a matter of psychological reality and is constantly changing, is the total opposite of the objective permanence of legal oughts. We will have reason to return again and again to this concept of will. But we can already note here that, for an examination of society that attempts to understand causal connections, the objectivity and permanence of a will that motivates the behavior of others is certainly ascertainable. The ruler who wishes to motivate his followers, who hopes to motivate each and every one, even at times when he is not actually thinking of commands, desires this command as soon as he attempts to reach its addressees. Perhaps he wants this command tomorrow, for years to come, even when he is sleeping. If I place a sign on my private property saying 'No Entry,' this is merely an objectification of my will using other materials. However, the separation of a specific will from a subjective course of experience and its concrete and relatively permanent objectification is a sociological necessity for the existence of any social order. The will of the military commander, like any other ruler, must objectify itself because it must motivate many wills, and do so for the future; it must make itself clear to his officers through numerous examples, in which it may be presented no longer as a concrete, actual psychological act, but as an ought—yet as an ought only because it was wanted individually for this case and this point in time. The juristic or military officer may never actually see the ruler's will and perhaps only experiences it as an ideal ought, behind which there is no longer any actual want.

Viewing law as will and as the purpose of the existing social order—that is, as social technology—obviously does not by any means exhaust the nature of law. A causal treatment of social orders does not subject itself to these orders, but observes them from the outside. As necessary as it is, a proper juristic analysis must separate the logical substance of law from all other social orders that support it and understand law as norms. However, it holds for juristic as for all kinds of knowledge that the fundamental principle is that the value of this separation of partial content from a totality is conditioned by the ability to see the separated part in the structure of the whole.

# III
## Sovereignty and Positivity

According to Bodin, the essence of sovereignty lies "in this supreme power for the giving and abrogation of the law" [*jubendae ac tollendae leges summa potestate*].[136] Bodin was right.

The reason for our agreement, however, requires a detailed explanation of the problem of lawmaking, which must in turn be undergirded with at least a preliminary agreement on the concept of law.

One of the peculiarities of present-day positivist legal science is that its most comprehensive and fundamental works begin by observing that the essence of law is a metalegal issue that is not their concern. The negative conflict of jurisdictions between legal science and legal philosophy would be unproblematic if legal scientists could and would use the findings of legal philosophy in defining their subject. But when not even preliminary attempts of any kind are made to determine what is the state of affairs designated by law—when one is satisfied to define law as the norm for any old substance—the possibility of any juristic discussion ends.[137]

We give the name law to a social order, created by communal authority, that provides normative boundaries to the mutually related—that is, social—behavior of bearers of will. We are provided with individual, varied bearers of will whose social behavior—that is, their acts, acquiescences, and omissions—may be normatively limited by an authoritative rule, as long as it expresses social effects and does not remain merely an internal psychological process or a process of conscience. A legal relationship is never a relationship between two individuals, but is always a triangular relationship—generally two individuals related by a rule that normatively binds their will to act: a legal principle.

Law, as an intersubjective normative binding of wills, has an objective existence; it is so, of course, not as a sensual natural phenomenon, but as a historically unique reality. It is no more a "mass conception of a norming"[138] than are the rules of German

136 Bodin, *De Republica* (see note 7), book I, chap. 10 (p. 155).

137 A classic testimony by Kelsen, *Problem der Souveränität* (see note 38), p. 13 f., note 1, for whom the question of what is just is "meaningless" within juristic epistemology and any such attempt by a jurist is in vain. Alfred Verdroß, *Die Verfassung der Völkerrechtsgemeinschaft*, Vienna 1926, p. 1 ff., undertakes this attempt, but at the same time leaves the pure theory of law with flags flying, in that he designates as a legal order any social order that is fundamentally oriented to the value of justice (ibid., p. 3).

138 Thus, Ernst von Beling, *Rechtswissenschaft und Rechtsphilosophie*, Augsburg 1923, p. 17. Correctly, see Gerhart Husserl, *Rechtskraft und Rechtsgeltung*, vol. I, Berlin 1925, p. 6f. On the structure of this intellectual objectification, which is not at all unique to law, Hans Freyer, *Theorie des objektiven Geistes. Eine Einleitung in die Kulturphilosophie*, Leipzig 1923, *passim*.

grammar; even the fact that the majority of those who speak the language confuse "I" and "me," yet are convinced that they are speaking correctly, cannot make a difference to the non-psychological, but objective, existence of linguistic rules. Of course, this psychological objectification is not only created but also destroyed by real psychological acts of individual subjects of law. But as long as it is valid—that is, exists—it is independent of the opinions of members of the community. This existence of law as a psychologically-substantive objectification with a particular nature is what we call its validity. Law possesses validity, social existence, and reality only within a given spatiotemporal legal community.

The fact that all law is connected to a concrete community is extremely significant. First of all, it involves a distinction between fundamental legal principles and positive legal rules; we call only the latter law. This (positive) law is always a piece of historical and individual reality, and has merely empirical validity everywhere and at all times. For this reason, at least, law's validity differs from the validity of logical principles that, despite the most recent efforts of dialectical logic, must be considered universally valid. But above all, legal rules are addressed to the will, while logical principles are addressed to knowledge. A legal rule does not apply because it is considered 'true,' but because it should be recognized as binding the will. The fact that the principles of logic apply to legal rules does not distinguish them from the principles of grammar or any other mental objectification. Like artworks or language, law, too, never possesses anything other than relative objectivity; in other words, it is an individual historical construct.

Awareness of law's linkage to a spatiotemporal community is in no way a denial of super-positive fundamental legal principles; on the contrary, it actually enables an understanding of the great juristic significance of such principles. One must first overcome the positivist utopia before one can recognize and distinguish the actual existence of both positive and 'natural law.' Far be it from me to claim that there are no principles of the absolute and general objectivity of logical rules that bind the will. There are indeed fundamental legal principles of that type; but they are not legal rules, not positive law. Such fundamental legal principles are either constitutive principles of the form of pure law, and thus significant for legal logic, or they are the foundational principles of legal content, which make an ethical claim. The former are universally valid, require no conscious affirmation, and are thus effective in any positive law. The latter can also be universally valid, particularly when they are affirmed by all cultures. Thus, they are basically dependent on culture. Ethical fundamental legal principles can be violated by willed revolt, and hence also by positive law. Both are legal possibilities vis-à-vis positive law; but only positive law is legal reality.[139]

The ethical fundamental legal principles refer to permanent or epochal ways of life, to institutions fixed by their nature, whose individually and arbitrarily determined, concrete manifestations are expressed in the positive norming of legal rules.

[139] See Hobbes, *De cive* (see note 9), chap. VI, 16 (p. 109) [86]; "*Theft, Murder, Adultery* and all *wrongs* [*injuriae*] are forbidden by the laws of nature, but what is to count as a *theft* on the part of a citizen or as a *murder* or *adultery* or a *wrongful act* is to be determined by the *civil*, not the *natural, law*."

A fundamental legal principle is assigned to a legal institution determined by a universal human or culturally-conditioned nature; in the case of a legal rule, a law determined by the existing power relations of the moment comes into force. Anything that positive jurisprudence can achieve that amounts to more than legal technicalities is directed towards exploring fundamental legal principles and institutions; in particular, juristic systemization is possible only with the help of both logical and teleological fundamental principles of law.

Thus, everything depends on showing how these fundamental legal principles differ from positive legal rules. Law is normative social order, conscious obligation, a binding of wills, and as such, it requires a decisive limitation of the will. Every legal rule must state that, under certain circumstances, a certain person should act in a certain way. This "legal certainty"[140] is the criterion for distinguishing between legal rules and fundamental legal principles. In Chapter 2, we explained that only decisive commands can require obedience and possess a social ordering function. Any kind of decision-making means either/or! If a norm is not definite enough that a decision-making norm of mutual human behavior can be derived from it, it is not a legal rule. This feature of sufficient individuation is as characteristic for positive law as its absence is for fundamental legal principles.

Thus, only decisive law deserves the labels positivity, existence, validity, reality—these expressions all refer to the same state of affairs. A concrete, individual decision-making unit is a requirement for this legal certainty. We know of one only in the guise of human will. Only through contractual or authoritative unification of the will, through an individuality of will, can legal principles be made decisive or positive. Super-positive norms and individuality of will are similarly "necessary conditions" [*conditiones sine qua non*] of positive law. Law is everywhere made, sustained, and capable of being destroyed through acts of human will.

Thus, all law, including customary law, is produced through decisions, made known in some way, by individual subjects, who in this way affirm a mentally objectified state of affairs as their norm.[141]

The doctrine of law-creation through acceptance of law[142] removes from the process of the genesis of validity the necessary activist character of an act of will, a decision. Passive acceptance can neither objectify a norm nor order relationships. Any law for human beings is created only by a willed evaluative behavior by human beings. That cannot and should not mean that law must be accepted by everyone for whom it is valid. It need only be accepted to the extent that it can be regularly

140 Erich Brodmann, *Recht und Gewalt*, Berlin 1921, p. 32 f.: "Legal security consists, aside from the certainty of execution, in legal certainty, that is, the meaning of law, on the one hand, and the facts to be judged on the other must be certain."

141 On the act-like structure of the creation of validity, Gerhart Husserl is quite instructive, *Rechtskraft und Rechtsgeltung*, p. 17 ff. His view, which revives the "social contract" [*Contrat social*] as a historical fact, is dubious. He suggests that in order to become a fundamental legal norm of the state association, the constitution requires "the voluntary recognition of *all* the legal subjects brought into community under this legal order," (ibid., p. 73).

142 As one of many, see Jellinek, *Staatslehre* (see note 3), p. 341 ff.; most recently, once again, Julius Hatschek, *Völkerrecht als System rechtlich bedeutsamer Staatsakte*, Leipzig 1923, p. 1 f.

asserted against those who do not accept it. The view expressed here is often met with the apparently compelling argument that such acts of will assume the existence of the very norm that is supposed to be created by their affirmation. This apparent problem can be resolved by a simple reference to the modern method of legislation, in which drafts produced by some ministry or other do not become laws and norms until they are sanctioned by the acts of will of a representative legislature.[143] Law thus only comes into being through announced acts of will that affirm the future substance of the norm. In order to create law, these acts of will must take effect by way of the fundamental legal principles identified above. A circumstance suited for normative content thus achieves validity and positivity only through the willed evaluative individuation bestowed on it.

But the validity, positivity, or existence of law is also maintained only through willed human activity. It is legal carping to assert against this the trivial truth that legal norms only bind 'the' legal subject, even against his will. What is under discussion is not the independence of legal validity from purposeful defiance by individuals, but rather its independence from norm-denying processes of will, whether of all or of a crucial segment of those subject to the law. As unsettling as it may be to the human need for security, it is indisputable that there is no earthly power that can prevent a sovereign self-determined will from breaking the law and replacing it with new law.

The positivity of law it thus grounded, on the one hand, in the ideal nature of fundamental legal principles, and, on the other, in the social facticity of an ultimately decisive unit of will that positivizes legal rules—that is, transfers them from the realm of countless legal possibilities, limited only by those fundamental legal principles, into the realm of unique legal reality.[144] The obligatory force of positive law can only be understood through the obligatory force of ethical fundamental legal principles and the obligating force of a communal authority. A fundamental legal principle alone creates only an ethical, but not a legal, obligation; the demands of authoritative power can gain obedience through fear and force, but they are not binding in themselves. Any one-sided bias towards ideality or facticity distorts the problem of legal obligation.

The concept of 'positive' law developed polemically in opposition to that of Enlightenment natural law. The dangerous errors of the belief in a rational "natural order," oblivious to individuality and history—the one-sidedness of the problem of

[143] This fact is completely overlooked by Hans Kelsen, *Hauptprobleme der Staatsrechtslehre, entwickelt aus der Lehre vom Rechtssätze*, 2nd edn, Tübingen 1923, p. 416 f., who gives every single act of legislation the same significance and portrays sanctions as merely the political and "unjuristic" consequence of the monarchical principle. His error is connected with his consistent confusion of logical and juristic validity, which is expressed on the same page in his discussion of the "truth of the judgment as to the legal rule." The fact that, under Art. 68(2) of the Weimar Reich Constitution, the determination of the content of the law and the sanction are in the same hands, while in the Bismarckian constitution the same authority was divided between the Bundesrat and the Reichstag, is obviously in no way determinative of our problem.

[144] Erich Kaufmann, "Die Gleichheit vor dem Gesetz im Sinne des Art. 109 der Reichsverfassung," in *Veröffentlichungen der Vereinigung der Deutschen Staatsrechtslehrer*, 3 (1927), p. 20 f., maintains that the state does not create "law," but that the "decision on the choice of the relevant principle of justice" must "absolutely" be reserved to the legislature, along with the "creation of the legal technicalities of forms and norms." But I do not know what one can call positive law before this activity takes place.

norm and individuality in a natural law that made a religion of statute—were nowhere more keenly recognized than by Friedrich Julius Stahl. "Philosophy," he said, "which only recognizes that which follows from reason, can seek this source of ethos nowhere but in reason. That is what natural law consists of."[145] "Reason, from which ethos is supposed to be deduced, now needs a basic concept from which it may be deduced, which is self-evidently what must remain after every abstraction. According to the subjective rationalist standpoint of natural law, this concept is the existence of those who think—that is, of human nature. In reality, this nature is always determined: determined by individuality, environment, fate, time, material, in short—by history. If it is so determined, however, it is not a logical necessity."[146]

In contrast to this rationalist natural law, we call the law that is "positivized" by an authoritative communal will positive law. The common will that makes the final decisions, that has the greatest power of legislation, is what we call sovereign.[147] An understanding of the sovereignty problem is fundamentally impossible if one believes in a "natural order" with a logical validity independent of human or divine will as a substitute for positive law, whatever form this belief takes, whether Grotian, Marxist, or liberal legal-rationalist. The same impossibility of understanding is also found where, as in today's dominant positivism, law is conceived of as a mere product of the will, without any suprapositive basis of legitimacy or any reliance on fundamental legal principles on the part of this will.

The relationship developed here between legal rules and fundamental legal principles is a priori. The close connection between positivity and sovereignty, however, only emerges with the formation of state power that is externally independent of Pope and Emperor, and internally independent of feudalism. In the feudal social order, with its largely decentralized creation of law, the famous words of Beaumanoir (died 1296) applied: "each baron is sovereign in his barony." However, the next sentence stated, "the king is sovereign above all."[148] The concept of sovereignty was comparative, and could become absolute only when the decentralized largely traditional modes of producing law were overcome. The growth of civilization required a heightened and territory-wide legal certainty, a uniformity and a greater scope for the central legislative body. The provisional conclusion of this development is embodied in Bodin's sovereignty, to which the same will is ascribed that is due to the highest legislative body. The essence of sovereignty thus consists in the positivization of fundamental legal principles into the most important, community-determining legal rules.

The grounding of legal positivism in the facticity of a sovereign unit of will is opposed today with particular energy by legal rationalists. This formalist rule-of-law

[145] Friedrich Julius Stahl, *Die Philosophie des Rechts*, vol. 1, 5th edn, Freiburg [1878], p. 111.

[146] Ibid., vol. 1, p. 117.

[147] On the common will that objectifies the "contracted law" [*lex contractus*] in the ruler-free contractual order, see below, p. 142 f.

[148] See Rehm, op. cit. (see note 2), p. 193; note 2 (Philippe de Beaumanoir, *Les Coutumes du Beauvoisin* (1283), ed. Comte Beugnot, Paris 1842, chap. XXXIV, 41 (vol. 2, p. 22); further, Rudolph Sohm, *Die altdeutsche Reichs- und Gerichtsverfassung*, vol. 1, Weimar 1871, p. 102.

liberalism, a child of Enlightenment natural law with its overestimation of norms vis-à-vis any individuality, is only reassured in its bourgeois need for security once it has eliminated any individualized units of will and replaced them with a norm, specifically a legal norm. But legal norms are individuated norms—norms that have achieved their determinacy, and only then their positivity, through announced decisions by individual wills. Today's legal rationalism, which, like Enlightenment natural law, would like to detach positivity from the individuality of a sovereign communal authority, thus finds itself in an insoluble conflict. On the one hand, it strives to be only 'positivist' and rejects natural law; in this way, it would have to arrive at a sovereign individuality that positivizes legal norms and is completely unbound by norms. On the other hand, there must be a legal norm, by no means merely a norm of morality or religion, that takes precedence over any individuality.

Let us now observe how this legal rationalism in its advanced form, represented by Kelsen, deals with the problem of sovereignty and positivism. To focus for the present on the state system of rule, Kelsen eliminated the socially effective decision-making unit, the legal-positivist sovereign will that positivizes legal principles into legal rules, and replaces it with a fundamental norm that apparently satisfied his legal logic. What creates positive law: the living, historically individual will, or the fundamental norm? Kelsen gives a logically incomprehensible answer to this question.

First, it is the original norm that "is applied by the constituent authority"; the constitution gets its "legally relevant *validity* from the presupposed original norm, but its *content* from the constituent authority's empirical act of will."[149] Thus, we first have a 'constitution' that already has legally relevant validity, and only then a 'constituent' authority—a feat of logic that I cannot follow! The simple solution to this convoluted reasoning is that there is no legally relevant validity without a will that positivizes legal principles, because there is no legal rule with individuated substance—that is, no positive legal rule.

Not only Kelsen's polemic against the doctrine of sovereignty, but the entire 'pure' theory of law, stands and falls on the claim that the validity of law has nothing to do with the facticity of an individual will that positivizes law. His polemics take on the appearance of justification because the dominant theory of the will of the state does indeed quite one-sidedly emphasize the law-guaranteeing power of this will, while not mentioning at all the logically more important function of individuation. However, because Kelsen entirely discards the individuality of will, not only is the concept of sovereignty left without a home, but the concept of positivity can no longer be realized. One is forced to admire the success of the pure theory of law in camouflaging its incorrect starting point by seemingly operating without contradiction, using identical words with ambiguous content, with two or more different concepts of sovereignty, positivity, law, norms, and so on.

What does positivity mean in a system of pure legal rationalism? First of all, Kelsen seems to agree with our concept of positivity, tellingly in those places where he presupposes the sovereignty of the state. His error consists in offering this

[149] Kelsen, *Probleme der Souveränität* (see note 38), p. v.

presupposition as one of two possible presuppositions, a point we will return to later. In any case, this is the only place in all of Kelsen's writings that positively states how one can recognize a norm as 'positive law.' His answer is "when it can be shown to be an element of the state's own legal order. This occurs through gradual return to the ultimate "sources," to the original norms that form the basis for the unity and unique features of the legal order and from which the legal system is derived . . . That the decision of this assembly (or for example the command of an absolute monarch) is to be obeyed: that is the not otherwise justifiable presupposition of the legal order that is called *positive* for that reason, the logical origin of the legal order that is considered the highest—that is, sovereign—for that reason."[150]

Here, Kelsen means the sovereignty of 'an' individual legal order vis-à-vis others of the sort. The concepts of the basic norm, law, positivity or validity, and sovereignty, however, suddenly become completely different when he says a little earlier that "nothing" can or should be expressed by the term "positive" but "the" law's difference from morality, politics, religion, nature, and so on, the independence of "the" law from other normative systems: "this is, however, nothing more than the *sovereignty* of the legal system."[151] Sometimes he speaks of "a specific legal system,"[152] at other times—and always in the same context, often in the same sentence—of "the law."[153] Sometimes he means a historically individual, concrete legal order positivized by an individual decision of the will of 'this' assembly; at other times the same word 'positivity' means exclusively the theoretical independence of the abstract concept of 'law' from other non-legal normative systems. To use Kelsen's own words: "If it were not naïve self-deception, such conceptualization could be branded shadowboxing."[154] Such confounding, found on nearly every page, is camouflaged by the introduction of the 'basic norm,' which is just as ambiguous as Kelsen's concept of positivity.[155]

[150] Op. cit., p. 93. [151] Op. cit., p. 87 note 1. [152] Op. cit., p. 93,

[153] Op. cit., p. 94. It should be noted that here, but especially in international law, many incorrect constructions would be recognized as such without difficulty if legal science were to distinguish clearly between law on the one hand, and a legal order or legal system on the other. Karl Bergbohm, *Jurisprudenz und Rechtsphilosophie*, Leipzig 1892, p. 62 and notes, already criticized this identification of law and the legal order, as well as Rudolf Stammler, *Theorie der Rechtswissenschaft*, Halle 1911, p. 384 ff.; Stammler, *Lehrbuch der Rechtsphilosophie*, 2nd edn, Berlin 1923, p. 274 note 1, who stated, however, that the question of what a legal order is was never raised in any of the literature on legal theory. Felix Somló, *Juristische Grundlehre*, Leipzig 1917, p. 98, who called the legal order "the totality of a multiplicity of legal norms born by a unified creator," identified it once again with law. Most recently, Friedrich Darmstaedter, *Recht und Rechtsordung. Ein Beitrag zur Lehre vom Willen des Gesetzgebers*, Berlin 1925, p. 60, attempted to separate the two concepts by speaking of a legal order only "if its norms determine the omission and cessation of self-help." This determination, however, only applies to a time when the legal order can be understood as a legal system. See below, p. 149.

[154] Kelsen, op. cit., p. 215.

[155] For a start, the basic norm is no different from a renamed state will (op. cit., p. 106). In this sense, the basic norm, first constructed by Walter Jellinek, *Gesetz, Gesetzesanwendung und Zweckmäßigkeitser wägung*, Tübingen 1913, p. 26 ff., is an impractical attempt by logistical nothing-but-positivism to get around the difficult problem of norm and individuality, law and power, through a merely grammatical reformulation of an 'is' authority into an 'ought'; the attempt to provide a logical surrogate rather than the required substantive justification is an expression of an inability to understand philosophically actuality of a normative fact. All the same, it is clear that the basic norm is in this case a renaming of the individual state unit of will and is supposed to justify the unity and uniqueness of "this" legal order. It is quite significant that, in the above-cited sentences, Kelsen (Kelsen, *Problem der Souveräntität*, p. 93),

It is clear that, where Kelsen speaks of a concrete, positive legal order, positivity and sovereignty are inseparable. But what does positivity mean in the second case, which Kelsen believes to be the only correct solution, although he appears to present an alternative? How can one distinguish natural law from positive law when the only criterion one maintains is the independence of the latter from the normative systems of morality and reason?[156] Kelsen gives no answer to this question, and cannot give one, because his distinction between natural law and positive law is historically and systematically incorrect,[157] and because he himself is indeed only formally a natural law scholar;—that is, because he does not base the validity of legal norms on individual acts of will within the framework of legal principles, but prefers to deduce it from contentless, logical abstractions. Only a 'fallacy of the four terms' [*quaternio terminorum*] camouflages the fact that the legal principles logically abstracted by Kelsen, which are supposedly sovereign, have no positivity, and thus represent legal sovereignty without law.

If Kelsen was correct to maintain that the dispute over state sovereignty was a dispute over the requirements for legal understanding, not a dispute over facts,[158] the state would not be sovereign, because Kelsen's jurist would be. In fact, the dispute involves the unquestionably juristic fact of whether a positive norm exists that creates and destroys the sovereign state, or whether, in contrast, the sovereign state as a historical fact has to be a logical given before the jurist can recognize a legal norm as positive. But Kelsen's idea that it seemed that "the point of state authority and state rule is not for a person to be subject to different *people*, but for people to be subject to *norms*, even though it is people—themselves in turn subject to norms—who establish these norms"[159] is, again, merely a not-very-graceful interplay between two different concepts of a "norm." But it is as correct to say that an authority's norms are only "positive" legal norms because it is legally competent to establish norms[160]

as always, uses the definite article as soon as he speaks of "the" legal order, although the issue here is undoubtedly the unity and uniqueness of "a" or "this" legal order, as can be seen with unquestionable clarity in the subsequent "decision of this assembly" (ibid.). He must permit this linguistic shift in order to conceal the fact that the basic norm that underlies the unity and uniqueness of "this" individual legal order is "altogether" [*toto coelo*] different from the basic norm that is the foundation of the unity and uniqueness of "the" legal order. The former says that you shall obey an individual will; the latter, that you shall obey if something within the scope of the logical constitutional principles of law commands—that is, you shall rightfully obey when you are rightfully commanded.

156 Kelsen, op. cit., p. 86 ff.

157 See the critique by Alexander Hold-Ferneck, *Der Staat als Übermensch*, Jena 1926, p. 39 ff. and Verdroß, *Einheit* (see note 96), pp. 80, 82, who in turn names as positive legal orders those that "realize themselves currently in acts of organs." Aside from the fact that this "circumstance, which must be precisely determined" also represents a leap from the pure theory of law to "metalaw," like Kelsen's principle of the economy of values, Verdroß here suffers the fate of all abstract idealism, which at a certain point always tips into the most naked facticity. See Verdroß, *Völkerrechtsgemeinschaft* (see note 137), p. 6 note 4, where positive law appears as "power" whose positivity, without any restrictions, ends with its implementation. Another "purer" theorist of law, Sander, fortunately arrived at the view that law dissolves into statements and predictions about power prospects, Fritz Sander, "Das Verhältnis von Staat und Recht. Eine Grenzauseinandersetzung zwischen allgemeiner Staatslehre, theoretischer Rechtswissenschaft und interpretativer Rechtsdogmatik," in *Archiv des öffentlichen Rechts*, 49 (1926), p. 168 ff.

158 Kelsen, *Staatslehre* (see note 46), p. 103; Kelsen, *Problem der Souveränität* (see note 38), p. 14f.

159 Kelsen, *Staatslehre*, p. 99.

160 Kelsen, *Problem der Souveränität*, p. 89 note 1.

as it is false to claim that some positive legal norm, or legal science, decides if the state has or does not have the authority to create law.

The view advocated here of the nature of sovereignty and its necessary links to legal positivism in the modern state is also opposed by the anti-centralist syndicalist view of the state. It refers to the positivity of the charters of small associations that are part of the state order. The rejoinder to this is that, for a legal understanding of the modern state, the positivity of the association charters that are part of it seem to be derived from the positivity of the state legal order. This is how the unity of the modern state is constituted—the state which, in certain circumstances, tries to destroy "legitimately" [*de jure*] the positivity of any orders that oppose it. Every will-bearing subject that is part of the state order is connected to all others at least through the fact that it wishes to influence the positivity of the state legal order, on the one hand, but, on the other hand, must also respect it, even if only by concealing its norm-violating behavior. The source of the failure of Laski's polemics against the doctrine of sovereignty becomes clear when he tells us, "A trade-union as such has no connection with the Mormon Church; it stands self-sufficient on its own legs. It may work with the State, but it need not do so of necessity."[161] However the concept of the state may be conceived, it always proves to be false that any legal subject could have no "essential connections" with the state. The legal subjects subordinated to the state may be as historically old, politically and economically self-sufficient, and as powerful as can be; nevertheless, the legal validity of their norms is ultimately based on the positivity of state norms.

In summary, we can say that we glimpse the nature of sovereignty in the ability to positivize the highest legal rules binding on the community. There is no legal positivity for the authority order of the modern state without sovereignty. The legal derivation and attribution that grounds legal judgments, administrative acts, and legal transactions in the law, and the law in the constitution, inevitably falls into a yawning void if it dissolves the connection between the positivity of law and the sovereignty of the state. The jurist must take as a starting point the fact of sovereignty; otherwise he loses the object of his science—positive law—and will be left hanging in the air with all his science and practice.

At this point, we must break off our discussion of the nature of sovereignty, and can only continue if we first explore the question of the person of sovereignty and its limits.

[161] Laski, *Studies* (see note 82), p. 10. When Laski continues by saying that, in monist theory, the individual derives his significance only from his relationship with the state, whereas "in the pluralistic theory, while his relations may be of the deepest significance, it is denied that they are the sole criterion by which a man ought to be judged" (ibid., p. 11), he thereby reads into juristically-meant monism the claim to a moralized judicial office. It has been well understood at least since Kant that one must carefully distinguish the good citizen from the good human being.

# IV

# The Sovereign Person

## A. The State of the Problem

Even in our account in the history of ideas, it became clear that the crux of the problem lies in the depersonalization of sovereignty today. Based on our discussion so far, we are forced to demand a sovereign person to positivize the supreme legal principles—in any event, to be capable of making consciously evaluative decisions. The person we are in search of must, on the one hand, eventually become a real bearer of the will, while, on the other, has to be an independent, law-creating authority. However, a person equipped with these characteristics is unknown to our present theory of the state.

The dominant theory in Germany since Hegel maintains that the sovereign person is the state; sovereignty is a characteristic of state power or, in a relationship that is not entirely clear, the state's will or state personality. The state can only be considered the sovereign person, however, if it is seen, with objective necessity, as a unified reality of will or decision-making unit.

The natural science epistemology of all contemporary theories of the state, however, allows only for a materialist concept of reality, as well as its correlate, in the form of an as-if idealism. On this metaphysical basis, some German theorists maintain that the state possesses only a fictional unity.[162] Long before Kelsen, one of them even advised, "Should one ... only attempt to do away with ... the personality of the state, or the concept of the state in general, in portraying the positive law .... of a state, one would see that it would work very well."[163] It is obvious that this fictional state will not do as our sovereign person.

But even the abstraction theory that seems to oppose this fiction theory, and which is advocated by the best minds,[164] necessarily ends in a fictionalism, and furthermore in internal contradiction. Häenel claims, with particular emphasis, that the state has, aside from its organs, "*no reality at all*, but is merely a *one sided abstraction* that we

[162] For example, Ernst Rudolph Bierling, *Zur Kritik der juristischen Grundbegriffe*, part II, Gotha 1883, p. 222 ff.; Sigmund Schloßmann, *Die Lehre von der Stellvertretung, insbesondere bei obligatorischen Verträgen*, part 1, Leipzig 1900, p. 125.

[163] Albert Affolter, "Studien zum Staatsbegriffe," in *Archiv für öffentliches Recht*, 17 (1902), p. 135.

[164] Aside from those mentioned in the text, see also Meyer/Anschütz, *Staatsrecht* (see note 2), vol. I, p. 17; Bruno Schmidt, *Der Staat. Eine öffentlichrechtliche Studie*, Leipzig 1896, p. 1 ff; Hermann Rehm, *Allgemeine Staatslehre*, Freiburg 1899, p. 156 f.

create in certain contexts to facilitate our thought and speech."[165] Triepel says essentially the same thing, though more cautiously: the organs are the state, and without them the state is "nothing."[166] It is, "though not a fiction, still always an abstraction. It is only the imagined unity of a human community constituted by many."[167] The formula "abstraction, not fiction" comes from Georg Jellinek: "Abstraction is based on actual processes in the world of external and internal events; fiction, in contrast, replaces natural facts with contrived ones, and equates them with the former."[168] According to Jellinek, the organs are even "the benevolent state itself... without the organs, the concept of the state itself has vanished."[169]

Jellinek's entire representation theory, as well as the dominant theory, are based on the proposition that someone stands behind private-law representatives, "but not behind the organs."[170] But if the state consists only of its organs, then its unity, like its will, is undoubtedly merely fictitious, according to Jellinek's own definition.[171] And this is especially so if, in accordance with Jellinek's insurmountable dualism of nature and mind and his warning against "methodological syncretism,"[172] one considers the state unity of will to be provided "never by the creative hand of nature," but only by "legal processes."[173] Elsewhere, Jellinek explains that there is no less scientific reason to view the state as a legal person than to see human beings as legal persons. Only on the basis of this theory can "the unity of the state, the unity of its organization and the will produced by it be made part of a juristic understanding."[174] It should be noted that this most promising statement takes as its starting point the "recognition of the state as a real phenomenon." Elevating a "collective unity" to the status of a legal person is "not the fiction of a nonexistent substance"; rather, "*all* unities" that law elevates to persons exist "in the same way"[175]—that is, in reality, as must be concluded from the aforementioned. In fact, however, Jellinek suddenly maintains precisely the opposite: the individual (and thus also the state) should not be seen as a material unit; it cannot be claimed that it "exists in reality—that is, outside of us."[176] Certainly, if what Jellinek says is true—"In the physical, natural world," the acts of will of members of a unity "are only the acts of will of individuals that occur; in the ethical-legal world, they are only the acts of will of the community"[177]—then the existence of unified state authority, which claims sovereignty as a characteristic, is an insoluble riddle. Alternatively, are state authority and state will not identical? A remarkable twilight has fallen upon the relationship between these two central concepts of the contemporary

[165] Albert Haenel, *Studien zum deutschen Staatsrechte*, vol. 2 (Das Gesetz im formellen und materiellen Sinne), Leipzig 1888, p. 231.

[166] Heinrich Triepel, *Völkerrecht und Landesrecht*, Leipzig 1899, p. 78.

[167] Ibid., p. 120.

[168] Georg Jellinek, *Das System der subjektiven öffentlichen Rechte*, 2nd edn, Tübingen 1905, p. 17.

[169] Ibid., p. 225. [170] Ibid., p. 30.

[171] See Kelsen, correctly, in *Hauptprobleme* (see note 143), p. 179; Carl Schmitt-Dorotić, *Die Diktatur. Von den Anfängen des modernen Souveränitätsgedankens bis zum proletarischen Klassenkampf*, Munich 1921, p. 141.

[172] Jellinek, op. cit., p. 17. [173] Ibid., p. 41.

[174] Jellinek, *Staatslehre* (see note 3), p. 172. [175] Ibid., p. 170 f. [176] Ibid., p. 171.

[177] Jellinek, *System*, p. 30.

theory of the state. On the one hand, there is the tendency, corresponding to the undialectical opposition between law and power, to identify state will with positive law and state authority with rule or power; on the other hand, the two concepts are themselves identified.[178] Here too, the relationship between ideality and reality is completely unclear. Most recently, Thoma provides an example that is surprising, given this scholar's significance: on the one hand, he repeatedly calls the state a "real entity" like every other association, and ascribes to Gierke's corporatist theory the lasting merit of having shed light on the "reality of the associations." In the sentence that follows immediately upon this, he speaks of an association as an "abstraction drawn from the realities."[179] Thus, the state, as a real entity, is ultimately once again elevated to the status, albeit relative, of a sovereign person. Elsewhere, shortly before this, Thoma said of the state that it was a "merely normative … unity," merely "an ideal entity and certainly not a social entity."[180]

The unresolved contradiction between nature and mind, will and norm, that characterizes the inorganic theory of the state is unilaterally resolved in Gierke's organic theory of the state in favor of nature and will. The authority of the state, but not its legal authority, can be understood on this naturalist basis. In associations, as in individual entities, Gierke glimpses "the heart of legal personality in the *will*, as the causal force of external movement."[181] This view makes it possible, where necessary, to comprehend the fact, incomprehensible in the inorganic theory of the state, "that the organic unity of a common will has formed from individual particles of will."[182] But a doctrine that likes to refer frequently to Darwin and Haeckel cannot credibly assert that the "causal force of external movements" has anything to do with law. The organic theory of the state is as incapable as sociology, working with the concept of reciprocity, mass psychology, and psychoanalytic data, of advancing without contradiction to a state unity.[183] For certainly no actual psychological connection exists between all the people who are members of the state in only a juristic sense.

In conclusion, it can be said that the theory of the state has not succeeded in comprehending the state as a sovereign person. It cannot conceive of a social decision-making unit that counts legally as the person of sovereign acts that intervene in causal reality. But the sovereignty of a fiction or an abstraction is unimaginable. Kelsen's claim that the dominant doctrine tends to see the state as being as real

[178] See Paul Laband, "Staatsrecht," in *Systematische Rechtswissenschaft*, 2nd edn, Leipzig 1913 (Die Kultur der Gegenwart, ed. P. Hinneberg, Part II, section VIII), p. 362 f.; Gerhard Anschütz, "Verwaltungsrecht," in ibid., p. 372.

[179] Richard Thoma, "Staat" (see note 96), p. 754 f.

[180] Richard Thoma, "Der Begriff der modernen Demokratie in seinem Verhältnis zum Staatsbegriff. Prolegomena zu einer Analyse des demokratischen Staates der Gegenwart," in *Hauptprobleme der Soziologie. Erinnerungsgabe für Max Weber*, Munich 1923, vol. 2, p. 55.

[181] Otto Gierke, *Die Genossenschaftstheorie und die deutsche Rechtsprechung*, Berlin 1887, p. 608 f.

[182] Hugo Preuß, "Über Organpersönlichkeit," in *Schmollers Jahrbuch für Gesetzgebung, Verwaltung und Volkswirtschaft*, 26 (1902), p. 562.

[183] See the critique, accurate in this regard, in Hans Kelsen, *Der soziologische und der juristische Staatsbegriff. Kritische Untersuchung des Verhältnisses von Staat und Recht*, Tübingen 1922, p. 4 ff.; (see also) Theodor Litt, *Individuum und Gemeinschaft*, 3rd edn, Leipzig 1926, p. 3 f. On the uselessness of category of "interaction," Litt (ibid., p. 226 f.).

as a human being[184] is thus entirely wrong. The merit of his 'pure theory of law' is, rather, that it recognizes the contradictory vacillation of the dominant doctrine and ruthlessly identifies the consequences of the assumptions specific to this doctrine. In his *Hauptprobleme*, he quite correctly shows how the premises of Jellinek's doctrine lead to the proposition that the psychological act of will of a state organ is "completely irrelevant" to a juristic approach.[185] "The concept of the state's will has nothing to do with any psychological facts of will."[186] But because the phrases 'state' and 'state will' proved to be disruptive,[187] he took account in later publications of Affolt's demands and eliminated both. Now that the state is identified with an ideal system of norms separated from any facticity—that is, with a legal or partly legal order—no one can doubt that the vanished state cannot be a sovereign person.

The vexatious fiction or abstraction of a state will, retained in the dominant doctrine only on pain of contradictions, would thus be eliminated, and we would return to 'the sovereignty of law.' Since the state as abstraction would be an unsuitable sovereign person, we would certainly not mourn for it, if only Kelsen's radical depersonification would help us to understand just what justifies him speaking of the 'unity and particularity' of this concrete legal order, and why and how an order is a 'point of imputation'—if one only knew what objective necessities, based on social reality or normative logic, oblige us to assume that it is the individual, the state, or humanity, and not the moon or Kelsen's theory of the state, that is being imputed. Is there nothing that obliges us to assume a real social unit as a substrate of legal personality? No, Kelsen replies: the sovereign jurist establishes the system's imputation points however he wishes; for him, there is not an iota of difference between order and imputation point, legal relationships and legal personality. Kelsen's argument is unquestionably correct: if one sees in the legal person "a construct that is subject to the jurist's discretion, with which one can, but need not, personify *any* legal relationship—that is, any total or partial legal order—then nothing stands in the way of sometimes personifying that very same legal relationship, and then sometimes renouncing its personification; that is, treating the legal relationship as a person in some directions but not others."[188] The question arises whether one—that is, first of all, Kelsen himself—can do public law given the fact that one imputes to the state the same legal personality as in, for example, compensation claims raised by a brawl. Of course, he cannot. According to Kelsen, the hierarchical construction of the legal order, starting with the individual legal act, flows through regulations, laws, and a positive law constitution, through a "peculiar parallelism between real facts and norms," and finally into "the *basic norm*, which is the foundation of the unity of the legal order in its self-motion"—why here in particular?—while a "psychological-physical act" must take place that "sustains a lower level of the norm."[189] Yes indeed,

[184] Kelsen, *Staatsbegriff*, p. 3.
[185] Kelsen, *Hauptprobleme* (see note 143), p. 184.
[186] Ibid.
[187] See the critique in G. A. Wielikowski, *Die Neukantianer in der Rechtsphilosophie*, Munich 1914, p. 163.
[188] Kelsen, *Probleme der Souveränität* (see note 38), p. 292.
[189] Kelsen, *Staatslehre* (see note 46), p. 249; see Hermann Heller, *Die Krisis der Staatslehre*, see above, p. 23 f.

this "specific self-motion of law,"[190] sustained by psychological and physical acts, is just as 'peculiar' as that parallelism of existing facts and norms. It is, namely, either terrible metaphysics, or it is not the basic norm that forms the basis of the self-propelled unity of the legal order, but the will, wrongly declared to be a basic norm, that appears again and that provides a foundation for this unity and motivates it. And the fact that Kelsen devoted an entire book to proving that state unity has no real existence, that the "group will" is nothing other than a "normative system,"[191] raises the self-refuting question: "Should class, national, and religious interests not be stronger than state consciousness? Should they not function to form groups across legal boundaries and thus call into question the existence of a group that coincides with the juristic state unity?"[192] What is battling here, ideal norm systems or real group units? But if, according to Kelsen, the constitution gains its content "from the empirical acts of will of the constituent authority,"[193] then this will may never be imaginable as anything but a collective will.

The contemporary theory of the state no longer believes in the reality of a "general will." Whether one then views the state as an abstraction, or an ideal system of norms absolutely separate from any facticity, an "ideal essence,"[194] or the "psychological conduct of a number of individuals, regulated by the contents of certain books,"[195] under no circumstances is there a viable sovereign person.

And yet, neither Kelsen nor anyone else can do without this state will without contradiction. When, for example, Laski, disputing the reality of state unity, argues "that you can never find in a community any one will which is certain of obedience"; when he refers to the fact that true authority cannot be found in a society, "but with the real rulers must go sovereignty; and if you cannot find them it too must be beyond the reach of human insight,"[196] one understands that he is ultimately advocating the view that "in actual political conflict the sovereignty of the state means the sovereignty of government."[197] Laski may still believe that, seen from within, the relationship between the state's elements may exhibit no unity, "neither in aim nor method. What the orthodox theory of sovereignty has done is to coerce them into a unity and thereby place itself at the disposal of the social group which, at any given historic moment, happens to dominate the life of the state."[198] But he thus also admits to an immanent unity of will, though a coerced one; otherwise, the antecedent would amount to incomprehensible mysticism: "The fact is that the state as an external unit seeking survival in a world of states is never the same to its members as that same state in the ebb and flow of its internal daily life."[199] Elsewhere, too, Laski does not resist the idea of "the constituent wills from which the

[190] Kelsen, *Staatslehre*, p. 248. [191] Kelsen, *Staatsbegriff*, p. 73. [192] Ibid., p. 10.

[193] Kelsen, *Problem der Souveränität*, p. v.

[194] Friedrich Meinecke, *Die Idee der Staatsräson in der neueren Geschichte*, Munich 1924, p. 72.

[195] Hans Driesch, *Wirklichkeitslehre*, Leipzig 1917, p. 204.

[196] Laski, *Studies* (see note 82), p. 16 f. See Duguit, *Traité* (see note 65), I, p. 100: the associations as such "do not have a personal reality . . . not having either consciousness or will."

[197] Laski, *Foundations* (see note 82), p. 28. [198] Ibid., p. 28 f. [199] Ibid., p. 28.

group will is made."[200] Laski's theory of government sovereignty—this view arising from a naïve, but also aesthetic, need to see state unity as real in the unity of an organ that can be sensually perceived—is familiar from the theory of the monarchist principle. Emerging in the French counterrevolutionary period, this theory found its last German advocates in Max von Seydel and Bornhak. Their claim to be more realistic than the theory of the fictional state personality cannot be accepted, so long as the juristic and sociological fact of constitutional limits on any such organs of the *Rechtsstaat*—in every situation—cannot be disputed away.

The sole, though highly significant, attempt to regenerate the dogma of sovereignty by substituting a person capable of will was undertaken by Carl Schmitt. Taking up the ideas of monarchist counterrevolution of the nineteenth century, as well as Sorel's syndicalism, Schmitt hopes to replace fictional state sovereignty with the sovereignty of an organ of state. This is an attempt to give depersonalized formal democracy a unity and a sovereign will by either integrating or replacing the separation of powers in the *Rechtsstaat* with a dictatorship—the attempt could not fail to make an appearance in either practical or theoretical politics. In Germany, Schmitt's dictatorship doctrine moves in this direction. In his view, the traditional concept of sovereignty has been significantly altered politically by the concept of class, and constitutionally by the modern freedom of coalition; and the concept of 'state sovereignty' still dominant today, which is held up in opposition to all other sovereign persons, is in many ways merely a paraphrase for an "equivocation" [*tergiversatio*] of the actual problem.[201] Quite similarly to Laski on this point, Schmitt sees in the doctrine of state sovereignty an effort to "hypothesize a fictitious higher unity as the real person of real power."[202] In contrast, his own observations lead to the conclusion, "If sovereignty is really state omnipotence—and it is so for every constitution that does not completely separate, that is, delimit, the powers—then legal rules can comprehend only the predictable content of their exercise, but never the substantive range of power itself. The question of who decides it—that is, the legally undecided case—becomes the question of sovereignty."[203] "Whoever decides on the state of exception is sovereign."[204] Carl Schmitt's critique of the dominant doctrine certainly revealed the deepest roots of its legal ineffectiveness by opposing decisionism to the rationalist belief in law. In this respect, Schmitt's critique is undoubtedly definitive, and in many ways a model for the study at hand. His construction of sovereignty, however, even if we ignore its shortcomings in international law, is full of internal contradictions and unsustainable. Its political background is evident when he says,

[200] Laski, *Studies* (see note 82), p. 13. [Heller appears to have quoted this phrase from memory or from notes, as he gets the quote wrong—it is corrected in the text—and the note reads "evidence not found."]

[201] Carl Schmitt, *Diktatur* (see note 171), p. x f.

[202] Ibid., p. 27 note 2.

[203] Ibid., p. 194.

[204] Carl Schmitt, *Politische Theologie. Vier Kapitel zu Lehre von der Souveränität*, Munich 1922, p. 9. Carl Schmitt had a very interesting precursor in Anton Menger, *Staatslehre* (see note 77), p. 166 f. He too finds the doctrine of state sovereignty "quite insufficient" domestically; in reality, he is sovereign who "is capable if necessary to impose his will [on the state] even against the law"; it is the prince if he can, "in an emergency," carry out a coup. At all times, this stratification of power relations is of crucial significance "as the 'most extreme case.'"

"The state, shaken by estate and class conflicts, is by its constitution in a constant state of exception, and its law is, down to its last elements, emergency law. Thus whoever controls the state of exception controls the state."[205] If we disregard other concerns, however, neither the lawyer nor the sociologist can dismiss the need to distinguish between states of exception and normal, legally formalized states, and to pose the question of who, in today's *Rechtsstaat*, controls the state of exception—which non-'fictitious' unity of will commands state omnipotence. The German Reich President under Article 48 of the Weimar Reich Constitution? Although an affirmative answer would be a consequence of Schmitt's explanations, he has nevertheless so far avoided a clear answer.

Most recently,[206] however, he has noted, criticizing Anschütz's interpretation of Article 48, that there must be "an authority" in every state that, exceptionally and "with sovereign power," undertakes actions that fall outside or break through the normal system of regulated responsibilities. Yet Schmitt keeps to himself an answer to the difficult question of who, under the Weimar Constitution, can undertake "such acts of sovereignty." But under his definition of sovereignty, he can only declare the president or a 'fictional unit' to be sovereign. Yet in the former case, obviously accepted by Schmitt, he contradicts both positive law and his own excellent distinction between commissarial and sovereign dictatorship. The former sets aside the constitution "in concrete" [*in concreto*] in order to protect that same constitution and its concrete existence, while the sovereign dictatorship sees the entire existing order as a state of affairs that it wishes to eliminate through its actions.[207] A few years ago, therefore, Schmitt still saw in Article 48 the "completely clear case of a commissarial dictatorship," and advised particular attention to the fact that "limitless empowerment" should by no means signify the dissolution of the existing legal situation and the transference of sovereignty to the Reich President.[208] Even in Schmitt's view, the positive constitutional provision in Article 48 hardly gives the Reich President 'state omnipotence,' but contains, in addition to an "inviolable organizational minimum," a limitation on "measures"—in contrast to acts—of legislation and administration of justice.[209] Furthermore, Schmitt himself pointed out that the president does not decide on a state of exception by himself, but only with the supervision of the Reichstag provided for in Article 50 of the Weimar Reich Constitution. One cannot simultaneously maintain that the dictatorship of the president is necessarily commissarial[210] and that the president is an organ that can undertake 'acts of sovereignty.' If we look at the regulation of states of exception in

[205] Schmitt, *Diktatur*, p. 18.

[206] Carl Schmitt, Review of Gerhard Anschütz, *Die Verfassung des Deutschen Reichs*, in *Juristische Wissenschaft*, 55 (1926), p. 2272.

[207] Carl Schmitt, *Diktatur*, p. 136 f. [208] Ibid., p. 201 f.

[209] Carl Schmitt, "Die Diktatur des Reichspräsidenten nach Art. 48 der Reichsverfassung," in *Veröffentlichungen der Vereinigung Deutscher Staatsrechtslehrer*, I (1924), p. 93 ff.; and Schmitt, *Diktatur*, p. 201 f.

[210] Carl Schmitt, "Diktatur des Reichspräsidenten," p. 89; the addition that it has the effect "in substance, not in its legal rationale . . . like the residue of a sovereign dictatorship of the national assembly," is incorrect according to Schmitt's own statements (ibid., p. 86 f.)

the Anglo-American states, under Schmitt's definition of sovereignty, interpreted in this way, any military commander or any court issuing or refusing a "writ of habeas corpus" would be sovereign. Ultimately, Schmitt cannot mean states of emergency or so-called state emergency laws when he speaks of extreme states of exception. For every state of emergency is based, in Schmitt's own, accurate definition, on the fact that "outside of or against constitutional provisions, in extreme, unforeseen cases, a state organ having the strength to act proceeds to rescue the existence of the state and to do what is necessary in the given state of affairs."[211] But who decides in cases of conflict is precisely the question Schmitt wants to answer.

Finally, Schmitt's definition of sovereignty must be termed untenable in regard to its political theology. Following Donoso Cortés, Schmitt teaches that states of exception have an analogous significance for jurisprudence as miracles do for theology.[212] Would not those who take seriously this analogy and Schmitt's definition of sovereignty need to identify belief in God with belief in magic or medicine men? God does not use miracles alone—or in the opinion of many, for example Schleiermacher,[213] not even to a significant extent; rather, He has an impact precisely in the overall legal context, which incidentally is no less marvelous than its breach. Schmitt is entirely wrong to refer to Bodin in regard to the conceptual connection between sovereignty and states of exception. Bodin saw the right to make law as the most essential characteristic of sovereignty.[214] Also very significant in this context are statements by the Huguenot Bodin in the *Heptaplomeres* to the very similar advocates of reformed Christianity. Curtius believed here that the state had to be fashioned according to the model of the world order set up by God: "Just as in a well-equipped state, there are certain stable laws of majesty and the Reich that are changed according to the various situations of the times and of things ... it also accords with reason that a God who provides for the future, the father of nature, would have sanctified certain constant and inviolable laws."[215] Bodin certainly believed that law, in nature as in the state, must sometimes be changed, and that in place of the usual authorities, extraordinary "curators" would need to be installed.[216] But the "perpetual power" [*perpetua potestas*] is and remains sovereign, and because dictators lack this mark of permanence, Bodin denies them the mark of sovereignty, with great force and many examples, in a passage from the *Respublica* that Schmitt himself cites extensively.[217] In conclusion, let us recall the significant fact that while Bodin believed, to a surprising extent for his times, in miracles, demons, and witches, in his *Heptaplomeres*

[211] Ibid., p. 83; see below, p. 130.

[212] Schmitt, *Diktatur*, p. 139; Schmitt, *Politische Theologie*, p. 37 (Donoso Cortés, Speech on January 4, 1849, in Alfred Maier (ed.), *Donoso Cortés. Briefe, Parlamentarische Reden und diplomatische Berichte aus den letzten Jahren seines Lebens*, Cologne 1950, p. 186 f.).

[213] Friedrich Schleiermacher, *Der christliche Glaube*, vol. 1, 2nd edn, Halle 1830, ß 47 (p. 199): "No need can ever arise from the interests of piety to interpret a fact such that, through its dependence on God, its conditionality is eliminated by the natural context." Very interesting remarks follow about miracles.

[214] See above, p. 62-3.

[215] Bodin, *Heptaplomeres* (see note 24), p. 29.

[216] Ibid., p. 30.

[217] Carl Schmitt, *Diktatur* (see note 171), p. 26. (Bodin, *Republique* (see note 19), book I chap. 8 (p. 77 ff.)).

he nevertheless had Octavius ask the question, "If God makes miracles, what is to prevent the great wizards from extoling themselves as gods?"[218]

After all this, Schmitt's doctrine of decisionism must certainly be given great credit for having on excellent grounds represented the sovereignty problem, in opposition to the dominant theory, as a problem of decision by an individual will. However, in seeing in the modern state a more or less voluntaristic dictatorship, he was as unsuccessful as Kelsen, the proponent of rationalist rule of law liberalism, in discovering in today's state a unit of will that could be considered the sovereign person. The theory of pure, ideal legal sovereignty has no conception of the essential importance of individual decisions for positive laws; in contrast, the doctrine of organ sovereignty ignores the decisive role played by law in the broadest sense for the sovereign individuality of will.

## B. State Sovereignty and Popular Sovereignty

The inability of German public law doctrine to establish a suitable sovereign person, and the bloodlessness of its concept of the state, are based in part in the historical and political situation. In a period when its entire intellectual basis pointed it towards democratic-nationalist legitimation and immanent explication of the state, it was forced by monarchist constitutionalism to be the public law of the monarchist principle, whose transcendent ways of thinking "consolidate the entire power of the state in monarchs."[219] In this way, the German concept of state sovereignty indeed became a paraphrase for an "equivocation" of the actual problem, that is, the ancient problem of popular or princely sovereignty.

The French counterrevolution undertook its attempt to protect the threatened monarchy from the democratic tendencies of the natural law doctrine of the state contract by elevating the monarch, by the grace of God, to the person of all state power. We know how the doctrine first formulated in Ludwig XVIII's Charter passed into Article 57 of the Final Act of Vienna, and from there was expressly adopted into most of the German constitutions. But even those constitutions that, like the Prussian, do not contain that formula explicitly were grounded in the theory and practice of the monarchist principle. It gained its substantive philosophical foundation in Prussian Germany from F.J. Stahl.

Since then, Germany's theoretical thinking on the state has suffered from contradictions; the liberal democratic efforts of 1848 failed, while the monarchist principle asserted itself in the organization of the state and did not end until 1918. Theories whose categories did not accord with this principle still had to attempt to process it. The founder of the doctrine of state sovereignty, Hegel, was a model; he

[218] Bodin, *Heptaplomeres*, p. 88. Cf. Salomos's remarks on miracles (ibid., p. 98).

[219] Erich Kaufmann, *Auswärtige Gewalt und Kolonialgewalt in den Vereinigten Staaten von Amerika. Eine rechtsvergleichende Studie über die Grundlagen des amerikanischen und deutschen Verfssungsrechts*, Leipzig 1908 (Staats- und völkerrechtliche Abhandlungen, vol. 7 I), p. 88; 79 f.; Erich Kaufmann, *Studien zur Staatslehre des monarchischen Prinzipes*, Leipzig 1906 (pp. 4, 38, 50); Hermann Heller, *Hegel und der nationale Machtstaatsgedanke*, in *Gesammelte Schriften*, vol. 1, p. 136 ff.

made the first attempt, in very convoluted ways, to reconcile Rousseau's popular sovereignty with the hereditary monarch's personal, non-derivative right to state power. He had nothing against the principle of popular sovereignty itself, to the extent it meant "that a people generally is independent *externally* and constitutes its own state"; and he had nothing against the fact that it was said about *internal* sovereignty "that it resides in the *people*, if one only speaks of the *whole*." One might presume that the immanent view of the state absolutely ruled out the monarchist principle. But the supposed reconciliation of the two should bring with it the following reflections: popular sovereignty must not be placed "in contradistinction to the sovereignty that exists in the monarch"; this "confused idea" was based on a "barren concept of the *people*"; for the people "*without* their monarch" are only the "formless mass that is no longer a state."[220] Hegel dismisses with a superior wave of his hand the idea that one could, without a monarchy, understand popular sovereignty to mean republic and democracy; such an undeveloped idea was no longer possible in face of the 'developed idea' of the constitutional monarchy. In a people that is "meant to be a truly organic totality, developed in itself, sovereignty is the personality of the whole, and this will be found in the reality that is appropriate to its concept—as the *person of the monarch*."[221] Thus, Hegel believed that, with the idea of state sovereignty, he had reconciled the sovereignty of the people with that of the monarch, whose byword shall be to be "not derivative but itself the origin."[222]

Like Hegel, but completely rejecting popular sovereignty, the dominant public law doctrine in Germany transfers all of state sovereignty to the personal monarchist government, and constructs the constitution as only a voluntary self-limitation by the monarch, who remains sovereign, and not as a basic law emanating from the state as a whole.[223] As long as the monarchy existed in Germany, one spoke of a 'bearer of state power,' who was often even entitled to state power in his 'own right.' Even when power in its own right was not claimed for the state power, this bearer of state power was claimed to be "an organ that fully represents the state and has on his side a presumption of exclusive right to exercise state power."[224]

Even those theorists who, like Georg Jellinek, rejected this bearer of state power felt compelled to acknowledge the "fundamental all-around authority of the monarch," to address the monarch as the "master" of public servants, and judges, in particular, as representatives of the monarch.[225] According to the dominant doctrine, the organs were the state—nothing stood behind them; they represented not a people connected to a political unit, but a point above the people, the monarch.

[220] Hegel, *Rechtsphilosophie* (see note 57), § 279 (p. 367 f.) and supplement (p. 370). That Hegel had clearly recognized the problem of sovereignty as a problem of the relationship between positive norms and individuality is very clear in these sentences. He believed, however, that he could only explain the 'I will' of the *Rechtsstaat* through sovereignty residing in the monarch.

[221] Ibid., § 279. [222] Ibid., § 279 (p. 367).

[223] Evidence in Kaufmann, *Monarchisches Prinzip* (p 42 ff.).

[224] Meyer/Anschütz, *Staatsrecht* (see note 2), p. 19 note 6a; See ibid., pp. 20, 272. Carl Schmitt's polemic against Anschütz (see note 206) is all the more suggestive since Schmitt's own definition of sovereignty apparently draws upon this bearer of state power as the highest organ of the state. Admittedly, Schmitt cannot refer to positive law, as Anschütz did in his time.

[225] Jellinek, *System* (see note 168), p. 158 f., note 3.

I maintain that German public law has paid for this localization of the state in the government with the unhappy consequence of a fictitious or abstract state. It might have been protected from this if, like American public law doctrine, for example, it had been able to identify the sovereignty of the state with national and popular sovereignty. In a remarkable statement, Erich Kaufmann feels it necessary to frankly confess, "in the sharp conceptual separation between 'state' and 'government,' American public law doctrine was ahead of us."[226] Certainly the naïve American equation of people and state is often based on theoretical ambiguity. But since the Americans, under the influence of European and especially German theory, have basically abandoned the natural law theory of contract,[227] that ambiguity has become less dangerous, and in most cases has even been overcome.[228] In any case, their "location of sovereignty in the body politic" is a more useful sovereign person than our idea of a conceptual phantom labelled the state.

In every epoch, explanatory and justificatory principles grow from the same root. Therefore, today a supporter of the monarchist principle or dictatorship may not without contradiction imagine a different legitimation or explication of state unity and sovereignty than one through organized popular will. The historical reason for the crisis of German public law doctrine lies in part in the contradictions between the available theoretical ways of thinking and the existing forms of state; the zeitgeist demanded the construction of the state from immanent forces, but political reality compelled construction from a point above the state, a construction from the top down.

The crisis of the concept of sovereignty and the state, whose roots are in the fictional and abstract understanding of the state, is however grounded even more deeply in the general history of ideas than in German constitutional history. Particularly in the places where this monarchist principle has been rejected politically and liberal democratic thinking has taken hold, it has been shown that the deeper roots of the crisis lie in liberal rule of-law rationalism, which has denatured the concepts of state, people, representation, sovereignty, and so on. It is astonishing but true that our current democrats could learn what democracy means from Bodin, Hobbes, or Hegel.

If the doctrine of state sovereignty is not to remain merely an "equivocation" from the actual problem, as it is today; if the theory of "sovereign state power" is to make comprehensible sense, it must be able to name a person of this sovereign power. But Georg Jellinek, for example, observes reproachfully that "the question of sovereign state power [is connected with] the question of the bearer of this power."[229] This opens the way for Kelsen: we have a sovereign state power, but we cannot ask what

[226] Kaufmann, *Auswärtige Gewalt*, p. 192.

[227] Charles Edward Merriam, *History of the Theory of Sovereignty since Rousseau*, New York 1900 (Studies in History, Economics and Public Law, vol. 12, no. 4), pp. 176, 179 f.

[228] See John W. Burgess, *Political Science and Comparative Constitutional Law*, Boston 1890, vol. 1 (Sovereignty and Liberty), p. 57 f. Westel Woodbury Willoughby, *An Examination of the Nature of the State. A Study in Political Philosophy*, New York 1922, p. 290 ff.; Westel Woodbury Willoughby, *Fundamental Concepts of Public Law*, New York 1924, p. 99; James Brown Scott, *Sovereign States and Suits before Arbitral Tribunals and Courts of Justice*, New York 1925, p. 7.

[229] Jellinek, *Staatslehre* (see note 3), p. 457.

the person of this power is. In that case, it would be more consistent to allow these state abstractions, equipped with the highest power, to disappear completely. But the true meaning of the doctrine of state sovereignty is, historically and systematically, none other than that of an antithesis of autocratic princely sovereignty. If the state is claimed to be sovereign, that means this 'state,' the 'corporate entity,' and not an individual person, is the supreme decision-maker. Here the state is conceived of as a unity of will resulting from a multiplicity of wills, which is subject to no higher unit of political decision-making.

Whenever we speak of state sovereignty, the idea of popular sovereignty is also somehow implicated. However, we must keep in mind that the idea of state and popular sovereignty can also have merely sociological or socioethical, non-juristic content. That the power of the state association always lies with the people was already familiar from natural law sociology, in Arumaeus and Limnaeus' doctrine of "real sovereignty" [*majestas realis*],[230] and in Hobbes as well.[231]

Frederick the Great meant the statement that the prince is "the first servant and the first magistrate of the state"[232] in a moral but not in any way juristic sense. But for all of the above, the state was substantively founded in an act of will by those represented, whose united power is placed at the disposal of their representatives. In this respect, there is no difference between popular and princely sovereignty, between democracy and autocracy.

In the autocratic state, those who govern can be bound by those who are governed only through sociological or socioethical bonds; but in a state under popular sovereignty, these bonds become a juristic concept—and state and popular sovereignty thus both first become indispensable concepts.

Now, in what way can the 'people' be conceived of as a suitable sovereign person? Something "logically impossible" is ascribed to liberalism with this conception, however. To liberalism, the people remained "the conceptually-grasped sum of individuals."[233] Hobbes knew better. He formulates with consummate juristic precision: "Whenever we say that a People or a number [of men] is willing, commanding or doing something, we mean a commonwealth which is commanding, willing and acting through the will of one man or through the wills of several mean who are in agreement; and this can only happen in a meeting [*conventus*]. But whenever something is said to be done by a number of men, great or small, without the will of that man or meeting, it means that it was done by a people as subjects, that is, by many individual citizens at the same time, and that it does not spring from one

[230] See Roderich v Stintzing, *Geschichte der Deutschen Rechtswissenschaft*, 2nd section, Munich 1880, p. 40 ff.; Otto Gierke, *Johannes Althusius und die Entwicklung der naturrechtlichen Staatstheorien. Zugleich ein Beitrag zur Geschichte der Rechtssystematik*, 3rd edn, Breslau 1913, p. 164 ff.; 6 note 9.

[231] Hobbes, *De Cive* (see note 9), chap. VII, I I (p. 128), derives both monarchy and aristocracy from the power of the people. See also ibid., chap. XII, 8 (p. 200): "In every commonwealth the People Reigns; for even in *Monarchies* the *People* exercises power." [137]

[232] Frédéric le Grand, *Mémoire pour servir à l'histoire de la Maison Brandebourg*, in Oeuvres, sec. 1 (Oeuvres historiques), vol. 1, Berlin 1846, p. 123. On the content of the idea of state sovereignty, see Rehm, *Staatslehre* (see note 164), p. 152 f.

[233] Richard Schmidt, *Allgemeine Staatslehre*, vol. 1, Leipzig 1901, p. 233.

will but from the several wills of several men, who are citizens and subjects but not a commonwealth."[234] On the representation that is necessary in every state and does not come into being except "this can only happen if each man subjects his *will* to the *will of a single* other [*alterius unius*], *to the will, that is, of one Man* [*Hominis*] or of one *Assembly* [*Concilium*], in such a way that whatever one *wills* on matters essential to the common peace may be taken as the *will* of all and each [*omnes et singuli*]."[235] In a democracy, two things must join this representation: "of which one ... constitutes a Δήμος [demos], and the other (which is majority voting) constitutes τό κράτος [authority] or power."[236]

Unification of wills through the majority principle and representation are the technical tools through which the people as a unity rule over the people as a multiplicity, and through which the people can become the sovereign person. But the prerequisite for both is the substantive existence of a "general will," which alone can ultimately make the minority submit to the appointment of representatives chosen by the majority.

The juristically precise difference between aristocratic or monarchic autocracy and democracy lies in the status of the representatives. In autocracy, we can find juristically unbound, sovereign representation; in contrast, the state of popular sovereignty invariably has only juristically-bound, magisterial representation.

Despite all the deformations and obfuscations of the popular will, the democratic idea corresponds to a concept of representation of the "general will" through juristically dependent magistrates, as well as to a situation of political power that has far-reaching juristic consequences. It is indeed remarkable how little our constitutional jurists have to say on the sentence 'State power emanates from the people.' Not a word do we hear about the fact that, ultimately, the entire Weimar Constitution, especially the positions of the Reich President, the Reichstag, the Reich Government, and so on, can only be understood through this sentence, as magisterial representation; that the only way to make juristic sense of the entire system of dependencies, such as elections, countersigning, parliamentarism, referendums, initiatives, and so on, is to juristically guarantee that power emanates from the people.

Of course, democratic representatives also possess independent decision-making powers that are inseparable from the concept of representation; in contrast to sovereign representatives, however, they exercise these not only within the scope of the constitution, but also within the scope of the constitution understood in the exclusive sense of the "general will." The objection that there is no objective knowledge of the relevant content of the "general will" is as shabby as it is correct; that is exactly why the idea that we are living not under the rule of men but under law is so foolish. Precisely because every individual is determined politically and socially in different ways, the text of the constitution can be interpreted very differently; the "general will" is supposed to be a corrective to this subjectivism. This is what the jurist means when he speaks of the spirit of the constitution, or of the will of the state or the will of the lawmaker in the normative sense. But the fact that all modern constitutions

234 Hobbes, op. cit., chap. VI, I (p. 92). [77]

235 Ibid., chap. V, 6 (p. 84). [72]

236 Ibid., chap. VII, 5 (p. 125). [94]

themselves are what binds the magisterial representatives juristically to the "general will" arises precisely from this formulation: 'The deputies are representatives of the entire people.' It means nothing that the dominant doctrine construes the deputy as an organ of state, since we know that 'nothing' stands behind the organ. For this view, this, like so many other constitutional provisions, must be nothing more than a political phrase with no legal content. In contrast, the deputy, as a magisterial representative of the people, is a theoretically and practically meaningful legal institution. Only in this way does the sentence 'The deputies are subject only to their consciences' gain a political and legal significance that goes beyond private morality. For a legal duty to subordinate my conscience to some ethic, be it the Sermon on the Mount or any other, is impossible. If conscience in that sentence is to have any legal meaning, it must point to something ethically and politically concrete, to an objective standard for which only the will of the people is adequate.

Thus, the exercise of that magisterial representation, not only that of the parliamentarian, must be conceived of as constantly dependent on the people, even in its independent decisions. In contemporary democracies, juristic dependency has reached such a high degree that one is forced to speak legally of the government of the people as a unity over the people as a multiplicity. In this way, any type of organ sovereignty is ruled out, and state and popular sovereignty are identified.

In the monarchical as in the democratic state, therefore, we only arrive at a serviceable sovereign person and a correct concept of the state by seeing the "general will" as substantively desired and unified by a representative institution, but also as substantively present, in order to be able to imagine it being represented and as supporting the representative.

## C. The Reality of State Unity and the Will of the State

The crisis of our theory of the state and the dogma of sovereignty, however, is ultimately merely a product of the overall crisis in our intellectual historical situation. The fact that theory today is unable to construct a state on either the monarchist or the democratic principle without contradiction lies in its philosophical and epistemological attitude. It does not know what to do with a popular will or Gierke's common will, because there is no path to social realism from their dogmatic individualism, which at best just barely considers the individual to be real. Furthermore, it cannot accommodate a real state, because it cannot handle its own doctrine of a state that is only real and capable of willing through its organs. How, from its own foundations, should it transcend the objections to the Jellinek/Kelsen doctrine, which, rejecting all 'methodological syncretism,' is no more willing to admit the link between psychological-empirical will and the normative authority of an organ than the link between a real popular will and positive state commands? Although it has already been shown that even Kelsen, not to mention others, cannot get by without this empirical will of the 'constitutive' authority, we must still show how this 'will,' and thus the sovereign state, may be imagined to be real and normative.

The problem of state and law in general, and of sovereignty in particular, is a problem of the connection between will and norm, is and ought. To the rationalist metaphysics of our jurisprudence, of which Jellinek is the most important representative but Kelsen the most consistent, such a connection is absurd. Their starting point is the contradictory opposition between nature and mind, will and norm—an idealism that considers the schoolmasterly deconstructed totality to be definitively compartmentalized, because it cannot find a way from the relatively justified analysis and from antithesis to a synthesis. Of course, the concepts 'value-blind empire of nature' and 'value-laden empire of the mind' are methodologically relatively justified oppositions, as long as one is aware that one is speaking of a dialectically self-dividing unity. An idealism, however, that at some point finally resolves the given tension in the direction of the mind is not one whit better, epistemologically or ethically, than a materialism that does the opposite. Only in the polarity of differences does the tension emerge that the religious experience is a restless longing for God. "Grace does not destroy nature, but perfects it." [*Gratia naturam non tollit sed perficit.*] In the epistemology of the historical-social world—including legal science—the insurmountable contradiction between nature and mind leads to a dualism that tears this world into two parts: there pure mind and the ideal ought, here the turmoil of a purely causal reality of is, which exists without being anything for us, and is thus completely senseless and incapable of imputation; it has no sociological imputability, and therefore no state as a sociological unity.

That the doctrine of the state worked with these ways of thinking in the nineteenth century was understandable at the time. In the meantime, however, both psychology and sociology have long since moved in other directions, and in philosophy, scholars from such varied schools of thought as Husserl, Rickert, and Simmel have met with Dilthey's students Spranger, Litt, and Freyer in acknowledging a sphere of the 'senses,' the meanings that are altogether appropriate for overcoming that rough dualism. It is now inexcusable for a legal scholar to take note only of purely natural science psychology and sociology that is incompatible with legal science, and to care so little for the results of contemporary thought that he does not even ask whether law can find its place in that sphere of the senses.

It is true that a concept of the will based in natural science and psychology—that is, meaning-free—constructs a world that is meaningless and, in every sociological and juristic regard, 'incapable of imputation.' But it is wrong when Kelsen, for example, instead of correcting the concept of the will, simply eliminates it and then operates with a mythic—in the worst sense—parallelism of is and ought, which in reality knows no imputation because it knows no will. The relationship between will and norm, state and law can only be explained when it is definitely established that neither sociology nor jurisprudence is interested in the will as 'psychological motivation,' as innervation. Only a will in the sense of socially correlated behavior, that is, announced through signs, and only a meaningful will, that is, behavior that means 'something,' is taken account of by every science of human society.[237] The issue is

[237] Litt, *Individuum* (see note 183), especially p. 151 ff.

therefore not one of behaviors, in which an individual only expresses himself, that is, his subjective emotional state, in signs; rather, it is one of process or signs that are fully located in causal reality and possess objective significance, an intersubjective meaning, a reference to something substantive, separable from the subjective course of experiences. In every gesture that, for example, invites one to sit, something extra-psychological and ideal is also seated—as Simmel once said, the turn to the idea is completed.[238] Such meaningful behavior reaches into natural reality, but at the same time reaches beyond it and, through the fact of being 'understood,' transcends the isolation of the self, thus creating the first condition of human society, unity of meaning. A meaning established in sensory signs has its own relatively objective existence, and can be named and understood apart from any psycho-physical reality—upon this fact is based the justified opposition between objective norms and subjective-psychological reality, and thus all jurisprudence. For the work of the jurist consists in selecting, interpreting and systematizing the sensory content or meanings that count as 'law' out of the behaviors that are significant for the ordering of human coexistence. However, jurisprudence inevitably reaches a dead end when it undertakes to establish as an absolute its methodological artifice—that is, the separation of sign and meaning, nature and mind, form and substance, act of will and norm. For as surely as the human individual is not a disembodied spirit, but is integrated into a sensory reality in which and on which it becomes mind, just as surely, sign and meaning form both a sensory and an unsensory whole, an "at a glance" [*uno intuitu*] comprehended dialectical unity of meaningfulness and meaning. Without insight into meaning's dependence on sign, without awareness of the internal relationship between substance and shape, content and form, one ultimately arrives, via our dominant jurisprudence, at Kelsen's pure theory of law, in which the ideal objectivity of law has finally liberated—that is, erased—the subject from the causal objectivity of natural reality. What remains is the thoroughly incomprehensible parallelism of ideal and causal objectivity, its peace of the graveyard no longer disturbed by any living subject. Note that the consequence of this 'idealism,' with its blatant tearing apart of is and ought, act and act's meaning, is the naturalistic concept of reality that is also dominant in our science. It is a highly ironic trick of reason that forces this idealism to neatly relegate the act to solely 'real' nature, while assigning meaning to the mind, so that nothing remains but for the latter to be unreal. The problem of a specific social reality cannot be comprehended by the undialectical dualism of nature and mind.

We can satisfy the stringent requirements of jurisprudence not by forcing upon it a mathematical concept of science that is not adequate to it,[239] but by comprehending

[238] (Georg Simmel, *Lebensanschauung*, Munich 1918, p. 28 ff.)

[239] According to Kelsen, who, following his teacher Hermann Cohen (*Ethik des reinen Willens*, 3rd edn, Berlin 1921, p. 67), labeled jurisprudence the "mathematics of the humanities." See Hermann Heller, *Die Krisis der Staatslehre* (see above, section 1, no. 1), note 44.

its unique linkage of reality and validity, that is, the social-historical world, as dialectically self-dividing unity and reality.[240] Wundt quite rightly noted, "Mathematical concepts arise from the abstract relationships of the forms of intuition, and they always lead back to elements of the simplest intuitive form Jurisprudence takes its concepts from the most complicated relationships of human intercourse and arbitrary behavior. Thus mathematics, in the nature of its problems, is the simplest and jurisprudence the most complicated of all the sciences."[241]

If we apply these insights to the problem of state and law with which we are concerned, we believe we may arrive at a synthesis of Gierke's doctrine and that of Laband/Jellinek, while avoiding each one's one-sidedness. To an ahistorical, individualistic understanding, getting from the individual act to the gigantic structure of the state certainly seems incomprehensible. But let us establish that human nature's formal predisposition to equality is expressed in typical, regular activity and, as an objective correlate of this regular, meaningful behavior, within the conditions of their individual cultural existence, objectivizes intellectual connections and orders such as language, art, and so on. These meanings, formed by human coexistence and the succession of human generations, include objective social orders, such as convention and law. Law is neither a system "of behavior"[242] nor the mass conception of a norming,[243] but norms, meaningful, objective norms, established, supported, and destructible by acts of human will, that aim meaningfully for legal effects. Legal institutions and fundamental legal principles, based in the sensory-ethical nature of mankind, and realized in the temporal and spatial situation of this particular culture, have been formed by the acts of will of the endless chain of generations. Now the individual act of realization discovers the world of forms that transcends it, built up over millennia in language, law, and so on, into which it flows, that forms it, but to whose form it has also contributed in its time.[244] Preserving and refashioning itself through tradition and revolution, this world of forms, despite its relative objectivity vis-à-vis individuals and individual generations—as centuries and millennia have given these entities their form—is nevertheless supported and determined in that moment by the fleeting acts of its realization, and gains its validity only from acts of will based on fundamental legal principles. Thus, we understand law as meaningful formed content. The reality of human associations that intervenes in causal reality, however, consists in its actuality. We call the unity of decision and action of these acts that realize this order state will or state authority: the first term emphasizes more the ordering legal function, the second more strongly the ordering power. The state association is not, as is generally claimed, a multiplicity 'of people.' Nor do solidarity

[240] From the standpoint of Rickert's philosophy of values, Julius Hatschek most recently, in *Einleitung in das öffentliche Recht*, Leipzig 1926, p. 28 ff., has advocated these ideas with some presuppositions and consequences that differ from my views.

[241] Wilhelm Wundt, *Logik*, vol. 2 (Logik der Geisteswissenschaften), 2d ed., Stuttgart 1895, p. 582.

[242] According to Max Ernst Mayer, *Rechtsphilosophie*, Berlin 1922 (Enzyklopädie der Rechts- und Staatswissenschaft), p. 55.

[243] According to Beling, *Rechtswissenschaft und Rechtsphilosophie* (see note 138), p. 17; correctly, p. 19.

[244] Freyer, *Theorie des objektiven Geistes* (see note 138), especially p. 52 ff.

and unity exist only "for human thinking."[245] The rationality of purposeful associative activity marks the beginning of the relative isolation of the individual, who can as a result no longer be seen as belonging to one or another association in his totality, but only in certain partial functions. Each human being is, as a rule, involved in the actualization of numerous associations. The state, in Friedrich Julius Stahl's words the 'realized legal order,'[246] is the unified interaction between certain human acts, and in this way the same as all other human associations; but it is fundamentally different from them in that the acts that it realizes guarantee the entirety of the interactions in this area. This universality of state decision-making functions is extremely important conceptually.

Just as contemporary psychology conceives of human beings as units of action and effect that are constantly evolving, but remain identical to themselves in structure despite all changes, we could in the same sense—endorsing Renan's words—call the state "a daily plebiscite" [*un plébiscite de tous les jours*].[247] For, like the ego, the state too can only be understood as a structure of a totality that remains relatively persistent in the fluctuation of acts; the totality of effect is found even where only its parts seem to be active. It would be thoroughly wrong to believe, once again returning to the ultimate separation of act and purpose, that the existence of the community is "independent of the individuality of the people who belong to it."[248] Just as the individual cannot exist without the individuality of his acts, the individual state cannot exist without these thoroughly individual acts. We cannot warn enough against the idea that allows a state to consist on the one hand of a bundle of human actions, and on the other of an ideal order. It is thus at least an unfortunate formulation when, following Max Weber, the idea of the state in "empirical reality" should be "an endlessness of diffuse and discrete human behaviours and indulgences . . . held together through an idea, the belief in norms and authority relationships of human beings over other human beings that actually apply or should apply."[249] This idea no more exists for us without the realizing act that is formed by it, than does the act established in this way without any idea.

Gierke rightly opposed Jellinek's doctrine, which maintained that there are "two species of unity: physical and purposeful units."[250] For the association is just as much a social unity of action, both physical and meaningful, as is the human individual. Yet Gierke's own claim that will and purpose cannot in the same way be considered constitutive elements of the concept of personality was erroneous, insofar as Gierke, in naturalistically one-sided fashion, called the living force of will, which

[245] As one of many, see Wenzel, *Begriff des Gestzes* (see note 124), p. 145. All those who see the state as consisting of 'people' have contributed a great deal to the misunderstanding of sovereignty (e.g., above p. 46 f.). See below, note 284.

[246] Friedrich Julius Stahl, *Die Philosophie des Rechts*, vol. 2, sec. II, 5th edn, Freiburg 1878 (Hints, p. 131 ff.).

[247] (Ernest Renan, *Qu'est-ce qu'une nation*? 2nd edn, Paris 1882 (Conference faite en Sorbonne le 11 Mars 1882), p. 27.)

[248] Wenzel, op. cit., p. 145.

[249] Max Weber, "Die 'Objectivität' sozialwissenschaftlicher und sozialpolitischer Erkenntnis" (1904), in *Gesammelte Aufsätze zu Wissenschaftslehre*, Tübingen 1922, p. 200.

[250] Georg Jellinek, *Gesetz und Verordnung* (1887), Tübingen 1919 (Neudruck), p. 193.

was to him the only significant content of that concept, "the causal force of external movements."[251] That the idea of the reality of the collective will is indispensable, on this we can agree completely with the corporatist theory. The opposing view, which, in the epoch of the world war of the imperial great powers, saw the states as fictions, abstractions, and ideal norm systems, will be quite amusing to future generations. What bellows could maintain parliaments, monarchs, presidents, and the entire state hierarchy in their ruling positions? The communalization of the individual will into the active unity of a common will is a problem that public law has so far dealt with in completely one-sided fashion. Until now it has been satisfied with a theory that maintained that this unity was a product of the legal order. In fact, however, the state will can only be understood as an effective decision-making unit, individuated by the entirety of the natural and social order and finally by state organs. The most important natural fact that determines the specific regularity of behavior is the neighborhood, the community of destiny of a territory.[252] Nevertheless, our newly fashionable geopolitics still has no idea of the problem at hand.[253] Of greater significance for the existence of a collective will, too, is without doubt the consolidation of blood, with the formation of a uniform anthropological type—facts that contemporary race theory nevertheless faces helplessly.[254] Mass-determined and imitative types of behavior are closely linked with commonality of territory; their influence on the unification of wills has already been examined more closely. However, all of these contexts and orders that seem unamenable to meaning are not in any way in a relationship of substructure and superstructure to meaningful behaviors, but operate at the apex as well as the base of the social pyramid. If we include the larger or smaller community of orders of an economic, conventional, moral, and religious nature, the result of all these natural and cultural conditions of social life is an individuated collective will, which manifests itself in the legal order as a counterbalance to all the other orders, an expression of the actual power relations. Each of these innumerable orders and valuations can have in common a larger or smaller shared culture than that which is determined by state borders; with this crystallization, which determines all of them, of a will that is finally individuated and decided by common institutions, each becomes unique. Certainly, the state will emerges and exists again and again only through the coming together of individual, meaningful particles of will. These wills have only become human, however, in and through the ancient world of forms of objective mind; without it, outside of it, we would be animals

[251] Gierke, *Genossenschaftstheorie* (see note 181), pp. 609, 631 note 2; see also Preuß, *Gemeinde, Staat, Reich* (see note 34), p. 153 ff.

[252] Jellinek, *System* (see note 168), p. 26: "The basis of this unity [of the state will] is first of all physical. The state evolves on a spatially limited part of the earth's surface."

[253] Instead of beginning by investigating the general meaning of the neighborhood for common behavior and following it with a detailed individual study of the specific effects of a part of the earth's surface on the economic and other commercial relationships, it prefers, in a highly unscientific short circuit in its thinking, to create a direct causal connection between land and state. Walter Vogel's assessment, *Politische Geographie*, Leipzig 1922 (Aus Natur- und Geisteswelt, vol. 634), p. 9, on Ratzel's works is still true today, despite valuable individual results, for this science as a whole: "One may cite excellent sayings from it as evidence for claims of all sorts, even if they contradict each other."

[254] See Hermann Heller, *Sozialismus und Nation*, in *Gesammelte Schriften*, vol. 1, p. 452 ff.

or gods. Individual and community are therefore correlative concepts, the one in juxtaposition with the other.[255] This is also the eternal core of the Marxist view of history: that the individual will finds social material whose iron construction and most rational part is the economy—material whose social will operates through its causal, but also normative, laws; a given world whose structure is only accessible at a few points. The bed of the subjective river of experience dug by history and society defines the most important individuation of the co`llective will, which a Canadian theoretician has rightly termed the "ultimate sovereign," "unformulated though very real."[256] The determination of the state will by the people as bearer of this order, while surely present in every form of state, is only in democratic states the crucial and juristically significant factor.

But this unification of wills only becomes the will of the state order of rule through the final individuation granted it by the state institutions. The representative bodies represent in themselves the values and powers of a community, joined in the unity of a will. Here, too, Jellinek's undialectical bifurcation is impossible. The will of the bearer of the organ is only a collective will in the physical-natural world as well as the ethical-juristic world as long as it can actually be expected regularly to have at its disposition the power of those it represents, and to generally be obeyed; but the fact that it is regularly obeyed lies in the fact that its acts of rule are considered acts of the collective will and are in fact determined by this collective will. "The law thinks and wants what the spirit of the people by a reasonable interpretation takes from it."[257] Absolutist legislative bodies, but especially democratic legislative bodies, find already present the essential values on which their decisions are based and the powers to implement them; they do not create fundamental legal principles, but at most reshape them. Thus, the dominant jurisprudence is right to believe that law can be more insightful than the legislative body; however, the law cannot be wiser than the state will. Certainly, the will and the views of the immediate authors of the law are not essential to the interpretation of the law. But to the extent that the authors are representatives of the state will, which is the values of the community smoothed into unity, their will and views are not altogether unimportant. The principles of the state, family, and property orders that apply in a legal community are, to a great extent, removed from the arbitrariness of the legislature. Bismarck had to engage to a certain degree in socialist and Lenin in capitalist legislative politics. The violation of this—in part culture-bound—"natural law" [*ius naturale*] will repeatedly occasion a reclaiming of the right to resist. Of course, there is no state omnipotence in this sense; understanding the concept of sovereignty in this way would be a foolish misunderstanding.

[255] Litt, op. cit. (see note 183) (p. 46 ff.).

[256] Robert Morrisson MacIver, *The Modern State*, Oxford 1926, p. 11 f.

[257] Karl Binding, *Handbuch des Strafrechts*, vol. 1, Leipzig 1885 (Systematisches Handbuch der deutschen Rechtswissenschaft, sec. VII, part 1, vol. 1), p. 456 f. See also Josef Lukas, "Zur Lehre von Willen des Gesetzgebers," in *Staatsrechtliche Abhandlungen. Festgabe für Paul Laband*, Tübingen 1908, vol. 1, p. 401; "The conceptual content of a law is determined by the average perception enjoyed by the relevant law in the social milieu into which it is placed."

If one goes no further than the nature–mind dualism and does not clarify for oneself, on the one hand, the habitual formation of the individual act of will by the world of natural-social legalities and, on the other hand, the fact that this world of forms is only actualized through these wills—then state will and state force will remain incomprehensible. The objections to the reality of the state will accordingly arise from the arsenal of a philosophy whose dogmatic individualism acknowledges only the reality of individual human beings, but, exhausting itself in its analysis of consciousness, ultimately corrodes the most certain experience, the experience of the self, as well as the human community. There are two primary objections raised against the presumption of a real state will. First of all, its existence is disputed because its abundance of prescriptions is found in no one's consciousness. Yet if we were socialized only through our consciousness, there would certainly be neither a state will nor a human community, nor even any individual wills. Essentially, I have just as little right to ascribe it to my will when the alarm clock I set for 7 a.m. wakes me, because I am asleep at the time. When it comes to the state, however, I ascribe to the will of the state, actualized in the regular behavior of its residents, the fact that those who oppose it consciously or unconsciously can expect very real coercive measures. Here we cannot speak of unconscious or coerced recognition; but nor should one fail to recognize that the coercion of will in particular cases in no way seeks to negate recognition of the order as a whole. The same is true for the second, at first seemingly irrefutable objection to the reality of the state will. It is undeniable that there are people in every state who find themselves in conscious opposition to the state will; as long as this conscious opposition amounts to nothing more than the occasional violation of certain norms, the objection can be easily overcome. The thief does not think of negating § 242 of the Criminal Code; first of all, he does not plan to steal always, and second, he does not want anything stolen from him. Where the legality of a state prescription is seriously contested, two cases must be distinguished. If, for example, the contestation is a purely internal judgment and does not affect the actual behavior required for the unity of the collective will, because, perhaps, the pressure of circumstance does not allow this assessment to become a deed, then we have no problem. For we are far from claiming that the state is an association based on the internal judgment and recognition of all its members. We are only claiming the regular unity of acts of will for which, where appropriate, the principle of "Though forced, I consent" [*coactus tamen voluit*] applies. If the individual will actively opposes the collective will, however, it is possible either that his judgment and power will assert themselves and create a new collective will, or that he will ultimately be destroyed, like Michael Kohlhaas. The fact that it is sometimes unorganized and sometimes organized force that ensures the existence of the collective will is a quite general phenomenon not limited to these cases. The entirety of the natural-social legalities and the acts of decision of state bodies are often enough experienced as the coercion of actual power relations. Ultimately, though, misunderstandings and objections to the collective will are based on nothing more than the fact that it is viewed not as a dialectic balancing of contradictions taking place within every individual, but as a substantive, socially directed will. Certainly, the collective will cannot be understood as I-consciousness; but as the habitual state of a more or less clear we-consciousness, it functions in every individual without exception. Let the worker battle the customs or tax laws, the military norms or whatever else in a state. As long as he accepts them, because he wants the same state's socio-political legislation, labor law, and so on, the state will is ensured——just as, conversely, a businessman accepts the form of state, social welfare laws, and so on, because he is guaranteed his private property and the customs policies he prefers. Let one avoid military service, another commit tax fraud, a third commit murder; as long as they all, a minute later, expect protection from the state and thus do not recognize it merely theoretically, but also, as a rule, contribute something or other to the constitution of the state will, this balancing is complete. In this sense, the individual sovereign state will is active in the individual and in the community, because it is active in both; but in the state it has, through individual decisions, become an artifact of unique character.

The results of this study of the concepts of state and law can be abundantly confirmed, even by Kelsen, who usually hastily leaves the halls of his pure theory of law when a genuine problem of legal science presents itself. In his view, namely, international law says, in a proposition that recognizes the individual state, "If A commands and B *usually* obeys, then A should command and B should always obey."[258] In other words, if A regularly meets with obedience from B, then this regular behavior by B should be considered rule-bound, lawful behavior and the corresponding acts should constitute the state. With this proposition Kelsen eliminates not only the entire pure theory of law and the most significant portion of its extensive polemic; he also determines with commendable precision that law means normative regulation of behavior, while state, in contrast, means not an ideal normative order, but a particular, actual regularity of behavior. All of a sudden, it becomes clear that it does not matter at all if all citizens share a real psychological relationship; it also becomes clear that (and why) the validity of the state legal order is independent of both the compliance of individuals and of whether or not the state officials, in behaving in accordance with the order, were consciously motivated by this order. It suffices for rule as a whole that those who are crucial 'usually' obey and that they regularly act as though they were motivated by these prescriptions. Theoretically, though not practically, their actual subjective motivation does not matter, as long as the regularity of their behavior is ensured. For like every other organization, the state originates and persists in no other way than by means of the collaboration of human beings, ensured by the organs, which in this way actualize an ideal legal order within a framework of fundamental legal principles. It is relatively justified for a jurist, for methodological reasons, to separate the "worthless remains" [*caput mortuum*] of the state, this ideal order, from the totality of state reality. However, he is completely unjustified in claiming that the validity of his order is independent of its actualization; and his doctrine becomes grotesque when he bluntly identifies the ideal order, which was established only through a methodological device of isolation, with the actual order of the highest imaginable social reality, which we call the

[258] Kelsen, *Staatslehre* (see note 46), p. 127.

state because it is actual. The only reason this identification accomplished by Kelsen does not reveal itself as nonsense simply from a linguistic perspective lies in the fact that all other German words ending in 'ung,' including the word 'order' [*Ordnung*], describe both an action and the results of this action—both regular subjective behavior and the ideal objective correlate of this behavior. Thus, even the spirit of the language confirms the dialectically divisive unity of sign and meaning.

## D. The Unity and Uniqueness of a Legal System as the Expression of a Sovereign State Will

The dominant jurisprudence treats the unity of the legal system, to which it dedicates its work, as something banally self-evident that is beyond any doubt. Detached from an actual legislature and from any social unit of will, the legal system seems, especially to the civil jurist, to be a logical whole. Give this logistical positivism a bundle of any positive legal precepts, and it will undertake to construct a complete system using logical reasoning. "The entire idea of gaps in the law," says Bergbohm, "should finally be abandoned. A law, even if it comprises almost no regulated material, is always something that exists in unbroken wholeness. Who could complete it, without setting himself up as a source of law? It never needs to be filled in from outside, for it is in every moment complete, because its internal fruitfulness, its logical [!] expansive force in its own area, meets any need for legal judgments at every moment."[259]

This idea of the unity of the legal system as a logical whole is wrong from top to bottom. This unity is teleological, historical, and sociological, based on the unity of a judging sovereign will. Before the unity of a legislative will and the unity of its requirement of validity existed, it was impossible to speak of the unity and coherence of a legal system.[260] However, a unified state will is the expression of a high degree of rational predictability of social relationships. Only when the ruling will can regularly expect obedience from everyone to whom it turns, without being dependent on the unpredictable consent of another unit of will—only then, and only from the value perspective of this will, can we speak of the legal system's logical structure. A development stretching over a millennium ultimately ended with the absolutist state and the unconditional legal validity of its state will. It began in our country with the capitulation of the Merovingians and Carolingians. Then took place a millennium-long struggle between state and peoples' law, between rational centralism and traditional, feudal law formation, fostered by the reception of Roman law in the form shaped by Justinian's centralized bureaucratic state and first made possible by a rational money economy and, connected with it, a bureaucracy that displaced the economically independent feudal lords. The absolutist elimination of intermediate legal powers now seems to be the condition for a will that can, "in one act" [*uno actu*], set the entire legal community in motion through the bureaucracy

[259] Bergbohm, *Jurisprudenz* (see note 153), p. 384 ff.
[260] Eugen Ehrlich, *Die juristische Logik*, 2nd edn, Tübingen1925, pp. 122 ff.; 138 f.

being able to count on obedience to its commands on the part of all legal subjects a condition for this, in turn, was the codification of the entirety of the law as an expression of the primacy of rational statutes through a will that asserts its totality over particular customs. The idea of the unity of law was promoted especially by natural law conceptualization, which believed it could deduce universally valid legal rules and concepts independent of any will, in mathematical syllogisms. Once state institutions had gained an enormous stake in legislation, justice administration, and enforcement and all other law, under the name of 'customary law,' was thought to be subordinated to statutory law, it was possible for the idea of the unity of the legal system to emerge. With the elimination of absolutism, finally, late-formalist liberalism believed it had eliminated every other law-creating will and had made the logical unity of the legal system independent of the will of its legal subjects. Now no one would ever again dare to 'set himself up as a source of law.'

For the conceptual jurisprudence that developed, the point of its logical-juristic harmonization of legal norms no longer lay in the ordering of social relationships, but was an absolute end in itself. It cannot accept that a uniform system of legal norms can only be understood as the expression of a sovereign order of rule, a correlate to a uniform system of acts of will independent of another permanent decision-making unit, and it therefore confuses logical validity with legal validity, logical unity with legal unity. Kelsen, once again a consistent representative of the dominant tendencies, sees in the unity of the legal system only the product of his supposedly completely sociology-free and ethics-free normative logic. "A norm system is a logically closed complex of norms whose inner consistency, whose unity one tends to express in figurative, fictive-anthropomorphic fashion ... by imagining that all normative content, simultaneously and side by side, is willed by a single subject."[261] This sentence contains all the fatal errors of logistical positivism. The assertion of the state as a logical whole—the historic-sociological pure theory of law must assert this for the feudal era as well—forces the further presumption that it is impossible "in one and the same order for content *a* and *non a* to be valid simultaneously."[262] This doctrine leads to particularly palpable impossibilities in Kelsen's international law. But in national law, too, from this point of view, contradictory final judgments and administrative acts cannot apply simultaneously, nor can state illegality exist. We understand that, to juristic rationalism, "the self-contradictory state will cannot be any more or less than self-abrogating legal science;[263] after all, it recognizes as the substrate of the person not a real, active unit of effect, but "only the consistency of its ideal existence."[264] One can no more ascribe contradictory action to a person than unlawfulness to a state. The ability of associations to commit delicts, especially the member states of a federal state; the numerous laws in the contemporary state that ascribe the unlawful acts of its organs to the state, such as civil servant liability; all this must be disputed away in order to claim that the state is a contradiction-free

[261] Kelsen, *Problem der Souveränität* (see note 38), p. 114. [262] Ibid., p. 110.
[263] Ibid., p. 173 f. [264] Ibid., p. 110.

norm system and its unity a logical whole.[265] The starkest immanent contradiction results, however, when Kelsen himself speaks of "the state person's capacity for unlawfulness and delict" under international law.[266]

No, the unity of a legal system can be understood only as the expression of a ruling unit of will. No one, be it an individual or collective unit of will, is a sophisticated book, but rather an individuality with its contradictions. Every order of rule is a hierarchical system of unification of wills, which at its apex demands consistency, in the sense of univocality. Even in the most technically perfect order of rule, the military, contradictory orders in the lower regions are not only necessary, but are harmless, and even essential, to the whole of rule and order. For social unity in multiplicity consists not of bricks, but of individuals, who can and should always independently interpret commands. The hierarchical structure of state unification of wills culminates today in the law. It is because of this, and not for some logical reason, that it is a justified demand of juristic construction that law in one and the same juristic system should be interpreted as consistently as possible. Even if we disregard the fact that historical categories are involved, even in the present, the unity and consistency of a legal system should not be understood as something essentially 'logical.' Statutory laws, like the laws of language, art, and so on, have their own logic, not identical to pure laws of thought, even though they are expressed in legal forms of thought. The jurist is involved in the creation of unity and of the consistency of the legal system only to the extent that he is not a pure normative logician, but also takes part, with the creative activity of his judging will, in the unified will constructed with all the other residents of the territory. This static unity of the legal order, as the individuality of this order in the multiplicity of its simultaneous norms, can only be understood as the expression of a unity of wills, and in fact, as we will soon note, as a sovereign unity of wills independent of the unpredictable consent of another.

This fact is even more vivid when we pose the question of the individuality of a legal system, within the multiplicity of its successively valid norms. For a certain type of positivism, state will is identical to positive law.[267] But all positive law is indisputably part of the flow of history; unchanging law means much the same as dead life. How, therefore, can the static unity of the legal order be released from its rigor mortis into the life of a historical ordering unity? To one who denies the existence of a real state will that constantly establishes new law, the historical individuality of a legal order will remain absolutely incomprehensible and impossible to construe. The exceedingly skillful, but thoroughly unsuccessful, attempts by Kelsen and his students to deal with this problem are interesting. In his *Hauptprobleme*, he makes it easy on himself by simply claiming that activity aimed at producing a state will

[265] On state unlawfulness, see Max Wenzel, *Der Begriff des Gesetzes* (see note 124), p. 212 f. and the sources mentioned there.

[266] Hans Kelsen, "Über Staatsunrecht. Zugleich ein Beitrag zur Frage der Deliktsfähigkeit juristischer Personen und zur Lehre vom fehlerhaften Staatsakt," in *Zeitschrift für das Privat- und öffentliche Recht der Gegenwart*, 40 (1914), p. 95 f.

[267] Affolter, "Staatsbegriff" (see note 163); Kelsen, "Staatsunrecht," p. 105 and passim; E. Hölder, "Das positive Recht als Staatswille," in *Archiv für öffentliches Recht*, 23 (1908), p. 359.

cannot be considered a function of the state, but should be characterized as a social process; without an imputation to the state, the factors participating in the legislative function, the representatives and their voters, parliament and the monarch, should not be viewed as state organs.[268] This unsurpassable "debacle" [*débâcle*] of juristic construction, which was charmingly supplemented by the later conception of the criminal as a state organ,[269] at least has the courage of consistency: "All juristic constructions have an unavoidable condition: the existence of a legal order; the fact that legal rules exist, and in them, a state will ready for action. This fact is the fixed point from which all juristic constructions go *out*—but which none of them can ever *go beyond*."[270] One sees where the radical dualism of will and norm leads us: in order to avoid falling into the "false doctrine of the psychological nature of the juristic will,"[271] any living will must disappear from state and law; an always-ready 'state will' stands at the apex, which is nothing but the sum of the legal rules positivized in this one moment.

Just as Mach conceived of everything psychological as substrate-less events, and ultimately resolved the unified structure of consciousness, here the substrate of the legal order is eliminated and the unified, temporal structure of legal norms becomes incomprehensible. In his later works, Kelsen attempted to cover up these all-too-obvious flaws with two constructions: the basic norm theory and the theory of legal hierarchy. But a basic norm that says to behave as this monarch or this parliament commands is not a 'legal rule,' and only because and to the extent that it is not a legal rule, but a redefined state will, can it act as that fixed point of juristic construction. It is remarkable how Kelsen's thinking is forced gradually to impute to this 'norm' all the features of a real will, until finally the concept of the norm is turned into its exact opposite. His rule of law rationalism had to assume, first of all, that the possibility of changing 'a' legal order can only be accepted if "the conditions for *how* it can be changed are established."[271a] These must be expressly fixed! But Kelsen stumbles over the question of "what is the actual nature of the fundamental principle of 'later law' [*lex posterior*] that guarantees the unity of the order despite a changing set of norms."[272] "Overcoming (!) the dynamic element that lies in the concept of norm change" is accomplished by demanding that every change, "in order to be comprehensible by the static normative-logical approach," is conceived of as being delegated by a higher norm "and thus *in nuce* [in a nutshell], as it were, already anticipated." Thus, every modifiable order already contains "every possible change in the blank form of the norm that lays down these conditions; it potentially contains within itself every imaginable variation of its normative content. In this sense, it is always the same, always unchangeable in its identity."[273] Thus we have really arrived at

[268] Kelsen, *Hauptprobleme der Staatsrechtslehre* (see note 143), p. 465.

[269] Kelsen, *Allgemeine Staatslehre* (see note 46), p. 262 ff.

[270] Kelsen, *Hauptprobleme der Staatsrechtslehre*, p. 466.

[271] Ibid., p. 467.

[271a] Kelsen, *Problem der Souveränität* (see note 38), p. 49.

[272] Ibid., p. 115.

[273] Ibid., p. 119 f. All of Kelsen's students also come to grief because of the static nature of a normative logic independent of a living unity of will; they therefore prefer to work with the concept of an unchangeable legal order. It is the substance-less "natural order" that breaks through here and becomes practical as the legal ideal of the *status quo*, see below, p. 178 ff.

the most marvelous example of a norm that any jurist has ever discovered! A critique of a norm that contains all imaginable variations of its content within itself is most likely superfluous. The only noteworthy aspect of this norm is its characterization by Kelsen, who thus very precisely describes the sovereignty of a unit of will.

The unity of a concrete legal system means the uniqueness of this system and every one of its parts. But a legal system can only be comprehended as such a unity, different from all others and unique in all its parts, as a consistent individuality, if at every point it is comprehended and constructed as the expression of a self-determining, concrete, individual state will. Like every individuality, this state will is at its core irrational and cannot be rationalized with any number of concentric definitions, and therefore cannot be rendered relational! For that very reason, it is a concept of juristic substance, and not a relational concept. Only as such is it suited to serve as a connecting starting point for social connections. The norms do not at all form a system because they have a logically systematic relationship to each other. The proposition 'Reich law breaks state law' is in itself no more 'logical' than its reverse. It possesses juristic logic only as the expression of a unique order of rule that represents a hierarchy of concrete superiority and subordination. Any rupture of the context of will and normative systems leads to a confusion between logical universality and juristic individual validity, and thus to the absolute impossibility of doing justice juristically to the individuality of this legal system. It is closed only for one who encloses himself voluntarily in the system, only for him; only he can bring closure. Each individual norm can therefore only be comprehended from the entirety of the system. Not that it would be impossible to detach property norms, for example, from the German and English legal systems and form a new norm out of them for the purposes of international jurisdiction. But it depends as much as anything else on realizing that this norm, first of all, would be substantively a new one that does not coincide with either German or English law, and second, that it would achieve legal validity only through a new act of unification of wills; that the formation of this norm, a thoroughly creative act, is not essentially an epistemological process, but a process of will. Only system unity as will unity allows us to explain the phenomenon—incomprehensible to legal rationalism—of differences between norms with the same wording in different systems. The fact that the Napoleonic Code applied differently and its content appeared in different form in the Rhineland and in France cannot be explained by the wording of the law or the logic that France and the Rhineland shared, but solely by the verbal meaning, which, in its realization through acts of will, was different in each place. The state will, as the product of all the conditions of nature and culture of state life, can never be gathered from the simple text of the law—least of all where the legislature purposely delegates norms that are in themselves indeterminate and to be determined by nothing but the "general will": such as reference to morality, general custom, the nature of the matter, implied declaration of intent, "good faith" [*bonne foi*], illegality, and so on. Only through the immanence of the state will in each individual norm does the individuality and unity of the entire normative system emerge. Those who fail to recognize this not only lack the bond that binds the norms into a concrete unity; they also never even grasp concrete pieces of that unity.

This fact of the pluralism of the individual legal systems and the individualism of every part of the system is misjudged from the ground up by legal rationalism, which makes the claim that "jurisprudence becomes science to the same degree that it meets the requirements of the postulate of the unity of its knowledge; that it succeeds in comprehending all law as a unified system."[274] "For the postulate of the *unity* of knowledge applies unconditionally at the normative level as well."[275] If we add the view, already familiar to us, that content *a* and *non a* cannot be true at the same time in one and the same system, then jurisprudence can only meet the requirements of Kelsen's concept of mathematical science if all people—Europeans and Bushmen, Americans and Chinese—were to possess the exact same legal norms in every particular. Mind you, it is only the "logical-epistemological character of the unity postulate"[276] that, for Kelsen and many other positivists from this school of thought, supposedly calls for the unity of all the law on this earth—and why only this one? Here the confusion between logical and normative validity, abstract theoretical and concrete social system unity, writing desk and life, is palpable. But here it must also be clear to the stupidest eye what theoretical and—to put it clearly—moral danger a jurisprudence of this kind represents. After all, it tears the heart from the universalist idea of law to replace its moral demand for unity, which appeals to our pure will, with the postulate of unity and purity of knowledge, which is moreover for Kelsen a mere economy of value and which satisfies only our intellect.[277] Don't they understand that it is precisely because the positive law of this world has no concrete systemic unity, that the postulate of universality, the unconditional harmony of all legal content, must be and remain immanent to the idea of law? Certainly, one can, with arbitrary hypotheses, prepare a system from all the legal norms in the world, and also argue happily about it.[278] It is possible that the construction of such an abstract unity could also have a theoretical purpose. Yet merely pointless confusion is sown when one confounds the abstract unity of 'the' legal system, which corresponds to no social reality, with the concrete unity of 'a' legal system whose substrate is the reality of a state will that pervades all norms. But the majority of German, French, and English attacks on the dogma of sovereignty are based on this confusion, as are Kelsen's polemics and his completely misguided construction of international law.

We now believe we have secured our sovereign person on all sides. As long as party and class struggles do not actually tear apart the state, the existence of a willing unity, albeit often quite meager, is unquestionably a given. Without the presumption of an actually present and represented "general will," we achieve neither a concept of law nor one of the state; but with it, the sought-after sovereign person presents itself to us.

[274] Kelsen, *Problem der Souveränität* (see note 38), p. 152. [275] Ibid., p. 105.

[276] Ibid., p. 152 note 1. [277] Ibid., p. 98 ff.

[278] Especially when one claims, in Kelsen's manner (ibid., p. 152 note 1), with great superiority, of an author (Fricker, "Das Problem des Völkerrechts," in *Zeitschrift für die gesamte Staatswissenschaft*, 28 (1872), p. 91) who speaks clearly enough about the "general idea" of law, that he speaks "more guessing than clearly knowing" of the task of legal science as "elaborating and bringing into unity" legal material through hypotheses. Opposing the theory of the tongue-in-cheek as-if hypotheses, see also Verdroß, *Völkerrechtsgemeinschaft* (see note 137), p. 2 ff.

# V

# The Nature of Sovereignty

## A. The Sovereign State Person

Sovereignty describes the characteristic of the absolute independence of a unit of will from other effective universal decision-making units; positively, we use this to express that the respective unit of will is the highest universal decision-making unit in this particular order of rule.

The jurist calls the state a person, an idea that is of course the result of juristic construction. When this construction is seen as a mere fiction, simply "at the discretion of the jurist,"[279] we can no longer speak meaningfully of the sovereignty of a state personality.

All valid juristic concepts are silhouettes of real social processes. Without constant reference to sociological-empirical fact, jurisprudence loses itself in a broad heaven of concepts. This reference should not of course belie its—incidentally also sociologically comprehensible—task of turning "pre-scientific" material into precise and practicable legal concepts. But this does not make these social realities either fictions or mere products of juristic method. After all, the material the jurist discovers to be dealt with is not a juristic "blank slate" [*tabula rasa*], but a cultural reality everywhere permeated by law; his task in dealing with it is essentially to continue the conceptual process of law formation that was already accomplished pre-scientifically; to perhaps even offer the life of law new constructions; to more strictly separate out the specifically legal aspects of other areas of life into which they are embedded; to bring it into a system. The isolation, construction, and systematization of juristic work has basically the same significance as the work of legislation: a just and reliable order of social coexistence. The juristic task is large or small, depending on whether the jurist makes himself the advocate of a higher or a lower order.

Despite all the relative freedom often given the jurist vis-à-vis the social substrate, it is made up of the highly real social conditions in whose normative likenesses he constructs his concepts of state will and state personality. A dominant tendency of our legal science, however, prefers to see in the state person a "fictional person" [*persona ficta*], a purely ideal normative subject, and to merge this with the impersonal legal order. Banished to an undialectical nature–intellect dualism, to this tendency

[279] Kelsen, *Problem der Souveränität*, p. 292; 164 etc.

the will of the legislature, for example, seems to be not a psychological fact, but "only a figurative expression of a thoroughly normative entity."[280]

But there can be no norm-logical imputation without constant reference to nomological knowledge, without insight into the regularities of causal connections.[281] Certainly, jurists should separate imputation and causation just as they do normative and psychological will; but for specific juristic reasons, these cannot be torn apart. The construction of the juristic person therefore means not spontaneous legal-scientific generation, as in the "let men be made as art" [*fiat homo secundum artem*] formula; rather, it draws, for the individual person as well as the person of an association on the unified bearer of actual enacted acts. Of course, jurists do not photograph the entire life of a human personality; instead, from a real unit of wills, a range of acts is chosen from particular juristic points of view, for which a continuous bearer of these acts is constructed. But where the jurist finds no continuous unity of will, he cannot create an artificial one. Even an "estate in abeyance" [*hereditas jacens*] or a foundation can only be meaningfully personified because, and to the extent that, they possess a real bearer of will. While in the latter case, however, an actual technical personification is present—the bearer of will is created by legal rule and therefore merges into a legal relationship—the situation for the individual persons and the persons of an association, who are real, social units of action, is quite different. Here the person is not a relation but relational; not merely juristically connected, but the connector; not function, but substance.[282]

The construction of a juristic person is always only an attempt at the relative, never the absolute, rationalization and relationalization of a real unit of will. Even for the jurist, the irrational totality of a living unit of will must remain visible behind the juristic mask (person originally meant mask). The specific juristic relevance of the real substrate of the personality is just as important in private as in public law. In all spheres of law, the unit of will as a person is not only the bearer but also the creator of rights and duties. This theoretically highly important situation generally goes unrecognized today. Erich Kaufmann, too, depersonalizes the private legal order when he states that, in private law, the will only begins to function on the basis of an objective order of competences; it is the "organ" of a super-individual order.[283] "As if the state," Husserl rightly responds, "as it constituted itself, had shattered the legal subjectivity of all the personalities found in its domain, with all their individual legal spheres, in order to then artificially revivify them, where it accorded

[280] As one example, see Radbruch, *Grundzüge der Rechtsphilosophie* (see note 135), p. 196.

[281] See Max Weber, "Die 'Objektivität' sozialwissenschaftlicher und sozialpolitischer Erkenntnis" (see note 249), p. 179. Kohlrausch, Radbruch, and Liepmann rightly emphasized that it is specific juristic principles that, for example, constitute penal imputation. The view that this juristic concept of causality is independent of a meaningful psychological causality concept goes back to the unfortunate dual-worlds theory of is and ought, which claims to see on the one hand a *purely* mechanical-natural causality and on the other a *purely* normative imputation. The intermediate empire of causal motivation and psychological imputation is, however, precisely the repressed cultural reality that the jurist alone is given as material.

[282] See Marck, *Substanz- und Funktionsbegriff* (see note 96), p. 89; 113.

[283] Erich Kaufmann, *Das Wesen des Völkerrechts und die clausula rebus sic stantibus. Rechtsphilosophische Studie zum Rechts-, Staats- und Vertragsbegriffe*, Tübingen 1911, pp. 175, 177; see below, p. 159.

with its purposes, by blowing *its* breath into them."[284] This Leviathan sovereignty of the state is what is fought by the corporatist-syndicalist idea. The idea of a state sovereignty that devours every personality is so incorrect, however, that its absolute opposite is the necessary requirement for a clarified concept of sovereignty.

Law is realized dialectically in a hierarchy that goes from the highest person through the constitution and laws, and only ends in the last implementing act.[285] This hierarchical structure of legal positivizing cannot at any point exclude the unpredictable human will. From the "private autonomy"[286] of civil law to the sovereign state person, a hierarchy is built of real units of will, of which not one is without law-creating power. Even if everyone in certain relationships seems to be determined by the will of the sovereign lawmaker, state sovereignty only gains its rich life from the wealth of personal acts that constitute it, which is in no way already foreseen by the law, nor can it be.[287] In the entire hierarchy of the will and positive legal rules, the unpredictable will is both indispensable for the sake of positivity as legal certainty, and cannot be excluded juristically for the sake of legal security.

In the separation-of-powers state, and even more so in other state forms, acts with law-creating qualities operate both "beyond the law" [*praeter legem*] and "against the law" [*contra legem*]; they can be attributed to the state and yet not to positive legal norms. The fact that there is no law-free space "within the law" [*intra legem*] is solely due to the fact that, as we are more than aware since the conflict over the Free Law doctrine, every space is constantly filled by the law-creating acts of state institutions.[288] Theoretically even more significant, however, is the existence of law-creating state actions "against the law." If one understands revolution as the process through which originally unlawful acts of will grow into legal validity, then revolution is a phenomenon that can be observed by jurists on pretty much a daily basis, and within which the great problem of the legal force of defective acts of state forms merely a special case.[289] Legal certainty requires that an order once created by an act of state, even if it is unlawful, has to count as a legal order, as long as no objections

[284] Gerhart Husserl, *Rechtskraft und Rechtsgeltung* (see note 138), p. 38. On this question, see Felix Stoerk, *Zur Methodik des öffentlichen Rechts*, Vienna 1885, pp. 30, 39; Brodmann, *Recht und* Gewalt (see note 140), pp. 47, 55; Ehrlich, *Juristische Logik* (see note 260), p. 81 ff.; Hans Nawiasky, *Der Bundesstaat als Rechtsbegriff*, Tübingen 1920, p. 14: "The obliged gathers ... the precise content of the obligation to which he is bound not directly from the will of the legal order, but rather from the will of the entitled party, and is thus subject to the will of the latter."

[285] Already stated by Ernst Rudolph Bierling, *Zur kritik der juristischen Grundbegriffe*, Gotha 1883, Part II; Oskar Bülow, *Gesetz und Richteramt*, Leipzig 1885 (p. 4); Ludwig Spiegel, *Gesetz und Recht. Vorträge und Aufsätze zur Rechtsquellentheorie*, Munich 1913 (Prager staatswissenschaftliche Untersuchungen, vol. 1) (p. 19 f.); Richard Thoma, "Der Vorbehalt des Gesetzes im Preußischen Verfassungsrecht," in *Festgabe für Otto Mayer*, Tübingen 1916 (p. 167); for an in-depth treatment, Adolf Merkl, *Die Lehre von der Rechtskraft, entwickelt aus dem Rechtsbegriff*, Leipzig 1923 (Wiener staatswissenschaftliche Studien, 15 II), p. 213. From the text it emerges that this 'hierarchy of law' must explode the pure theory of law.

[286] Andreas v. Thur, *Der allgemeine Teil des Deutschen Bürgerlichen Rechts*, vol. 2.1, Munich 1914, p. 143 ff.

[287] See above, p. 81. [288] See above, p. 118 ff.

[289] Walter Jellinek, *Der fehlerhafte Staatsakt und seine Wirkungen*, Tübingen 1908; Kelsen, "Staatsunrecht" (see note 266), p. 1 ff.; Ernst v. Hippel, *Untersuchungen zum Problem des fehlerhaften Staatsakts*, Berlin 1924.

are raised on the part of those entitled to raise them. The presumption of legality exists not only for the acts of the highest state organs,[290] but also for all acts of state.[291] But while in the lowest institutions, someone with the right to object can regularly raise legal objections to such acts and have them declared ineffective by higher institutions, even this rarely-utilized possibility is not always available for the flawed decisions of the highest institutions. Even if we overlook the impossibility of juridifying all the acts of the highest institutions, there remains the not at all rare case—think of the development of the English constitution—in which the communal will's recognition is bestowed upon an unlawful state act.

However, not every creation of law by persons integrated into the state, whether implemented "within, beyond or against the law," can be imputed to be a norm in the state legal order. And yet, as York von Wartenburg also argued, it is not just the filling of law-free spaces, but often enough also the breach of law "according to the demands of the case, of the times and of persons" that constitutes the living state will.[292] The fact that the norm formalist cannot come to grips with either phenomenon—except perhaps with a 'norm' of unlimitedly variable content—is simply a sign that the jurist must imagine at the apex of the state legal system not a dead norm, but a sovereign, living unit of will. Confronting the impersonal legal order with the sovereign state personality, endowed with will, thus reflects an unavoidable juristic interest.

However, deeper juristic insight into the nature of sovereignty can only be expected with an understanding of the specific social function of the state. A theory of the state whose positivism essentially frowns upon the highly positive question of the meaning of the state can reveal neither its own concept of the state body politic, nor the full import of the absolutely unique function of the sovereign state.[293]

Through the institution of the 'state,' the interaction of all social acts in a particular territory is ultimately guaranteed. A more comprehensive explanation of this proposition must await another study. Suffice it here to note that the state function, at times superseded by the Church, consisted in essence of carrying out the ordering tasks that cannot be achieved by custom, morality, interests, and the like. The state at first leaves it to other social orders to deal with the frictions that arise through this interaction, but guarantees those orders, for its part, by holding out the prospect of intervention in case they should fail. Because human life is only possible as ordered communal life, the state aids in both psychological and metaphysical self-preservation. Established traditional societies without a great deal of intercourse require smaller state institutions; growing civilizations, in contrast, growing

[290] According to Georg Jellinek, *Staatslehre* (see note 3), p. 18 f.; see also the examples in ibid., p. 340.

[291] Walter Jellinek, *Gesetz, Gesetzesanwendung und Zweckmäßigkeitserwägung* (see note 155), p. 115; Radbruch, *Grundzüge der Rechtsphilosophie* (see note 135), p. 172 ff.

[292] (See above, note 19.)

[293] See the highly unclear statements by Georg Jellinek, *Staatslehre*, p. 396: only one state can exist in a territory, that is the basis of the state's "impenetrability"; only the spatial extension of its rule and the exclusivity connected with it affords it the possibility of complete "fulfillment of purpose." On the misunderstood meaning of territory in the organic theory of the state, see Kelsen's critique, correct in its negative aspect, in *Problem der Souveränität* (see note 38), p. 77 ff.

intercourse and therefore growing areas of friction require increased security and predictability of interaction with neighboring territories. The sovereign state, with its thoroughly rationalized organization, stands before us as a modern product of this need. Aside from some cases of quite secondary importance, self-help has been eliminated for reasons of legal certainty; instead, the regulation of the conditions under which force should be used for purposes of the smoothest possible interaction of residents has been centralized. In the words of Max Weber, it successfully claims a "*monopoly of legitimate* physical force."[294] This monopoly of force, however, is only the technical side of a phenomenon in which the sovereignty of the modern state is actually rooted, and through which alone its nature can be recognized: the characteristic, belonging only to the sovereign state, of being a universal territorial decision-making unit. The universality of state decision-making is of course only potential, not actual. But the essence of sovereignty can be found in the possibility of finally and effectively deciding any issue involving the unity of social interaction in the territory, even sometimes in opposition to positive law, and of imposing this decision on everyone—not only members of the association, but absolutely all residents of the territory. The unit of territorial decision-making is the dialectical counterbalance to the human variety of social acts on the territory, and thus always the expression of actual power relations.

There is quite simply no other social institution that possesses the characteristic of making the ultimate decision in every conflict of interest occurring in its domain. The issue is not only that the contemporary state does not know the refusal of justice or law. The concept of decision-making must be more broadly interpreted and not limited to conflict resolution through the use of existing law. The sovereign state, and it alone, also does not know a refusal to decide. If it does not want to abolish itself, it must in all circumstances ensure, through its decisions and efficacy, the minimal amount of order that is indispensable for the self-preservation of the residents of its territory. The interactions of its residents would be threatened most seriously by any violent conflict unregulated by the center. It is this type of territorial sovereignty, and not the capability of "changing itself . . . substantially (or dissolving itself),"[295] which flatly rules out the claim that the state is "a consubstantial link in the chain of human community."[296] The sovereign makes decisions about predictable conflicts, first of all through its ordinary and constitutional rules; in a democracy, the people, indirectly through their representatives or directly through referendum; in an autocracy, the autocratic institutions. All state institutions are then directed to decide any cases of conflict that occur within the scope of these supreme legal rules. But all predictable, calculable legal rules refer to the normal case that is amenable to a legal rule. Yet the contemporary state must decide, for the aforementioned reasons of legal certainty, even if no legal rule is available. In fact, it must even decide, weighing the

[294] Max Weber, *Wirtschaft und Gesellschaft* (see note 124), vol. 1, p. 29. Quite characteristic of the zeitgeist, Weber argues that one cannot define the state by its "purposes," but only by its means of physical force, which are not even appropriate to it alone.

[295] Preuß, *Gemeinde, Staat, Reich* (seen note 34), p. 406; see above, p. 69ff.

[296] Ibid., p. 208.

greater against the lesser interest, against law. And these cases are the ones that show us that even today, in some circumstances, the "highest authority" [*summa potestas*] as a universal decision-making unit is and remains "legally free" [*legibus soluta*], as long as it is impossible to make people and history fully predictable.

To remain for now with decisions "beyond the law," it is most likely readily apparent that a state that refused, in the absence of a legal rule, to make a decision in only a single case would consign those demanding a decision to civil war and would abolish itself. Georg Jellinek, who never tired of emphasizing that state power is "not power per se, but power wielded within legal bounds, and thus legal power," was still too little the formalist not to note at least once that state power does not merge into positive law. Without recognizing the great systematic significance of the problem for the concepts of state, law, and sovereignty, he nevertheless noted, "where extraordinary circumstances themselves disrupt the legal context, or a decision in concrete cases cannot be reached through legal norms, the factual supersedes the legal, and thus itself becomes the basis for the formation of new law."[297] The case of the disruption of legal structures holds no public law interest for us, as we must understand sovereignty as a legal term. The second case, however, is present, for example, when the sovereign people decides, through its representatives or through plebiscite, on the assets that princes possessed in their earlier capacity as heads of state; there is no legal rule for these thoroughly non-'civil' disputes, which is why judges, who have no right of legislative representation, may not decide these cases.[298] So the sovereign is whoever has decided on the normal situation through a written or unwritten constitution and, because he intentionally maintains its validity, continues permanently to decide. And only the one who makes decisions on the normal constitutional situation can also make juristic decisions on the state of exception, sometimes "against the law." Only he is reasonably entitled to make the final decision on whether his law must give way to the exigencies of the moment or not. If one were to assume two units of will that are independent of each other, of which one would make decisions on the state of exception and the other on the normal situation, one would be presuming two sovereigns in the same state.

For an autocracy, this proposition would be obvious. But it also retains its validity in the state with popular sovereignty. Article 48(2) and (3) of the WRV [Weimar Constitution] must be interpreted in conjunction with Article 1 (2) of the WRV. The fact that the technique of momentary decisions requires the law of small numbers, and accordingly that the Reich President—as the magisterial representative of the people—is the first to decide on the state of exception, should not obscure the fact that the institutional process under Article 48(3) WRV leads from the Reich President to the Reichstag, and that the latter, as the normal representative legislature, is superior to the Reich President on this point. But the constitution does not stop here. For a longer state of exception, the people also have the ability to decide

[297] Jellinek, *Staatslehre* (see note 3), p. 387. The clarity of the formulation is marred only by reservations against the normative strength of the 'factual' that can, in Jellinek's usual intellectual views, be all too easily misunderstood as a natural-causal facticity.

[298] See Hermann Heller, *Der Begriff des Gesetzes in der Reichsverfassung*.

on the state of exception, in the final analysis, through referendum and plebiscite. In the German Reich, Carl Schmitt's formula[299]—that the sovereign is whoever definitively decides whether a normal situation really prevails—would hold true; not for the president, however, but for the people. In every state where today only magisterial representatives—in England and the United States, the courts as well—may decide on the continuation of a state of exception, this definition would only apply in this sense.[300] The only immanent explication and legitimation of state power that is possible for our contemporary way of thinking would force us to conclude that, even in monarchical or dictatorial absolutism, the 'real sovereignty' lies in the whole. But in the separation-of-powers *Rechtsstaat*, not even a "personal sovereignty" [*majestas personalis*] can be localized in a single state representative.

*Sovereignty that is not localizable in any single representative is, by its nature, the conceptual symbol for the unity, which cannot be dissolved into positive law, of an act of will that constitutes the law and the power of a territorially universal decision.*[301] This is what Hegel means when he says that two stipulations "make up the sovereignty of the state—that the particular affairs and powers of the state are not independent and are not established by themselves or in the particular will of individuals, but are ultimately rooted in the unity of the state as its simple self."[302] A basic stipulation of the state appears to Hegel to be "substantive unity as the *ideality* of its moments"; in this substantive unity of the state, "the particular powers and affairs of the same are just as much dissipated as maintained, and only maintained such that they have no independent justification, but only a justification that goes as far as is determined by the idea of the whole; they begin with its power and are its fluid limbs coextensive with its simple self."[303] Hegel learned from Rousseau, as he himself noted, that the sovereign state should be understood as an immanent act of will.[304]

[299] See above, p. 101 ff.

[300] Some examples from continental constitutions shall suffice here: under French law (Law of 3 April 1878), the imposition of a state of siege is exclusively the purview of parliamentary legislation; only if Parliament is not in session can the President, with the agreement of the Council of Ministers, decree a state of siege; but the Parliament meets two days later, without being called, and makes the definitive decision. In Switzerland, the Bundesrat is initially responsible for intervention by the Confederacy (see Fritz Fleiner, *Schweizerisches Bundesstaatsrecht*, Tübingen 1923, p. 72 note 27). In Holland, under Art. 5 of the Law to Implement Art. 189 (formerly 187) of the Constitution of 23 May 1889 on the State of Siege Law, Parliament makes the definitive decision. In Czechoslovakia, under the Law of 14 April 1920, a decision by the Council of Ministers, approved by the President, is necessary to impose a state of exception; but the decree must be submitted to the Parliament within fourteen days, or if it is not in session, to the Standing Committee of the Parliament, which then makes the definitive decision.

[301] Only Erich Kaufmann, *Wesen des Völkerrechts* (see note 283), p. 135 ff., correctly saw that a 'purely formal' concept of sovereignty (Jellinek, *Staatslehre*, p. 475) is meaningless. However, the "materially substantive element" worked out by him (based on Albert Haenel, *Deutsches Staatsrecht*, vol. 1, Leipzig 1892, p. 110 f.) must be rejected on epistemological, ethical, and especially juristic grounds. From the point of view of 'the idea of power,' the state will never become 'a moral institution.' The 'particular' universality and totality of the state of which Kaufmann speaks is exclusively juristic—the universality of the decision. Therefore, the superlative 'highest' is not, as Kaufmann claims, 'relative and meaningless,' but is—in the juristic sense and only in that sense!—quite an absolute and meaningful concept. See below, p. 173 ff.

[302] Hegel, *Rechtsphilosophie* (see note 57), § 278 (p. 363).

[303] Ibid., § 276 (p. 362).

[304] Ibid., § 258 (p. 314).

The idea that the state, as a universal decision-making unit that does not by any means derive its decisions solely from positive law, must be sovereign cannot, of course, be understood by a legal rationalism that promulgates legal sovereignty without positive law and a doctrine of the state without the state. We have been assured until the point of exhaustion that the state, being subject to the legal order, cannot be superior to the legal order; that like every legal person, the state, too, is nothing but "the law as person";[305] that the "metalegal" state standing above "the" law is a figment of the imagination that "sinks away under the microscope of critical analysis"; that the state, in fact, "thoroughly merges into law."[306] How would this doctrine deal with the problem of the legal force of unlawful state acts?

In considering this problem, we will also stay with the representatives of the pure theory of law, although essentially the same sources of error can be found in most other authors of the dominant legal science.[307] For Kelsen, of course, the imputation to the state cannot succeed; if any state of affairs is to be seen as a state act, that is, as imputable to the state, then we would need to examine, according to Kelsen, "whether it corresponds in form and content to the requirements for imputation established in the legal order. And if even *one* requirement is lacking, then according to general principles of logic, a judgment of imputation cannot be made."[308] The invalid state act, or "not-state act,"[309] is always present when some error occurs, for to Kelsen, all positive law rules are equivalent. For the pure theory of law, a distinction between nullity and an appeal "from the weight of the violated norm"[310] is obviously "completely and totally unjuristic"[311] as a value judgment. To the question "who will decide?" [*quis iudicabit*?] however, juristic rationalism must answer that the question of nullity or not nullity is "a question of legal logic; it is decided through the reason of every judging *individual*, but not *in authoritarian fashion* by the state."[312] This argument is self-contained, round, and nice. Suddenly, however, Kelsen seems to be overcome by horror at the "reason of every judging individual"; for the problem of decision seizes him once again, and he sees unexpectedly the possibility that it is "essentially" incorrect, when giving a theoretical treatment of the problem of the defective state act, to always start with the unspoken premise "that the error in question can be determined or is determinable with absolute certainty."[313] And now, once again, the "pure" theory of law is unstoppable. Now it is suddenly "apparent" that one gives preference to the "state" in the dispute over the material rightness of its own claims, and not to the opinion of "Mr. Everyman."[314] "It is undeniable that, in this way, the state places its own authority over the individual's sovereign reason. But if one gives the state the right to punish the thief, one *must* also give it the right

[305] Kelsen, *Problem der Souveränität* (see note 38), p. 109, and everywhere in his and his students' writings.

[306] Verdroß, *Einheit* (see note 96), p. 70, 38.

[307] See Ernst v. Hippel, *Untersuchungen zum Problem des fehlerhaften Staatsakts* (see note 289) (p. 54 ff).

[308] Kelsen, "Staatsunrecht" (see note 266), p. 85 f. [309] Ibid., p. 86.

[310] Ibid., p. 69. [311] Ibid., p. 74.

[312] Ibid., p. 55; on this, see Walter Jellinek, *Der fehlerhafte Staatsakt* (see note 289), p. 103 f.

[313] Kelsen, "Staatsunrecht," p. 92. [314] Ibid., p. 93.

to authoritatively determine whether someone is a thief."[315] One more step and the disaster has happened—the state that cannot be merged into any positive legal order as a sovereign decision-making unit has been identified!

Adolf Merkl undertook to prevent this disaster and, on the base of the pure theory of law, to cut off one of the many heads of the wretched Hydra of the "state" that is still not identical to law. He finds strong, if not always linguistically correct, words in the struggle against the "chimera," against both of these two sides of "the dichotomous state creature, which the jurists have only created or invented in this grotesque form, reminiscent of a mythological creature, purely in order to practice convenient politics with it on the pretext of jurisprudence."[316] It is ultimately also the fault of this concept of the state that legal science, in the doctrine of legal force, "so shamelessly, though also—this must be said in their defense—generally unwittingly prostituted itself."[317] He resolves the contradictions of his teacher Kelsen such that, in a difference of opinion between state institutions and subjects, he places legal science above both as the deciding institution, as the "only competent authority."[318] He does recognize that the "awkwardness" of contradictory views in legal science is increased by the fact "that it lacks a factor to authoritatively determine *who is right*."[319] Nevertheless, he thinks it can be said, not materially but formally, and not for individual cases but abstractly: "law is what legal science recognizes as true."[320] Yet there exists "the most urgent need for legal policy" to ascribe defective state acts to the state. But according to Merkl, legal science cannot do this on its own, but only "on the basis of a *positive law* determination that we will call a *mistaken calculation*."[321] Thus, the *enfant terrible* now has a name. But it is not at all clear what a jurist can do with it. Unfortunately, Merkl also says nothing about how to articulate the 'explicit' positive legal norm that permits us to recognize as law, despite their defects, acts that do not conform to positive law.

If we remain with the school's mathematical-natural science ways of thinking and speaking, we must formulate the relevant legal rules more or less as follows: all legal rules in this legal order are only valid if the sovereign state will is taken into account, which, following its decision, can allow errors of calculation—that is, defective acts—to merge into the totality of imputation. "Thus it has been demonstrated!" [*Quod erat demonstrandum*!]

The meaning of the sovereign state person as a universal decision-making territorial institution—sometimes even "against the law"—can finally be shown using the example of a constitution that was fathered by Kelsen. The fact that the federal constitution of the Austrian Republic contains no state of exception is thus self-evident. Kelsen notes proudly that the Constitution Law (Art. 149(2)) removed "any possibility" of imposing a state of exception.[322] Despite the short life of the Austrian constitution, the government nevertheless had the opportunity to carry

315 Ibid. 316 Merkl, *Lehre von der Rechtskraft* (see note 285), p. 160.

317 Ibid., p. 168 note 1. Because the pure theory of law, as we know, cannot exactly distinguish between logical and ethical-juristic validity, one may ask whether shameless prostitution, witting or unwitting, is to be found in the violation of logical or ethical norms?

318 Ibid., p. 286. 319 Ibid., p. 289. 320 Ibid., p. 290. 321 Ibid., p. 293.

322 Hans Kelsen, *Österreichisches Staatsrecht*, Tübingen 1923, p. 92.

out an unconstitutional state act, during which they referred to a "state of emergency": their offence earned them a motion to be charged with a legal violation, though it was denied by the majority. The complicated facts are only interesting to us as follows: on the evening of June 30, 1926, the government was notified by the president of the national bank that, if it did not intervene immediately, a newspaper article that had appeared that evening could spell the collapse of the Central German Savings Bank, and thus a danger for many savings and cooperative banks throughout the entire state that had deposits with the Central Bank. To avoid the expected 'catastrophe,' the government decided that same evening, without asking the Lower House of the Parliament to back the bank in the amount of 62.5 million shillings—a sum, as the opposition emphasized, that was almost a tenth of the entire state revenue. The government claimed that summoning Parliament in time to authorize the act would not have been possible. The opposition speakers called this behavior "a true attack on the entire embodiment of our federal constitution."[323] The Chancellor, in defending himself, referred in turn to a "state of emergency of the most serious kind";[324] the government did not "act arbitrarily, but under the pressure of the most dire necessity."[325] There was no time to summon the Lower House of the Parliament if catastrophe was to be avoided. "A danger was posed to our credit, a danger to our currency, a danger to the trust placed in us abroad, in short, a danger to our entire economy."[326] In addition, however, the government and the majority also referred to Article 6 (XII and XIII) of the Federal Law of July 21, 1925[327] on the Simplification of the Administrative Law and Other Measures to Relieve the Administrative Authorities. Such an interpretation of the law, which might not be outrageous on its face, was, however, as the opposition speakers noted, a violation of this administrative reform law in its spirit and attitude. "The law would otherwise have gone beyond the infamous § 14 of the old Austrian constitution."[328]

If, as we presume, the other conditions claimed by the federal government were true, we have the case of an unconstitutional act of state, the validity of which is unquestionable, but for which the pure theory of law would not only have to condemn the government, but also to declare the act itself absolutely null and void. The magisterial representation of the people, as the executive, would have had to decide here whether the interest protected by observing one of the most important constitutional norms should be placed higher or lower than the interest that could only be protected by a violation of that constitutional norm. But only the representative unit of will, not the legal order itself, can balance interests and sometimes decide against the legal order. Thus, despite the Kelsenian constitution, even in Austria there is a state that is not identical to the legal order, and that is sovereign as a universal decision-making unit.

[323] *Stenographische Protokolle des Nationalrates*, Vienna, 11 (1926/7) 4, p. 3810 (156th sitting, August 31, 1926).
[324] Ibid., p. 3806. [325] Ibid., p. 3805. [326] Ibid., p. 3807.
[327] BGBl. 1925, I, p. 970. [328] Op. cit., p. 3812.

## B. Sovereignty as a Characteristic of the State

State means a decision-making unit that is universal in a specific territory, and therefore necessarily unique and sovereign. It is possible for two armies to fight over sovereignty on the territory in question, and the jurist must accept the suspension of sovereignty until the outcome of the battle is decided. But it is impossible to have two sovereign decision-making units on the same territory; this would mean two supreme units of will working against each other would cancel the unity of the state, and would ultimately result in civil war.

The concept of the state characterized in this way would need fear no contradiction if, in the middle of the last century, the federal form of organization had not appeared and given our theory of the state a dominant new category that could not be reconciled with our definition of the state—namely, that of the non-sovereign state. It seems completely unnecessary to once again present the literary dispute over the problem of non-sovereign and federal states, which has been reproduced a thousand times, since today it should be clear that the disputing parties have refuted each other in outstanding fashion.[329]

I believe the starting point and the questions in the discussion miss the point. We should start with the fact, which cannot be doubted today, that in any case the federal state as a whole constitutes a sovereign state that decides universally on its territory. Otherwise, one would have to denature the concept of the state to such an extent that it would be useless as a characteristic of all states that are termed unified states by the dominant theory. Wherever a universal territorial decision-making unit is found, however it may form its unity of will, the term 'state' is in all cases indispensable and to be retained.

The problem presented to us should be correctly theoretically formulated thus: can the same concept of the state that is indispensable for the universal territorial decision-making unit be applied to the so-called member states of the federal state? If "only *one* state can unfold its power" on one and the same territory, then the federal state, composed of a number of 'states,' is in no way, as Georg Jellinek believes, only one of the "apparent" exceptions, but is an actual and completely incomprehensible one. Only a theory of the state whose concept of the state can cover two fundamentally different phenomena and which does not recognize the true meaning of regional authority can reassure itself with the obvious sophism that the member states that unfold their power on the same territory as the federal state contradict "the proposition presented above no more than does the quality of the municipalities as regional authorities."[330] Thus, the member state is by its nature a particular territorial decision-making unit, just like every province and municipality, while the federal state is, like all unified states, by its nature a universal decision-making institution.

[329] The latest in-depth summary of the state of the dispute is found in Nawiasky, *Bundestaat* (see note 283), p. 196 ff.

[330] Jellinek, *Staatslehre* (see note 3), p. 396 f.

For political reasons, it can be understood that one would give certain particular territorial units the same names as the universal decision-making units. Theoretically, however, both the state and the sovereignty concepts are distorted if we include the member states and the federal state in the same conceptual category and ascribe sovereignty to both of them. Either the member state is potentially responsible for every decision, without exception, on its territory—then it is not part of "the association of the federal state by which it is ruled,"[331] it is a state and is sovereign; or it is at some point subject to the decisions of a different universal unit, in which case it is not sovereign, and the term state has an essentially different meaning for it than for the unit to which it is subject.

We will not go into the fact that the emergence and continued existence of the so-called member states are fundamentally subject to different juristic conditions than they are for the sovereign state.[332] But the member state can possess neither true legislative autonomy nor true constitutional autonomy; its administration must be subject at critical points to Reich oversight of whatever sort, and the justice system, too, must at certain points be centralized beyond its own territory. All these unavoidable structural necessities arise from the nature of the federal state as a unified decision-making institution. As much as one may try to construe the member states as being coordinated with the supreme state,[333] the attempt will always be recognized as a failure as soon as one realizes that the total constitution standing above both is coherent only because it is filled by a living unit of will, but that the limits of this unit of will are decided in situations of concrete conflict only by a universal decision-making unit and cannot be limited once and for all by a constitution, no matter how carefully calculated. The federal state is only a state because it can make authoritative decisions, whether through its courts or its president or some other federal institution, regarding which party to a conflict is in the right. Therefore, in a federal state, violent action against a state that is not fulfilling its legal duties, whether on the basis of a court or a presidential decision, is always federal execution and never war; but violent insurrection by the member states is always rebellion. An institution that may under no circumstances refuse to make a decision, which has the right, both "within" and "beyond the law" and even "against the law," to at least temporarily give its decisions validity, is always superior to all other institutions on its territory. Nawiasky believes that any use of force by the federation against the member states without a positive constitutional basis, taken by itself, that is, as long as no other norms of federal law oppose it, leads to the same "international law consequences" as force used against an independent state; if this view, which is today incidentally the only existing opinion, were correct, then the federal state would certainly not be a state or a universal decision-making unit.[334] The Swiss federal constitution, for example, does not regulate federal execution.

[331] Ibid., p. 397. [332] See below, p. 160f.

[333] See Nawiasky, op. cit., p. 25 ff.; Hans Kelsen, "Die Bundesexekution," in *Festgabe für Fritz Fleiner*, Tübingen 1927, p. 132 ff.

[334] Nawiasky, *Bundesstaat*, p. 90; see p. 98. Kelsen ("Bundesexekution," p.175 f.) hopes to avoid the above consequences by way of equal execution against the federal government and the states. This parity is to be achieved by having a court composed of the constituent and the federal states make the judgment, having a similar organ or at least one independent of the federal government execute the

The theory nevertheless found itself forced to interpret confederate execution into the text of the constitution.[335]

The view of state and sovereignty advocated here can find no better confirmation than the transformation of theory and practice that has emerged in the concept of federal states in the United States—in the wake of the Civil War! In 1793, a well-known judgment found that "Every state in the Union in every instance where its sovereignty has not been delegated to the United States, I consider to be as completely sovereign, as the United States are in respect to the powers surrendered. The United States are sovereign as to all the powers of government actually surrendered. Each state in the Union is so sovereign as to all the powers reserved."[336] In 1879, however, we hear the judge describe the universal decision-making function of the regional authority with the apt words, "We hold it to be an incontrovertible principle, that the government of the United States may, by means of physical force, exercised through its official agents, execute on every foot of American soil the powers and functions that belong to it. This, necessarily, involves the power to command obedience to its laws, and hence the power to keep the peace to that extent."[337]

In the Union Constitution, which ensures to its states an especially high degree of autonomy, the federal government is not just a universal legal institution, but in addition not only a "within," but also a "beyond" and even "against the law" decision-making unit. Despite the Tenth Amendment to the Constitution, the Supreme Court has continuously expanded federal powers by expanding the "implied powers."[338] A constitutional act of Congress of course takes precedence over a contradictory state law. Should there be two rival governments in a state, with each claiming to be the rightful one, the federal president can recognize one of them or the other, and if called upon can support it with federal military assistance,

judgment, and above all by ensuring that "collective and strict liability is replaced by individual and fault-based liability of Reich organs that violate the overall order." This pure theory of law has yet to accomplish anything more grotesque. Let us disregard the fact that executions are often necessary in the moment, that the organ independent of the federation must be a federal organ and might itself require execution. But how does Kelsen, even with the help of the pleasant idea of a court commanding an army of execution, imagine these institutions representing individual and fault-based liability? Apparently, first the Reich Chancellor will be locked up, then the ministers, then parliament, and finally the voters. In a certain analogy, individual liability of the state governor and the state authorities subordinate to him in case of indirect federal administration (Art. 102 (1)) is in fact regulated in the Austrian Reich Constitution by its father, Kelsen. If the governor does not follow the orders of the federal government or individual federal ministers, he can be charged under Art. 142(2) lit.d of the Constitution and possibly neutralized under Art. 142(4). This can continue until all the members of the state government (Art. 101(4)) are taken care of; what then? On this, see Kelsen's completely confused explanations, *Staatslehre* (see note 46), p. 310 ff., of the representation problem.

[335] See Fleiner, *Schweizerisches Bundesstaatsrecht* (see note 300), p. 56 ff. (62); Walther Bruckhardt, *Kommentar zur schweizerischen Bundesverfassung vom 29 mai 1874*, 2nd edn, Bern 1914, p. 699; Jakob Schollenberger and Otto Zoller, *Das Bundesstaatsrecht der Schweiz*, 2nd edn, Berlin 1920, p. 115 f.

[336] *Chisholm v. Georgia*, 2 Dallas (U.S. Supr. Ct.), 419 (435).

[337] Ex parte Siebold et al. 100 U.S. 371 (395).

[338] Of great importance to the expansion of federal powers through constitutional amendment, see *United States Reports* (Supreme Court), vol. 253 U.S. 350 (1919).

depending on the decision he makes on their legality.[339] Theoretically and practically of great importance is the fact that an unlawful act of federal power is subject only to review, and this can only be done by the federal judiciary, whereas an act of a member state that violates federal law is considered "by operation of law" [*ipso iure*] invalid, and obeying it is sedition against the Union, which must quell it by force.[340] We cannot speak of the constitutional autonomy of the member states in the strict sense, because Article IV (4) of the Federal Constitution prescribes a republican constitution to the states, and Amendment XV additionally prohibits limiting the right to vote on the basis of race, color, or previous condition of servitude. If the Union is to be a state, the North American member states must be subject to it on the crucial points.[341]

But if the member states can only be particular decision-making units subject to a universal one, how is it possible to separate them conceptually from other particular territorial associations? Is there a juristic criterion through which the 'non-sovereign state' can be fundamentally distinguished from a municipality or province? Given the libraries that the best minds of the two previous generations have devoted to this problem, and given the results they have brought to light, one must answer the question in the negative. Any attempt to separate the state conceptually from other territorial entities should be considered a failure.[342] When Georg Jellinek, for example, says of "non-sovereign" states that their state power is "the irreducible power of a ruler, the power of a ruler from his own power and thus in his own right"; when he defines sovereignty as the capacity for "exclusive" legal self-determination and adds that even non-sovereign states can determine and obligate themselves through their "own" will;[343] when Laband, in the first edition of his *Reichstaatsrecht*, already finds a distinction between a state and a municipal association in the fact that states possess public law authority "by virtue of their own right,"[344] "their own rights of rule,"[345] and an "independent will to rule ";[346] in all these characteristics, repeated in endless variations, the issue is what one means by the expressions "own," "irreducible," "independent," and so on. Gierke and Rosin have shown that the opposite of "own" can only be "alien" right—that therefore the municipalities also have their own rights within their own sphere of activity.[347] But if, with Laband, it is not their own right but their "own right of rule" that is decisive,[348] this own, irreducible,

339 See Address by President John Tyler to the House of Representatives, vol. 10, April 1844, in the case of Rhode Island, in *The Congressional Globe*, Washington, XIII (1844), p. 504.

340 James Bryce, *Amerika als Staat und Gesellschaft*, vol. 1, Leipzig 1924, p. 195, 198.

341 On current American views, see Walter Thompson, *Federal Centralization. A Study and Criticism of the Expanding Scope of Congressional Legislation*, New York 1923, and especially Harry Pratt Judson, *Our Federal Republic*, New York, 1925.

342 In this regard, see Kelsen's critique, *Problem der Souveränität* (see note 38), p. 56 ff.

343 Jellinek, *Staatslehre* (see note 3), p. 489, 495.

344 Paul Laband, *Das Staatsrecht des Deutschen Reiches*, 1st edn, Tübingen 1876, vol. 1, p. 106; 5th edn, Tübingen 1911, vol. 1, p. 65.

345 Ibid., 5th edn, vol. 1, p. 66.

346 Ibid., 5th edn, vol. 1, p. 57.

347 Otto Gierke, "Labands Staatsrecht und die deutsche Rechtswissenschaft," in *Schmollers Jahrbuch für Gesetzgebung, Verwaltung und Volkswirtschaft*, 7 (1883), p. 1163 ff.; Heinrich Rosin, "Souveränität, Staat, Gemeinde, Selbstverwaltung," in *Annalen des Deutschen Reichs*, 1883, p. 279 ff.

348 Laband, op.cit., 5th edn, vol. 1, p. 66.

independent right of rule must either mean sovereignty, in which case the stated features are true, but are not true for the member states; or it concerns only the 'own' sphere of activity of a municipal association. Only the latter can be right if, according to Laband, the member states "are rulers looking down and subjects looking up"[349]—a correct statement that applies without exception to every legal subject that is subordinated to a universal decision-making unit. As great as the member state's right to self-determination may be, in the hierarchy of the unification of wills that we call the state, there is nevertheless only a quantitative difference in the extent of discretionary power from the individual to the member state. Only at the final point in the pyramid, solely in the universal decision-making unit, does the heretofore quantitative difference turn into a juristically qualitative one. The sovereign state alone is only a ruler looking downward and no longer a subject looking upward. Up to this universal decision-making unity, all legal subjects have their 'own' rights and rights of rule; but they are all derived juristically, if certainly not historically, from the universal decision-making unit. Without this juristic conceptualization, the aforementioned relationship of submission of the member states to the Union could not be articulated. Without it, too, it would be impossible to fathom the momentous fact that, within a universal decision-making unit, there can be no legal subject whose existence might not fall victim to extinction if the existence of the sovereign state was endangered. As obvious as this fact seems to be to the modern theory of the state for all other legal subjects, it has been little emphasized for the member states.[350] If, however, in the correct view, a federal execution is never war, but instead the execution of a legal rule decided by the universal decision-making unit, then the lawful extinction of the member states is both a juristic-theoretical and a thoroughly practical possibility.

Given the entire state of affairs characterized here, it is a scientifically clear requirement that the name 'state' should be reserved solely for a universal decision-making unit. Of course, it cannot be the critical task of legal science to begin dealing with nearly every problem by "destroying the linguistic usage provided by unscientific practice."[351] On one hand, a test of such an undertaking would yield nice results. On the other hand, however, it is theoretically untenable to designate with the same words two concepts so fundamentally different in their juristic natures as the particular and the universal territorial decision-making unit. It should be an acceptable suggestion to call the particular territorial association the "state" [*Land*], or at least always the member state, and never the state *per se*; and it should be agreed upon once and for all that the state and the member state are two fundamentally different entities.

If we are serious about the concepts of state and sovereignty, we cannot ascribe the features of a state to the sub-state units [*Länder*].[352] The concern that a federal

349 Ibid., 5th edn, vol. 1, p. 59.

350 In contrast, see, e.g., Erwin Jacobi, *Der Rechtsbestand der deutschen Bundesstaaten*, Leipzig 1917, p. 110 ff.

351 Kelsen, *Problem der Souveränität* (see note 38), p. 54.

352 See Heinrich v. Treitschke, *Politik* (ed. Max Cornicelius), Leipzig 1897, vol. 1, p. 40; vol. 2, p. 323 ff.; Philipp Zorn, "Streitfragen des deutschen Staatsrechts," in *Zeitschrift für die gesamte Staatswissenschsft*, 37(1881), p. 317 ff.; and Zorn, "Neue Beiträge zur Lehre vom Bundesstaat," in *Annalen des Deutschen*

state can now no longer be juristically articulated is not really understandable. The organization of such a "decentralized" state offers sufficient positive law rules that guarantee to the sub-state units a juristic position going beyond that of a normal province; it is first of all in the influential part that the sub-state units play in federal legislation, and second in the institutions that are quite varied in positive law, but are found in all federal states, that certain affairs that would otherwise be discharged by central state institutions are here left to the self-administration of the sub-state units.

*Reichs*, 17 (1884), p. 461; 480; Eugène Borel, *Étude sur la souveraineté et l'état féderatif*, Bern 1886, p. 173 ff.; Louis Le Fur, *État federal et confédération d'État*, Paris 1896, p. 589 ff., 673 ff. More recently, aside from Kelsen, see Thoma, "Staat" (see note 96), p. 737 ff.

# VI

# The Sovereignty of the State and the Problem of International Law

## A. Sovereignty and Positivity in International Law

Any study of international law that does not take the existence of a plurality of sovereign units of will as its starting point is doomed from the start to fundamental failure. International law exists only as long as there are at least two universal and effective territorial decision-making units. The sovereign state is a necessary part of juristic thought but international law is not. The "world state" and the state that isolates itself behind a Chinese wall would exist as sovereign decision-making units even without international law; international law without sovereign states, however, is a conceptual impossibility. A universal-planetary, effective decision-making unit would change any international law into state law—and would be sovereign in the most eminent sense. The following will show that the sovereignty of the state is not an obstacle to international law, but an essential requirement for it.

That the state is sovereign means that it is a universal territorial decision-making unit, internally and externally. The potential universality of territorial decisions implies both its juristic supremacy and its independence. If a state is sovereign, it is the universal decision-making unit in its territory; this existentiality of the decision-making unit prohibits splitting sovereignty into the sovereignty of a state law and a separate international law sovereignty.[353] Insofar as such a division merely means two relationships of the same sovereign unit, there would be no objection to it. The highest independent decision-making power is, however, always the mark of one and not two facts.

The sovereignty of the state is a juristic-political phenomenon, and of course not a naturalistic one. It describes something that has been misunderstood to an incredible extent by jurists and non-jurists alike—the relationship between a unit of will and positive law—and says absolutely nothing about the relationship of this unit to other norms and societal powers. It has yet to occur to anyone to view the sovereign state as "first cause" [*prima causa*].

[353] Most recently, see Jean Morellet, "Le principe de la souveraineté de l'état et le droit international public," in *Revue générale de droit international public*, 33 (1926), p. 109 ff. See also Walther Schücking and Hans Wehberg, *Die Satzung des Völkerbundes*, 2d edition, Berlin 1924, p. 181, where it is thought possible for a state to be "completely free internally, but completely independent externally."

Seeing sovereignty as the universality of decision-making on a particular territory also makes it easy to comprehend that juristic-political supremacy in no way necessarily implies sole supremacy. Only to legal rationalists—who deny the spatiotemporal connection of all positive law, dissolve the state into law, and moreover confuse 'a' concrete, individual legal order with 'the' abstract idea of law in legal science—must the sovereignty of one state rule out that of another.[354]

The universality of territorial decision-making also implies the absolute and superlative character of sovereignty, which almost the whole of contemporary theory seems no longer to understand. And yet it is the "unbound power" [*soluta potestas*], even in regard to positive law, that constitutes the essence of sovereignty. The dialectical relationship between sovereignty and positivity, inaccessible to formalist logic, causes the juristic difficulty of imagining the sovereign decision-making unit as both bound by positive law and at the same time, in a certain way, free of it.

All the problems of international law, from Grotius to Locarno, are based in the indispensability of the concept of sovereignty, on the one hand, and the necessary concept of the sovereign person's normative binding through international law, on the other. With the creation of the League of Nations and the establishment of an international court and arbitral tribunals, our fundamental problem merely became more complicated, but did not fundamentally change. Placed before the dilemma of absolute state sovereignty versus the absolute validity of international law, the positivist jurist can have no doubt which part is more sociologically and juristically problematic: the existentiality of universal territorial decision-making units or the fact that they are absolutely bound by international law. One may imagine a "world state" for the contemporary nation state, or a future one; in every case, it is at least clear that the social situation that has been achieved creates a positive legal order whose positivity and legal certainty is inconceivable without the absolute unit of territorial decision-making. It may sound paradoxical, but it is absolutely true: the existence or positivity of a legal order is determined by the existence or facticity of a decision-making unit that can violate that legal order if necessary. If the existence of a unit of will that individuates law and maintains its validity is recognized as an absolute requirement for the positivity of the law, this is therefore an admission that the decision-making unit, when threatened in its existence, may violate law for the law's sake; it must therefore at some point become "a power unbound by law" [*legibus soluta postestas*]. That unit of will, which brings law into effect and validates it by its decisions, is certainly in turn determined by fundamental legal principles, but it is and invariably remains the determiner. This can only be disputed by the belief in miracles held by rationalist metaphysics, whose omniscient and omnipotent *deus ex machina* one day individuated, for all time, every positive legal rule that could ever, in the most unpredictable transformations of history, have been useful for the preservation and development of mankind and its laws. As long as we do not cling

[354] See Kelsen, *Problem der Souveränität* (see note 38), p. 188; even before him, Leonard Nelsen, Die *Rechtswissenschaft ohne Recht. Kritische Betrachtungen über die Grundlagen des Staates- und Völkerrechts, insbesondere über die Lehre von der Souveränität*, Leipzig 1917, p. 60.

to this disbelieving belief, we cannot dissolve the state into law; as long as this is the case, the state remains sovereign even vis-à-vis positive law.

In international law, state sovereignty first of all proves itself through the fact that there is not and cannot be any positive legal rule that decides the existence or non-existence of the state. Before a single international legal rule can exist, there must first be at least two states. The international legal rules that are individuated and objectified by the common will of the two states can by nature exist only as long as both states, in their capacity as universal territorial decision-makers, exist independently of one another. These rules thus take the sovereignty of both states as a prerequisite for both their validity and their transformation into legal form. But if the existence of one of the two states would be threatened if it follows a legal rule, no legal rule can be found or created in the entire legal world that would form the basis for a decision that would allow anyone to determine the threatened state's right to exist, against its own will. In state law, such a legal rule is, of course, impossible; nor can it exist in international law, because both states would have had to agree in advance which of them would make decisions in case of an existential conflict. But then one of them would be raised above the other as a superior decision-making unit, which would nullify the requirement for international law and ultimately justify the "world state."

Well-meaning peace lovers who see sovereignty as an obstacle to the development of international law should read Kant's "Perpetual Peace": "The idea of international law requires the *separation* of many neighboring states that are independent of each other." And anticipating later debates, we can continue, with Kant, "Although such a situation is actually already a state of war (if no federal association prevents the same from breaking out into hostilities): even this, according to the idea of rationality, is better than fusing together the same through a power that grows over the others and merges into a universal monarchy; because with the expanded scope of government, the laws lose ever more of their vigour, and a soulless despotism, after eradicating the germ of the good, ultimately declines into anarchy."[355]

## B. The Special Features of the Problem of the Validity of International Law

The validity or positivity of all law is based, on the one hand, in the ideality of fundamental legal principles, and on the other, in the facticity of an ultimately decisive unit of will that, within the bounds of the fundamental legal possibilities, bestows upon a legal rule the legal certainty that first makes norm-conforming behavior possible. The validity of international law is different from state law in this regard, in that the decision-making unit that gives validity to the law, maintains its validity, and destroys its validity, is not a norm creating and norm implementing unit that differs from the addressee of the norm and stands above it; rather, it is formed by

[355] Immanuel Kant, *Zum ewigen Frieden. Ein philosophisches Entwurf* (1795), in *Sämtliche Werke* (ed. K. Vorländer), vol. 6, 2nd edn, Leipzig 1922 (Meiners Philosophische Bibliothek, vol. 47 I), p. 147.

agreement among the addressees of the norms themselves. To this extent, we must agree with Triepel's often contested formulation: "Only the *common will* of several or many states, coalescing in a *unit of wills* through *agreement of* wills, can be the source of international law."[356] It is correct that this sentence, considered in itself, contains the risk of a misleading one-sidedness in the validity problem, on the side of facticity. But the fact that Triepel, in contrast to his critics, correctly viewed the issue in light of the dualism of will and norm is shown in his remark that his concept of consent should be understood "as a declaration by the consenting parties that a norm should be a legal norm,"[357] and especially in his excellent formulation: "The 'legal basis' for the validity of law is not a legal one."[358] With this remark, he pointed far beyond the erroneous positivism of his day.

The validity of international law is thus grounded in the common will of states, and in the validity of fundamental legal principles. It is as obvious that the legal norms individuated by the common will are above the will of the jural community, as it is obvious that they are generally available to the whole jural community. This hardly exhausts the problem of the validity of international law, but merely identifies its starting point. For now, we aim simply to establish that no positive international law can be achieved using the doctrine of voluntary obligation or the pure theory of law. The former claims that the state in international law is "only subject to its own will";[359] it fails to recognize the nature of all law as an intersubjective, normative binding of wills and is unable to construe the objective validity of international law. The pure theory of law, which argues, in opposition to the theory of a common will, that declarations of will by various states may only be bound together as a legal unit "on the basis of a legal rule,"[360] cannot demonstrate such a 'legal rule,' and thus also fails to arrive at international law positivity. The doctrine of voluntary obligation spells an equally unacceptable one-sidedness on the problem of validity, on the side of facticity, just as the pure theory of law is one-sided on the side of abstract ideality.

The creation and implementation of international law presupposes the existence of independent states. Since Grotius, Bynkershoek, and Vattel, one also tends accordingly to ascribe the validity of customary international law to a tacit contract, a "tacit pact, tacit convention" [*pactum tacitum, convention tacite*].[361] The apparent contradiction between this contract theory and the so-called submission theory is

[356] Triepel, *Völkerrecht* (see note 166), p. 32.

[357] Ibid, p. 63, note 1. Kaufmann correctly opposes the distinction between contract and consent, see Kaufmann, *Völkerrecht* (see note 283), p. 160 ff.

[358] Triepel, op. cit., p. 82.

[359] Jellinek, *Staatslehre* (see note 3), p. 479. See Triepel's critique, op. cit., pp. 77, 166.

[360] See Verdroß, *Völkerrechtsgemeinschaft* (see note 137), p. 20.

[361] Grotius, *De jure belli ac pacis* (see note 27), introduction; Cornelius van Bynkershoek, *Questionum juris publici libri duo*, 2nd edn, Lugdunum Batavorum 1752, book II, *cap.* X (p. 251); Emer de Vattel, *Le droit des gens ou principes de la loi naturelle*, London 1758, vol. I, préliminaires § 25 (p. 14). Among the more current, e.g., Triepel, op. cit., p. 95, and Triepel, "Les rapports entre le droit interne et le droit international," in *Recueil des Cours*, I (1923), p. 83; Charles Calvo, *Le droit international théoretique et pratique précédé d'un exposé historique des progrès de la science du droit des gens*, 3rd edn, Paris 1880, vol. I, p. 119; John Bassett Moore, *A Digest of International Law*, Washington 1906, vol. I, p. 5; Arrigo Cavaglieri, *La consuetudine giuridica internazionale. Saggio critico*, Padua 1907, p. 56 f.; Dionisio Anzilotti, *Corso di diritto internazionale*, Rome 1923, p. 42.

easily resolved by the fact that those acts of will of the state that are meant to become legal practice may connote fundamental legal principles and neither mere "comity of peoples" [*comitas gentium*], nor a legal rule that still needs to be produced. As long as the exercise is intended merely as ordinary usage, it lacks any legally binding character. The first legally intended practice therefore does not yet apply a 'legal rule,'[362] but instead positivizes a legal rule within the scope of fundamental legal principles, on condition that the other states act in the same way. Thus, we observe only in international law the otherwise everyday process by which a social custom grows into law, through the addition of the idea of its socially and ethically binding force—a process that Georg Jellinek incorrectly called the normative power of the factual.[363] Facticity that is not grounded in any normative principles can never be normative.

A requirement for the validity of customary international law is, however, uncontested and incontestable: its exercise through the actions of independent states. The decision as to whether this action should be taken and if it should be taken with "legal opinion of peoples" [*opinio juris gentium*] is entirely up to the state, represented through its institutions, and to no one else. According to the dominant doctrine, customary international law also applies only to the 'recognizing' states.[364] The question, already in dispute between Suarez and Vitoria, whether customary law can be objectified and changed by majority decision or only through unanimous consent must be answered fundamentally to mean unanimity. Making law through majority decision requires a positive legal rule.[365] It is also decisions of state will that are capable, through desuetude, of quashing the validity of even expressly agreed-upon, treaty-based international law. Thus, under Article 11 of the Berlin Treaty of July 13, 1878,[366] the Donau fortifications were to be demolished and the construction of new fortifications prohibited. This provision, which was never obeyed, lost its positivity through tacit agreement.

It is clear from general contract principles that no treaty-based international law can come into being without the agreement of all treaty parties, and that it is, as a matter of principle, only objectified by units of will that are subject to no universal decision-making unit. The act of a state subjecting itself to any international norm is to be construed juristically as a free decision of will. It makes no difference whether a subject of international law is capable, politically or economically, of withdrawing itself from all international law interactions. All that matters juristically is that there

362 Verdroß, *Einheit* (see note 96), p. 104, goes in a circle, because he wants to prove at all costs that the fundamental legal principle that first made its legal exercise possible is a legal rule.

363 Jellinek, *Staatslehre* (see note 3), p. 337 ff.

364 See the discussion on Art. 3 WRV and the protocols of the 3rd and 36th meetings of the Constitutional Committee. In the latter, Kahl states that, in the unanimous view of the Constitutional Committee, "only a rule also recognized by the *German* Reich can be considered a binding element of German Reich law" (*Verhandlungen der verfassungsgebenden Nationalversammlung*, vol. 336, Appendix no. 391 (Bericht der Verfassungsauschusses), Berlin 1920, p. 406. See Max Wenzel, *Der Begriff des Gesetzes* (see note 124), p. 468 ff.; Verdroß, *Einheit*, p. 111 f. See also Art. 38 (2) of the Statute of the Permanent Court of International Justice: "International custom, as evidence of a general practice accepted as being law," Société des Nations (ed.), *Cour Permanente de Justice Internationale, Documents*, Geneva 1921, p. 258 ff. (p. 264).

365 Gerhart Husserl, *Rechtskraft* (see note 138), p. 75 f.

366 RGBl., p. 307.

is not a single international legal rule for a state that wishes to remove itself from the international law community. No state is forced by international law to enter into diplomatic relations or to conclude particular treaties. But if it does so, it subjects itself to the legal rules that apply to diplomatic intercourse or to legal rules objectified by the treaty. In this sense, international law, like all law, is a law of subordination.

Both the fundamental impossibility of being outvoted in the creation of law and the fundamental possibility of denouncing an international treaty are the characteristic features of a treaty order that is free of rule, created from and for sovereign legal persons; for the constitution of the concept of sovereignty, however, this is not enough. In this regard, the concept of sovereignty would mean little more than full capacity to make law and act in international law.[367] If it indeed means nothing more, its opponents would be right: it would be unnecessary, at least in international law. The problem of the validity of international law would then be just as simple as the legal rationalists like to portray it: international law would be valid only to the extent that it was created by acts transformed into norms by international law. 'Law,' they say, can only be established by 'law.'

Now, outside of grade school primers, this type of world history and legal history continues to exist only in certain international law textbooks, which try to remove any excitement and intricacy from the problem of international law's validity by coyly disguising, as "something to be ashamed of" [*pudendum*], in the veil of their abstractions the reality of lawmaking through lawbreaking that characterizes all of international law. The literature of international law is familiar with a sort of juristic untruthfulness, a "Can't" [in the original] that is presently in particularly full flower, which for more or less laudable purposes uses all sorts of terminological and logical tricks to make invisible the gap in international law, at whose precipice this warning sign should be posted. International law offers every international law person the opportunity to rid itself of all its legal obligations towards other international law persons by completely eradicating the other persons. "Save himself who can!" [*Sauve qui peut!*] Apart from this extreme and, even at the present time, the quite practical case of "complete destruction" [*debellatio*], the making of law through lawbreaking in international law is a phenomenon that will disappear once and for all only when international law ends with the establishment of the "world state" as a universal unit of decision-making and effect. Sentimental abstractions that disguise this phenomenon suffice only to diminish its diabolical magnitude; God knows they are unable to sweeten its bitterness; and world peace is not realized, but only disgraced, by it.

Apart from everything else, the silence around this situation and its juristic redefinition have proved to be a scientific mistake that has serious consequences for the theory of the validity of international law. This is the gap in international law that

[367] For example, in Franz von Liszt and Max Fleischmann, *Das Völkerrecht*, 12th edn, Berlin 1925, p. 91 ff. But the correct idea breaks through here involuntarily when they say (p. 95) that the evidence for continuing sovereignty of the constantly neutralized state lies in the fact that the obligated state can act against the obligation it has taken on. See also Hans Gerber, *Die Beschränkung der deutschen Souveränität nach dem Versailler Vertrage*, Berlin 1927 (Völkerrechtsfragen, vol. 20), p. 10 f.: Sovereignty is the expression for the "legal capacity of the state as such, but this is its legal capacity."

gives birth to war, because there is no universal unit of decision-making and effect above the sovereign states—this gap is not only, and not essentially, a product of hunger for power or of the cowardice of certain politicians, but an expression of the fact that, in these areas, there is an absence of both law and of power to close the gap. The gap exists for law because, for certain issues in international life, there are not even fundamental legal principles that would be equally acceptable to both parties to a conflict. Whether Crusaders or Turks, Germans or Frenchmen, Bolshevists or capitalists, have a greater or lesser right to exist, on this question there is no fundamental legal principle, and we know that persuading them to get along does not work in every case. It is cheap to accuse the statesmen of 1919 of "not having the courage to resolutely lay aside the concept of state sovereignty in favor of the concept of the common good of all states."[368] Like all law, international law is the product of a community of culture and interests, which no statesman can artificially produce, though he can and should certainly promote it. It depends on the intensity of this community whether it succeeds at all in objectifying fundamental ethical, fundamental legal principles, and whether the objectified fundamental legal principles prove to be sufficiently effective to be positivized by states' acts of will into rules of international law. Finally, the more or less firm anchoring of these principles in community consciousness decides whether they, like the legal rules, are capable of triggering acts of will that set aside the tempting possibility of decisions of sovereign power, a lawmaking through lawbreaking, while forgoing greater prospects and accepting subjection to positive law.

Thus, even if both fundamental legal principles and legal rules exist in a given case, under international law it is nevertheless possible that interests and moral pressure are not enough for them to assert themselves, and the lack of a powerful, law-implementation unit leads to the formation of new valid law through the breach of the old. We have heretofore deferred consideration of the question of power, both because the question of decision-making is the primary juristic one and because, when it comes to the problem of validity, the question of power tends to be emphasized one-sidedly. Today, however, it appears in German international law literature that a type of resentment of power has again led to an underestimation of the systematic significance of the lack of force in international law. It should not on any account be overlooked that, in contrast to domestic law, the realization of law by international law can in each individual case be decisive for the positivity of a rule of international law. Law and power need not, but certainly can, coincide in sovereignty, as long as there are sovereign states whose breach of law creates new law. Thus, from the aspect of power, a new connection results between sovereignty and positivity, which positive jurisprudence should recognize. In the process, it must be careful not to simplify the law–power dualism in the shallow fashion of an undialectical nature–mind dualism. The facticity of a unit of power is just as much founded

[368] Hans Adolf Harder, "Souveränität der Staaten und Aufgaben des Völkerbundes," in *Völkerbundfragen*, vol. 3 (1926), p, 233. On the following, see also Max Huber, "Beiträge zur Kenntnis der soziologischen Grundlagen des Völkerrechts und der Staatengesellschaft," in *Jahrbuch des öffentlichen Rechts*, 4 (1910), p. 56 ff.

in a community of fundamental legal principles and a commonality of interests, as conversely the positivity of law is founded in that community of fundamental legal principles and in the existence of a unit of effect that creates and implements the law. The potential universality of decision-making, and the power that asserts itself against any rebellion, are inseparable attributes of the sovereign state, and the execution of international law is therefore an insoluble problem. Either set up a state above today's states, or stop manipulating the assertion of the interests of a power group to look like execution of law! But the construction of war as a legal act may satisfy insubstantial legal rationalism. Where legal problems are still taken deadly seriously, one must pose the question of whether a state can summon up enough moral selflessness, or if its representatives are permitted to summon it up, to rectify, through its own, generally grave sacrifice of goods and blood, a breach of law in which the state is uninterested ideally or materially? What guarantee is there that, if the execution succeeds, the executing power group goes no further than law allows? What happens if the lawbreaking state remains victorious vis-à-vis the execution? Does one now comprehend the absolute character of sovereignty? Or does one believe that the problem "who will guard the guards?" [*quis custodet custodem*] is ultimately easier to resolve than the squaring of the circle?

The unit of decision-making and effect that is universal in its territory is sovereign. One who does not also possess the instruments of power that guarantee law is never sovereign. But positive law can never be sovereign. It requires one or more lawmakers for its existence or positivity, but for its ultimate guarantee also needs a law executor. To describe this "highest power" [*soluta potestas*] vis-à-vis positive law, no concept but that of sovereignty will suffice. In the following we will explain in detail the limits of the validity of international law that arise from this concept.

## C. Legal Rules and Fundamental Principles of Law in International Law

If the indissoluble nexus between legal positivity and state sovereignty in the area of international law is so often misunderstood, generally not even seen, this is the fault not least of the lack, which we have already criticized, of clear distinctions between the concepts of legal idea, fundamental legal principle, legal rule, legal order, and legal system, which are tossed together indiscriminately, especially in the international law literature.[369] The consequences show themselves in the highly confused doctrine of the sources of international law; in the construction, as erroneous as it is consequential, of an 'international law system'; and, finally, in a lack of clarity, which is also dangerous in practice, regarding the bases and limits of international jurisprudence.

All the blurriness and mingling have their final source in the fact that the theory is unclear on the meaning of the concept of sovereignty, or even attempts to eliminate it.

[369] See above, note 153.

Incorrect civil law analogies, pacifist wishes, and epistemological errors block insight into the fundamental contradiction between order of rule and contractual order.

One does not find the right synthesis in the justified reaction against the positivism of the nineteenth century, which took contempt for natural law so wonderfully far. Moreover, it begins once more to blur the border between natural law and positive law in an impermissible fashion. Especially when one is firmly convinced that the entire legal world is not at any point independent of super-legal standards, one must place the greatest importance on not disgracing those fundamental legal principles through short circuits in thinking. What has been called genuine natural law, I call constitutive ethical principles of law, or fundamental principles of law, which must be clearly separated from both positive legal rules and logical fundamental principles of law.[370]

I hope I will not meet with any misunderstanding if I state emphatically that international law knows no legal rules but those positivized by the intentional behavior of sovereign decision-making units. The hierarchy of the legal rules positivized and maintained in validity by a universal unit of decision-making and effect ends exactly where the sovereign decision-making unit ends. The only thing standing above the sovereign unit of will is, necessarily, fundamental legal principles, and legal rules only to the extent that it is fundamentally subject to them. The "world state" could only be subject to fundamental legal principles, but not legal rules. As long as there are still two sovereign decision-making units, the legal rules positivized between them, no matter how large a number there is, will never form a legal system; for that is always the expression of a universal decision-making unit. All theories of 'the' unified international legal order, all constructions of an 'international law system,' are arbitrary speculation. There is no such system, and cannot be one; not because there can be no praetor over the states, but because a universal decision-making unit, which would be a requirement for the system, would have to change international law to state law. Any praetor over the states would necessarily find a legal vacuum, and in certain cases would declare a "no applicable law" [*non liquet*] that is impossible in state law. How lacking in clarity is the thinking about this object is shown by Lapradelle's demand: "It is not possible to admit the possibility of a 'no applicable law' by an International Court; the denial of justice must be excluded from the international domain as it is from the national domain."[371]

It is believed that international law can be understood juristically by grounding it in "super-positive legal rules" or even constructing it as a unified system. In contrast, we adhere to the fact that all international law rules can only be positivized by means

[370] A treasure chest of such confusion is the survey "Jus naturae et gentium" in Niemeyer's *Zeitschrift für Internationales Recht*, 34 (1925), p. 113–89. An example from the newest international law literature can be found in Jahrreiß, *Rechtliche Liquidation* (see note 126), p. 86, which speaks of "law that must be brought into validity." Thieme, *Schiedsgerichtsbarkeit* (see note 95), p. 62, which is aware of an "international law" that "never applies as positive, but has long been an influence." See the text of the following pages above; see also Kaufmann, "Gleichheit vor dem Gesetz" (see note 144), p. 10 ff., and my comment, op. cit. (Diskussionsbeitrag), p. 57.

[371] Lapradelle, at the 14th session of the Jurists' Commission on July 2, 1920, in Societé des Nations (ed.), *Cour Permanente de Justice Internationale*, Comité Consultatif de Juristes, *Procès-verbaux des séances du comité, 16. juin-24, juillet 1920*, The Hague 1920, p. 312, 14th Session. See also Loder, op. cit.

of tacit or express treaties, through international law persons that face each other in formal freedom and equality. It is, however, the juristic stability of this very rule that legal rationalism believes to be impossible, unless the equality of states, the observance of treaties, and the fact of international law subjects are just as much 'legal rules.'[372] One then takes some or other 'legal rule' as a basis, at one's own discretion, and from them weaves a range of other legal rules or even an entire international law system. Thus, Liszt, for example, starts with the "basic idea" of the equality of states and concludes from this "directly a whole range of legal rules, which determine states' rights and duties to each other that need no treaty-based recognition in order to possess binding force."[373] This does not at all mean "natural law delusions, but legal norms that follow from the concept of the international law community, according to the rule of non-contradiction, and do not require the form of express lawmaking, because international law would not be conceivable without them."[374]

Just as the pure theory of law is, on state territory, nothing but the one-sided execution of Laband's legacy, on international law territory they must be understood as the implementation of Liszt's program. After all, Kelsen also believed he had arrived at the hoped for "natural order" according to the rule of non-contradiction—the 'legal rules' that "possess the character of complete objectivity—like a mathematical proposition derived from the axioms. ... "Recognition" of this norm on the part of the subject to whom they apply, as a condition for its validity, would be meaningless, because it would completely contradict its objectivity."[375] This is a question of those 'legal rules' of which Verdroß claims they "appear to even the *first* international users to be complete *legal rules*."[376] Apparently we have here those absolute barriers that 'law' places on the sovereignty of states, and because of which we may no longer call the state sovereign, but only 'law.' The pure theory of law comes to this conclusion, as we know, by revealing the system-forming state unit of will to be a fiction and depersonalizing the sovereign decision-making unit into a basic norm. Nothing more, then, stands in the way of portraying the relationship between state and international law as a relationship between two 'orders,' which could ultimately be made part of a globe-spanning 'system' through a basic international norm apparently analogous to a basic state norm. "Through the delegation by the state legal orders undertaken by the basic norm or source of international law, these should be viewed as subordinate to the international legal order and ultimately, with it, brought together into a unified system of norms."[377]

This juristic 'systemic unity' can be achieved only if one somehow eliminates the state as a sovereign person and dissolves it into positive law, whereupon it can be claimed: "The relationship between international law and the state is thus only possible as a relationship between international law *and state law*."[378] The only difficulty

[372] See, in part, Karl Gareis, *Institutionen des Völkerrechts*, 2nd edn, Gießen 1901, p. 34.
[373] Liszt/Fleischmann, *Völkerrecht* (see note 367), p. 115 f. [374] Ibid., p. 115.
[375] Kelsen, *Problem der Souveränität* (see note 38), p. 215
[376] Verdroß, *Völkerrechtsgemeinschaft* (see note 137), p. 39. [377] Kelsen, op. cit., p. 137.
[378] See Verdroß even in his *Verfassung der Völkerrechtsgemeinschaft*, p. 14, which was otherwise quite cleansed of Kelsenian purity.

is the basic norm that is supposed to be the basis of every universal system. Behind the basic state norm, as we have seen, stands a substantive state will; but what is behind the basic international law norm, what does it mean? Does it command something, or is it an example of the species of 'norm' that has unrestrictedly variable content—that is, no content whatsoever? All that is clear, first of all, is that that 'norm' must at all costs be a "legal rule"; the unity of the legal system can only be established by one or more *legal rules* that form the tip of the legal pyramid."[379] In contrast to the 'old doctrine,' with its 'artificial system,' this new doctrine certainly knows of "no meta-legal foundation."[380] "The problem of the unity of international law hinges on the problem of international law's basic norm."[381] We should take note!

The 'legal rules' that have heretofore been taken as basic international law norms are the principle of the equality of states, for some, and the rule of "agreements must be kept" [*pacta sunt servanda*] for others. If we first examine the formula of the equality of states for its quality as a legal rule, we find at first glance that this rule, as we might suppose, has no content whatsoever; it is not even an ethical fundamental principle of law, but merely a logical constitutive principle of international law, the voluntary acceptance of which would, however, be just as meaningless as the recognition of a mathematical proposition. For the very reason that it applies completely independently of our will, because it does not call on our will at all, it has logical and not juristic validity; it is a logical presupposition of law and not presupposed law. Upon closer examination, it appears that the equality of states—no more precisely defined!—is nothing but a tautological paraphrase of the subjectivity of international law; according to Hegel, the personality "constitutes the abstract basis of abstract, and therefore *formal*, law. The command of law is thus: *be a person and respect others as people.*"[382] Such a logical fundamental legal principle cannot be recognized if it cannot be violated. It says only that, if law is to exist between you and me, we must view each other mutually as bearers of rights and duties.[383] The equality rule only becomes a norm that calls upon my will when certain normative content accrues to it from a concrete historical epistemic community.[384] The answer to what should be considered equal or arbitrary, "reasonable" or "unreasonable," is always determined by history and culture. The formation of the ethical world is never given to us as a "natural order," but is always the result of a decision.[385] Thus, in international law, it completely depends on whether the concrete international

[379] Verdroß, *Einheit* (see note 96), page 58. [380] Ibid., p. 51 f.

[381] Verdroß, *Völkerrechtsgemeinschaft*, p. 12.

[382] Hegel, *Rechtsphilosophie* (see note 57), § 36 (p. 75). See Grotius, *De jure belli ac pacis* (see note 27), book II, ch. XII, § 8.

[383] See Friedrich v. Martens, *Völkerrecht* (German trans. by C. Bergbohm), vol. 1, Berlin 1883, p. 390: "The states must recognize each other as legal subjects, they must recognize their rights mutually, otherwise no relations at all are possible between them." Kaufmann, *Völkerrecht* (see note 283), p. 195, and those mentioned by him are similar to the text. In contrast, Max Hüber ("Die Gleichheit der Staaten"), in *Rechtswissenschaftliche Beiträge. Juristische Festgabe des Auslandes zu Josef Köhlers 60. Geburtstag*, Stuttgart 1909, p. 106 ff.) tries to show the rule of equality to be a positive rule of law.

[384] See above, p. 81.

[385] See Kaufmann, "Gleichheit vor dem Gesetz" (see note 144), p. 16; Hans Nawiasky (Mitbericht), in op. cit., p. 30, also does the only thing possible to interpret the equality rule in the German constitution, by trying to determine its precise meaning from "the *total content* of our existing legal order."

law community has reached sufficient intensity to develop substantive fundamental legal principles about how equality should be understood. Ask the colonial peoples of any century what they think of the character of the European equality rule as a legal rule or merely a fundamental legal principle. But to see how little it means even within the contemporary community of international law, one must be aware that international law also presumes that respect for another as a person requires that the other has not been destroyed by me or by a third party.

The situation is no better for the character of the often referred to principle of "agreements must be kept" as a legal rule. Like the former rule, this too has never—taken by itself—made normative action possible for a legal person. Where the former is a tautological paraphrase of legal personality, this one is a tautology of legal objectivity, in that it states nothing other than: if you have concluded a lawful treaty, it is lawful—that is, binding. This rule, too, considered in itself, is merely a logical, not an ethical, fundamental legal principle, let alone a rule of law; for immoral treaties, as we are aware, are not to be enforced. The valid conclusion of a treaty, which can only occur through the interaction of will and fundamental ethical principles, was characterized succinctly by F. J. Stahl: should a treaty be legally binding, he says, "it must serve a lawful purpose"; "while agreement of will is thus the actually binding element, it is only binding on the condition of that content."[386] Until two or more legal persons positivize "a law of the contract" within the framework of fundamental legal principles or legal rules, there is no legal rule. Thus, while the rule of "agreements must be kept" may be immanent to all lawful treaties, and may be abstracted from them with logical validity, it only attains legal validity through and with the conclusion of a valid treaty.[387] Likewise, its express inclusion in a treaty does not make it a legal rule, but makes the parties to the treaty legal theoreticians.[388]

[386] Stahl, *Rechtsphilosophie* (see note 145), vol. 2, part 1, 1st edn, 1845, p. 415 f. Also correctly, see E. v. Ullmann, *Völkerrecht*, Tübingen 1908 (Das öffentliche Recht der Gegenwart, vol. 3), p. 249: "In applying the legal form of the treaty, the states express and bring into effective validity the knowledge of the general nature of the treaty and its logical consequences."

[387] It is claimed to be a rule of law by, e.g., Heinrich Lammasch, *Das Völkerrecht nach dem Kriege*, Kristiana 1917 (Publications de l'Institut Nobel, III), p. 95 f.; Kelsen, *Problem der Souveränität* (see note 38), pp. 158, 171, 186, 192, etc.; Strupp, *Theorie* (see note 95), p. 3 f.; Alfred Manigk, Besprechung von Theodor Niemeyer, *Völkerrecht*, 1923, in *Juristische Wochenschrift*, 32 (1923), p. 487; Verdroß, *Einheit*, pp. 61, 104, 105 note 1; Verdroß, *Völkerrechtsgemeinschaft* (see note 137), p. 139 believes, in contrast, that "the supranational norm 'agreements must be kept' is a precondition to all international law"; Verdroß thus seems to return to his original opinion that that rule, whose efficacy was massively overestimated even then, represented a logical principle of law; see Verdroß, "Zur Konstruktion des Völkerrechts," in *Zeitschrift für Völkerrecht*, 8 (1914), p. 347. Verdroß himself (*Völkerrechtsgemeinschaft*, p. 49) notes that before the point at which sufficiently definite promise and acceptance is present, nothing juristically binding exists whatsoever, and he proves it with good international law examples. Wenzel, too, *Begriff des Gesetzes* (see note 124), p. 504, considers it possible for "agreements must be kept" to be a legal rule. See, in contrast, Triepel, *Völkerrecht* (see note 166), p. 224 f., and now, in detail, Husserl, *Rechtskraft* (see note 138), p. 38 ff.

[388] See, e.g., the protocol of the London Conference of January 17, 1871, in Georges Frédéric Martens, *Nouveau recueil général de traités*, vol. 18, Göttingen 1871, p. 273 ff. Of course, the positive law provisions of the London Protocol of February 19, 1831 had a crucially different significance, see Martens, *Nouveau Recueil de traités*, vol. 110 (1826–32), Supplement vol. 14, Göttingen 1836, p. 197, which provided for the continuity of treaties regardless of constitutional change in the treaty states.

The rule of "agreements must be kept" is thus just as little a rule of law as is the principle of state equality.[389] If the dogma of legal sovereignty were to be built on such rules, we would in turn come to the conclusion that this legal sovereignty is without law, and that positivism is without positivity.

But how do such rules succeed in constituting a 'system of international law' and robbing the states of their sovereignty? To understand this, one must keep in mind the typical manner of argumentation of individualist legal rationalism, which constantly proceeds in the pattern familiar to us from Politis.[390] First, it has established that the sovereign decision-making unit is a fiction or abstraction. But if the state is only an abstraction, the contemporary community of states is an equally justifiable, though more comprehensive, abstraction—both, after all, consist only of 'people.' Expressed in terms of normative logic, this means, according to Kelsen, that the state is nothing but a legal order, and therefore "the hypothesis that the norms of international law are a universal legal order standing above the individual states, as partial legal orders, and encompassing all of them" is identical with the hypothesis of a "comprehensive universal polity that, because it has fundamentally the same nature as the individual states, can be described as a personification of the universal or world legal order, as a universal or world state, as a "world state". In this concept formation"—as Kelsen calls it—"the recognition is expressed with particular clarity of the *definitive* consubstantiality, from a *juristic* point of view, and ultimately the unity, of the international legal order and the individual state legal orders."[391] Certainly, it all depends on one's point of view! There is undoubtedly a point of view, for example, the anarchistic one, for which the difference between the state and the world legal order is as much "of completely incidental, purely terminological importance"[392] as, for example, the fact that a chair and a table are made of wood is enough, for a certain point of view, to blur their other differences. Permit me this drastic comparison, which is, however, fitting down to the last detail: for one who deals in old furniture for scrap, different contexts and differences undoubtedly exist than for those who would like to sit on a chair and not on a table.

The same opposition of viewpoints is characteristic of the opposition between a legal doctrine of the above-described type, and jurisprudence. For the latter, a legal system can only be discerned where a sovereign decision-making unit acts in system-forming fashion. For Kelsen, the content-less fundamental legal principle of state equality is enough[393] to form a system; for, he argues, just as one can act, with the hypothesis of the primacy of state law, 'as if' the state is a sovereign person, one can just as well act, with that basic norm, 'as if' the treaty community is a sovereign state. It is interesting that this fictionalism, which prefers not to recognize that this is not about the as if hypothesis of a sovereign normative logician, but about a concrete unit of will, on the one hand, and material, fundamental social, and

[389] We will return at length to the fact that no legal rule decides on the existence of an international law person.

[390] See above, p. 74 ff.

[391] Kelsen, *Problem der Souveränität* (see note 38), p. 249 f.

[392] Ibid., p. 250.

[393] Ibid., p. 251 f. However, he does not wish to resolve "in detail" the "origin of international law."

ethical principles on the other, allows legal positivism, along with state sovereignty, to slip away at this decisive point. Kelsen does not wish to contest the "natural law" character of his fundamental principles of international law, but believes, "in this sense"—in what sense?—that there is "no contradiction at all between natural law and positive law."[394] A nice example of the necessary relationship between positivity and sovereignty!

Kelsen's student Verdroß saw correctly that Kelsen would not exactly succeed, as he promised, in establishing the "correct and inalienable core of all the changes" that the concept of sovereignty had undergone in history.[395] He also saw that this concept comes to roost homelessly upon a logical principle, but that Kelsen was forced, despite his methodological syncretism, to have recourse to "metalaw."[396] Verdroß then tried, eschewing any "metalaw," to show the connection "in accordance with law" between the two spheres of law, international law and state law; for him, too, "the unified legal system is not a mere postulate, but a legal reality."[397] He too believed in the system-forming power of a "legal rule." Verdroß hopes to establish an "international law constitution," "analogous" to state constitutions, which would define "that legal rule or complex of legal rules" "which is the condition of all others, without itself being conditioned by them."[398] The principle of "agreements must be kept" presents itself to him as such a legal rule, that is, as expressly positive.[399] In a monograph appearing soon after and devoted to the same theme, however, Verdroß himself admitted between the lines that the undertaking had failed categorically; unfortunately he did not draw the appropriate conclusions. In any case, that fundamental legal principle is expressly termed an "ethical norm";[400] but Verdroß seeks to avoid the consequences that arise from this for the international *law* community through the following arguments; once again, he supposes that the 'legal community as such' is first founded not through a treaty, but already through the "norm" of "agreements must be kept". "Treaties can only further develop it. Here it is without significance to our question whether or not the norm of "agreements must be kept" is considered a legal or an ethical norm. The difference consists merely in the fact that, in the first case, law is understood as a self-contained unit, and in the second case, in contrast, as a partial order derived from ethics"[401]—a difference, we must add, with which the pure theory of law stands or, in this case, falls. The entire book is after all devoted to the 'constitution of the international *legal* community,' and the pure theory of law once again places us in the tragicomic situation of earnestly preserving the purity of legal epistemology against itself. An international law constitution is never based on an ethical norm—an insight that would have to be brought

394 Ibid., p. 252 f. 395 Ibid., p. 3 f. 396 Verdroß, *Einheit*, p. 13f.
397 Ibid., p. 136 f. 398 Ibid., p. 59. 399 Ibid., p. 61.
400 Verdroß, *Völkerrechtsgemeinschaft*, p. 28.
401 Ibid., p. 128. On the basis of this norm, the states "are from the very beginning *potential* members of the community of states; they are able to do no more than to develop them into *actual* ones." What could this be: a 'potential' member of the community of states? If, according to Verdroß, a distinction must be made "between the state community founded through the basic norms, and the linkage of states through positive norms of international law," this would be an immanent admission that the former is not an international law community (ibid.).

home on every page and even in the title of Verdroß's work, if he did not constantly confuse legal rules and fundamental legal principles.[402]

Nevertheless, Verdroß's work deserves our sincere thanks. Not only because it immanently finishes off the sovereignty of Kelsen's legal logic, but above all because it strongly renounces that destructive fictionalism and makes room, at least upwards, in the ethical-political sphere for life and living science. If this breakthrough could be completed downwards as well, toward the sociological and political sphere, jurisprudence would have found the synthetic way to overcome the crisis of the doctrine of the state. Then, distinguishing legal rules and fundamental legal principles, positivity and sovereignty would once again become justified, and international law would no longer simulate a 'universal legal order' or 'universal system.'[403]

A legal system has sovereignty as a presupposition; it only exists where a unit of universal decision-making and effect constitutes the systematic unity of legal rules within the scope of fundamental legal principles, and guarantees their validity. But there is no unified international legal order, or even just general international law, in the sense of law that governs all existing states equally,[404] although today there are already a number of more or less general individual legal rules, and a much greater number of fundamental legal principles that must be positivized into legal rules.

## D. The General Fundamental Legal Principles of International Law Jurisprudence

The distinction I propose, and which pervades the entire legal world, between logical and ethical fundamental legal principles, on the one hand, and legal rules positivized by an authoritative collective will, on the other, today finds its most practical, excellent test in the international courts and arbitral tribunals. Under Article 38(3) of its Statute, the Permanent Court of International Justice in The Hague is supposed to apply, in addition to customary international law and treaty law, "The general principles of law recognized by civilized nations." Similar provisions are found in numerous international conventions regarding arbitral tribunals that have since been concluded.[405] In these principles of law, we recognize our fundamental legal principles.

To logistical positivism, however, both the character of these fundamental principles of law, as well as their relationship to customary and treaty law, on the one hand,

[402] See, e.g., ibid., pp. 27, 57 (in the same sentence); 61 f.

[403] Kelsen, *Problem der Souveränität*, pp. 120, 122, 205, 229.

[404] For agreement, see, e.g., Triepel, *Völkerrecht* (see note 166), pp. 83, 283; Husserl, *Rechtskraft* (see note 138), p. 32; Wenzel, *Begriff des Gesetzes*, (see note 124), p. 391 ff., with extensive bibliography.

[405] See, e.g., Article 5 of the Treaty on Arbitration and Conciliation between the Swiss Confederation and the German Reich of December 3, 1921, reprinted in Société des Nations (ed.), *Recueil des Traités*, 12 (1922), p. 271; the German-Swedish Treaty on Arbitration and Conciliation of August 29, 1924, in ibid., 42 (1925/6), p. 111; the German-Finnish Treaty on Arbitration and Conciliation of March 14, 1925, in ibid., 43 (1926), p. 347; also Art. 4 of the Netherlands–Germany Treaty on Arbitration and Conciliation of May 20, 1926, in ibid., 66 (1927/8), p. 103; the German–Danish Arbitration and Conciliation Treaty of June 2, 1926, in ibid., 61 (1927), p. 325.

and decisions "according to equity" [*ex aequo et bono*], precedents, and the teachings of publicists,[406] on the other, must be fundamentally incomprehensible. A clarification of this question will also decide the position that international judges should take in regard to these general principles of law.

The history of the origins of Article 38(3) first of all permit a clearly negative judgment. The deliberations of the committee of jurists charged with drafting the Statute make it unquestionably apparent that not a single member imagined positive legal rules as part of those "principles" [*principes*].[407] Much more emerges from the discussion: despite all the contradictions and ambiguities, all the members agreed that, were Article 38(3) to be adopted, the judges would have the task of further developing positive law. For this very reason, Root and Ricci-Busatti opposed these "principles," while Descamps, Lapradelle, Loder, Hagerup, Fernandes, and Phillimore supported them.[408] Root stated, "The States would not accept a Court which had the right to settle disputes in accordance with rules established by the Court itself, and by the interpretation of more or less vague principles." "The Court must not have the power to legislate."[409] Ricci-Busatti agreed, "notably in regard to the impossibility for the Court to act as legislator." In the absence "of a positive rule of international law," the "Court" [*Cour*] would have to deny the claim. "If a case is brought before it and if it finds no applicable rule, it will declare that there are no rights that one party can assert against the other, that the conduct of the state that is the subject of the action would not be contrary to any recognized rule."[410] This is the decisive point, practically and theoretically, that the majority of the Committee very clearly expressed on this issue in opposition to Root and Ricci-Busatti. Hagerup first remarked that, in Root's view, "if there are no rules of positive law, the Court lacks jurisdiction"; but it would then be impossible for it to fulfill the task "of contributing to the development of law."[411] Likewise, Loder believed that a "denial of justice" must not be possible,[412] and Lapradelle agreed with him, against Root: "It is not possible to admit the possibility of a 'no applicable law' by an International Court; the denial of justice must be excluded from the international domain as it is from the national domain."[413]

In conclusion, President Descamps observed that when positive treaty and customary law is silent, it is "in truth impossible, and it would be above all odious, to say to a judge confronting a solution that manifestly conforms to justice: 'your task consists in committing a veritable denial of justice' under the pretext that one has not found a determinate convention or custom." The President expressly stated that

[406] Art. 38(4) states: "Subject to the provisions of Article 59, judicial decisions and the teachings of the most highly qualified publicists of the various nations, as subsidiary means for the determination of rules of law. This provision shall not prejudice the power of the Court to decide a case *ex aequo et bono*, if the parties agree thereto."

[407] *Procès verbaux* (see note 371), p. 129.

[408] Regarding Lord Phillimore's view, in addition to his remark (ibid., p. 311), his statement should be noted: "These divergences arose from the continental idea of justice ... The English system is different: the judge takes an oath 'to do justice according to law' " (ibid., p. 315).

[409] Ibid., pp. 286, 309. [410] Ibid., p. 314. [411] Ibid., p. 307 f.

[412] Ibid., p. 312. [413] Ibid.

this question was a point of controversy.[414] Finally, Fernandes attempted to make the majority's viewpoint acceptable to the opposition by answering as follows the question whether the judge could, if necessary, act as legislator and create a rule of law: "Definitely not. It merely highlights a latent rule, in accordance with Jhering's term. And this rule is legitimate since it is contained logically in the principle to which national consent had been acquired."[415]

Based on our distinction between legal rules and fundamental legal principles, and considering the discussion presented here, we are now able to determine that all the members of the committee of jurists were first of all in agreement that the "general principles of law" in Article 38(3) were to be understood not as legal rules, but as fundamental legal principles in our sense; second, that all, however, shared the view that it was the international judges who would first positivize these legal principles into legal rules.[416] Thus, the history of the origins of the Article in question not only presents no obstacle, but also gives highly valuable support to the integration of those fundamental legal principles into the systematic structure of our basic conception of state and law.

We can discard, with the help of the history of its origins, the view that Article 38(3) is a legal source coordinated with treaties and custom. According to the available material, it is simply impossible to place "international justice as a source of international law" next to the first two, to claim that it is through justice that the international legal community is founded "in accordance with law"[417] and to declare that section 3 also concerns "norms that directly obligate states in their mutual intercourse and therefore must also be applied by the Court, and not principles that the Court first creates to settle a dispute."[418] In this case, the Court creates not the principles, but the legal rules, which are once again confused here; so that, however, there is the possibility that "states are judged subject to obligations that no legal rule had previously bound them to," but not the possibility that a fact situation will be "subjected to different principles than the ones that are applicable to it."[419] This is exactly the situation that Root and Ricci-Busatti wished to prevent and all the others hoped to bring about. The former wanted only to permit decisions bound by legal rules under Article 38(1) and (2); the latter also wanted to permit decisions bound by principles of law under Article 38(3). The difference between decisions bound by principles of law and "equitable" decisions (sec. 4) results clearly enough, even aside from the positive law differences, from the fact that in the former case the judge is bound by objective legal principles imposed upon him;[420] but in the latter he is, at the express wish of the parties, deliberately allowed broad discretion for subjective

[414] Ibid., p. 323. [415] Ibid., p. 346.

[416] Fernandes only gave this process a different theoretical interpretation. For the above reasons, Verdroß's interpretation of Art. 38(3) (*Völkerrechtsgemeinschaft*, p. 60 ff.) is already wrong based on the history of its origins.

[417] Verdroß, *Einheit* (see note 96), pp. 120, 124.

[418] Verdroß, *Völkerrechtsgemeinschaft* (see note 137), p. 61 f.

[419] Ibid., p. 61. The confusion is particularly instructive here.

[420] See Descamps, in *Procès verbaux* (see note 371), pp. 318 f., 323. On decisions *ex aequo et bono*, see Thieme, *Schiedsgerichtsbarkeit* (see note 95), p. 22.

judgment. Let us not forget that the judge, by applying those fundamental principles of law, imposes an "exact law" [*ius strictum*] that is in no way different from positive law, and whose possible "equitable" mitigation is provided for by section 4. It is therefore self-evident that the Court does not thus obtain "an arbitral character that makes an absolute abstraction from legal rules."[421]

Thoroughly incorrect, but very typical, is the view that "international justice" represents a third source of international law, "next to" or "in addition to" treaty and custom.[422] One almost sees logistical positivism, roused from its rest, suddenly rubbing its eyes and glimpsing, "next to" its positive law, something the existence of which it could not heretofore have imagined. Article 38(3) means, prudently, something very different from "international justice"; it speaks of principles of law that are not yet positive international law, but upon which individual national legal orders are based—"recognized by civilized nations" [*reconnus par les nations civilisées*]—and which are to be positivized into legal rules by a unit of will, "the Court." International justice must, even in decisions based on treaty and custom, be envisaged as authoritative; only legal rationalists believe the judge is, by a logical subsumption, an automaton and place justice 'next to' positive law. On the basis of Article 38(3), the judge absolutely has the status of law-creator, who positivizes a rule of law within the scope of fundamental principles of law. Even the legislator normally cannot do more; even the sovereign decision-making unit is subject to fundamental principles of law. Before there is a judgment based on section 3, no legal rule exists. This view, which follows from all of our observations so far, brings us into gratifying agreement with an authority as important as Anzilotti; "This norm," he says, "does not exist in the international order; it is the judge that creates it."[423] In this case, too, as in all creation of law, the dualism of will and norm must prove effective.

The basis for the legitimacy of international judges as law-creators is formed, however, exclusively from the treaty-based agreement of wills of sovereign decision-making units; the Permanent International Court and its decisions owe their existence and validity not to some 'international law constitution,' but to the sovereign acts of will of the states. This fact, in its eminent juristic importance, is also expressed in Article 38(3) in the fact that only principles of law "recognized by civilized nations" are named as bases for decision-making. It is, in turn, a fundamental misunderstanding of the difference between logical and juristic validity when the "teachings of the most highly qualified publicists of the various nations, as subsidiary means for the determination of rules of law"[424] denoted in Article 38(4) are described as sources of law. A doctrine can appeal to the judge's cognitive function and act as an aide to clarifying, in his mind, the normative content appropriate for lawmaking; but it can never be a "method of lawmaking."[425] The pure theory of

[421] Antonio S. de Bustamente y Sirvén, *La Cour permanente de justice internationale*, The Hague 1923, p. 59.

[422] See, e.g., Verdroß, *Einheit*, p. 120; Verdroß, *Völkerrechtsgemeinschaft*, p. 57 ff.

[423] Anzilotti, *Corso* (see note 361), p. 64.

[424] See above, note 406.

[425] Verdroß, *Einheit*, p. 125; he calls scholars of international law subsidiary "lawmakers" in international law. Yes, if these scholars were only able to form a decision-making unit! Herbert Kraus is also

law, for example, which to some extent advocates fundamental principles of law that are by no means "recognized by civilized nations" should thus not in this respect be applied by judges. The judge always has the final decision of will, above all of this, in any case generally quite contradictory, theory.[426]

The relationship between will and norm is expressed in theoretically irreproachable fashion in the above-mentioned arbitral treaties, which are listed at the end of the well-known article in the Swiss Civil Code[427] as bases for decision-making: treaties, customary law, and the "general principles of law recognized by civilized peoples," but which then continues: "To the extent, in individual cases, the aforementioned legal bases contain gaps, the arbitral tribunal shall decide according to the legal principles that in its view are the rules of international law. In the process, it shall follow established doctrine and jurisprudence."[428] Here the arbitrator doubtless has available other bases for decision-making than the judge has under Article 38(3) of the Statute. The juxtaposition is instructive precisely because it shows that judges of the Permanent International Court must declare a "no applicable law" if they find no generally recognized principle of law, and are not to create principles of law.

From this alone, it follows that the Hague Court is a particularist decision-making institution whose lawmaking attains positivity only because it derives its authority from the sovereignty of the states, and whose substantive jurisdiction is likewise based on treaty-based agreement among universal decision-making units. It was the Permanent International Court itself that, in an advisory opinion regarding the Russian–Finnish dispute over Karelia, spoke of the principle "which is at the very base of international law: the principle of the independence of states."[429]

completely incorrect, *Gedanken über Staatsethos im internationalen Verkehr*, Berlin 1925 (Schriften der Königsberger Gelehrten Gesellschaft, geisteswissenschaftliche Klasse, 2 III), p. 83; he wishes to see in Art. 38(4) a type of "subsidiary blank slate reception of the speculations of natural law, and therefore also ethicizing, international law scholarship into international law."

426 Anzilotti, op. cit., p. 59: "The truth is that the Court applies the rules of law and may use jurisprudence and doctrine to define them."

427 (Of December 10, 1907, Art. 1, *Eidgenössische Gesetzessammlung*, 1908, p. 233.)

428 (See above, note 405.)

429 Société des Nations (ed.), *Publications de la Cour Permanente de Justice Internationale*, Série B (Recueil des avis consultatifs), no. 5, July 23, 1923, p. 27.

# VII

# State Sovereignty and International Law Personality

Neither international law positivity nor the concept of the international law person can be constructed without the concept of sovereignty. Basically, the only international law persons are sovereign territorial decision-making units. There are certainly individual exceptions. But if there is any case in which the exception proves the rule, this is it;[430] especially when one understands an international law person correctly as not only a bearer, but also as a creator of international law rights and duties.[431] This concept of the international law person is built upon the historical fact that, for a few generations, pretty much the entire ecumenical world has been divided among sovereign decision-making units. There are exceptions to this fact, however, and thus the possibility of international law persons that, without being states, "are not subject to the authority of any state."[432]

These include, first of all, cases in which the unity of territorial decision-making is still being contested; that is, the case of rebels recognized as belligerent parties. Strictly speaking, this is not an exception at all, as under customary law, the recognition of rebels as international law persons occurs only on condition that they have already established themselves as a sovereign decision-making unit on their piece of territory, with the intention of gaining independence from the motherland.[433]

An exception that proves our rule is represented by the international law personality of the Apostolic See. Since the defeat of the Papal State, the Apostolic See is not a territorial decision-making unit, but merely a decision-making unit on a personal basis. Under the "Code of Canon Law" [*codex juris canonici*], it claims "supreme and complete power of jurisdiction over the universal Church both in matters pertaining to faith and morals and in those pertaining to the discipline and order of the Church spread throughout the world." [434] In the case of faith and ethics, the state, which has gradually become secularized since the Renaissance, can without difficulty recognize

[430] Very well formulated by William Edward Hall, *A Treatise on International Law*, 8th edn (ed. A. P. Higgens), Oxford 1924, p. 17: "Primarily international law governs the relations of such of the communities called independent states as voluntarily subject themselves to it. To a limited extent, as will be seen presently, it may also govern the relations of certain communities of analogous character." See Arrigo Cavaglieri, "I soggetti del diritto internazionale," in *Rivista di diritto internazionale*, 17 (1925), p. 175 f.

[431] See above, p. 125 f. [432] Cavaglieri, op. cit., p. 184.

[433] See Moore, *Digest* (see note 361), vol. 7, p. 158 ff.

[434] *Codex juris canonici*, Rome 1917, can. 218, § 1.

a decision-making unit independent of itself, even if it does not recognize the justification for the canonical right for the Papal claim "independent of any human authority whatsoever."[435] But this Papal authority has nothing necessarily political or international law related about it. Where the Pope is an international law person, what matters is his "power pertaining to the discipline and order of the Church," that is, the collective organization of social acts.[436] This political world power was able to ensure that the Apostolic See is "independent of any human authority whatsoever," also as a matter of social territory, and that it could assert its independence vis-à-vis the universal territorial decision-making power of the Italian state.[437] Far too little importance is placed, in the international law literature, on the theoretically as well as practically important fact that the Apostolic See has its seat on Italian state territory, but possesses universal territorial decision-making power, analogous to sovereignty, on its territory. It is through this very exception that the crucial importance of territory for the concept of sovereignty first becomes clear. As the behavior of the Italian state during the World War showed, the Pope can only exercise his international law "right to appoint and receive ambassadors" [*ius legationis*] because, and to the extent that, he can grant the protection required by international law on his territory to the envoys accredited to him.

If even in this exceptional case, a certain correlation can be seen between state law and international law sovereignty, we can presume this necessary correlation even more so in all other cases. Only someone who is able to be a subject of duties can be a legal person. International law obligations, however, in principle can only be taken on by sovereign decision-making units; for only they are able to impose on their members the obligations they have entered into without another decision-making unit getting in the way, and can if necessary change their constitutions for this purpose.

The recently much-discussed question of whether individual 'international law persons' other than the states can exist must be answered fundamentally in the negative, if we do not intend to expand the concept until it is systematically worthless. Individuals undoubtedly lack the ability to create international law duties and rights. They are also doubtless not bearers of international law duties. The pirates who again became relevant with Article 3 of the Washington Treaty of February 6, 1922 are objects of international law, but on no account subjects of duties. These provisions only empowered all states to intervene against the pirates.[438] Even if one

[435] Ibid., § 2.

[436] See, however, Pius X's first consistorial allocution, in Carl Mirbt, *Quellen zur Geschichte des Papsttums und des römischen Katholizismus*, 4th edn, Tübingen 1924, no. 647, p. 502: "But every impartial observer sees that the Pontiff *can by no means separate political matters from his rule over faith and morals.*"

[437] Italian Guarantee Law of May 13, 1871, Art. 7, in Karl Strupp, *Documents pour server à l'histoire du droit des gens*, vol. 1, 2nd edn, Berlin 1923, p. 399 f. On this, see Hubert Bastgen, "Papst," in *Wörterbuch des Völkerrechts und der Diplomatie* (ed. K. Strupp), vol. 2, Berlin 1925, p. 239 ff.; Anzilotti, *Corso* (see note 361), p. 81 ff.

[438] Treaties and Resolutions approved and adopted by the Conference on the Limitation of Armaments, November 12, 1921 to February 6, 1922 (Treaty in Relation of the Use of Submarines and Noxious Gases in Warfare, in *American Journal of International Law*, vol. 16 (1922), Supplement, p. 59.)

does not see these courts as state institutions,[439] the individual's right of action before the mixed arbitration tribunals appears, on strict legal consideration, to be a power delegated to the claimant by his state. Certainly, the state is obligated to delegate in this way by international law, but the treaty that binds it is not only the basis for that delegation; it also destroys it, one-sidedly through the state's will, in both cases without the consent of a third party. There would of course be no objection to this if the jurisprudence that wishes to find such a right of action were to establish a special category for bearers of international law trial powers. But to coordinate this case with the exceptions described above would mean completely hollowing out the concept of the international law person.[440]

Since J. J. Moser, the concept of the semi-sovereign state has been adopted into international law in order by dint of careful language to camouflage rather than express certain power situations. This expression aims to describe certain international law powers accorded to dependent polities, such as the member states of a federal state, protected states, and vassal states. 'Semi-sovereignty,' this concept of convenience, is an obvious symbol of the fact that jurisprudence finds itself in a dilemma, as in the question of the state character of member states of the federal state.[441] From a theoretical point of view, the solution to the problem cannot be in doubt; just as there can be no divided sovereignty in state law, there can be no semi-sovereignty in international law. There is either a sovereign legal person, or a subordinate polity that can be construed not as an independent, international law person, but only as an organ of such a one. Practically, however, the question of actual subordination can be quite uncertain. Jurisprudence must all the more emphatically strive for clear concept formation. Nothing keeps it from noting the uncertainty of the factual issues at stake, and if need be rejecting the postulated construction. Under no circumstances, however, do ordering ideas exist to legitimize the political aspirations or resentments of one or another power. The insight that the states of a federal state possess neither state law nor international law semi-sovereignty has gradually taken hold. In contrast, it is still the dominant doctrine that a vassalage or protectorate relationship is a basis for semi-sovereignty on the part of the protected or vassal state. The wish of the protector or suzerain not to be called sovereign, understandable politically in certain circumstances, should, however, not lead the jurist to believe that it is not. Such more or less good faith is costly, theoretically; it is paid in internal contradictions, such as the claim that, on the one hand, the proposition that the promise of protection "in no way" affects the sovereignty of the protected state is true—"protection does not involve subjection"—but, on the other hand, the protecting state possesses supreme authority.[442] Calling the protected polity "sovereign," while at the same time noting that it has granted another state the right "at least" to control its foreign

[439] Anzilotti, op. cit, p. 163.

[440] See the discussion of this problem at the 7th annual assembly of the German Society of International Law, in *Mitteilungen der Deutschen Gesellschaft für Völkerrecht*, 7 (1926), p. 30 ff.

[441] See above, p. 134 ff.

[442] For one of many, see Liszt/Fleischmann, *Völkerrecht* (see note 367), p. 106; 99.

policy by way of an approval or veto right, means turning the concept of sovereignty into its opposite.[443]

Here we must judge according to substantive criteria and distinguish whether the protected polity is indeed a universal unit of decision-making and effect that is merely limited by treaty, and in this case is not semi-sovereign but simply sovereign; or if the form of a treaty is just a more gentle method of colony creation. To force both of these cases, which are worlds apart juristically, into the category of protectorate is to blur the most crucial juristic differences.

Without in the least wishing to exhaust the tangled subject, let us merely emphasize the viewpoint that most directly touches upon our topic, and which must be crucial for a correct presentation of the problem. The deciding factor must be the legal and power situation. If a state, based on written or unwritten law, is capable and has the necessary power to mandate something state law related for another polity, then the latter must be construed under international law not as a legal person, but as a dependent state that is in no way sovereign, and its other international law responsibilities—for example, in the area of trade policy—must be juristically understood as a sphere of activity delegated by the supreme state. As soon as a state can rightly claim that, because of the legal and power situation, it has no state law means at its disposal to induce the polity in question to abide by its international law obligations, this polity is sovereign and neither in a vassalage relationship nor protected. These questions gain practical significance in regard to liability in international law. The fact that an act or omission contrary to international law by the member state counts as an international law delict on the part of the federal state[444] determines both the state law and international law sovereignty of the latter. Under the principle "no one can transfer more right than he himself possesses," the exact same thing must be true of suzerains and true protectorate states, though it must be firmly emphasized that this sovereignty cannot be dissolved into either state or international law, and means far more than ability to act under international law.[445]

The view developed here must consider the international law position of the English Dominions. Until the World War, they were undoubtedly to be viewed as dependent countries, and their ability to act under international law, despite the extensive trade policy independence of Canada since 1907, to be construed as delegated by the mother country. This found its most striking expression in the fact that the Dominions entered the World War without their own declarations of war, at the same time as the English declaration. What the legal and power situation is today cannot, or cannot yet, be said. At the Paris Peace Conference, the representatives of the Dominions and India still appeared with powers of attorney signed

443 See Verdroß, *Völkerrechtsgemeinschaft* (see note 137), p. 120 f.

444 See Triepel, *Völkerrecht* (see note 166), p. 358 ff; Paul Schoen, *Die völkerrechtliche Haftung der Staaten aus unerlaubten Handlungen*, 2d supplementary volume to *Zeitschrift für Völkerrecht*, 10 (1917/18), p. 100 ff.; Anzilotti, *Corso*, p. 269 ff.; Moore, *Digest*, (see note 361), vol. 6, p. 663 f.

445 See, quite characterictically, Karl Strupp, *Das völkerrechtliche Delikt*, Stuttgart 1920 (Handbuch des Völkerrechts, ed. F. Stier-Somlo, vol. 3, sec. IV a), p. 24 ff., who considers the concept of sovereignty in international law to be only confusing (see above, note 94), but is forced, in establishing the capability to commit delicts under international law, to have recourse to sovereignty.

by the English King. Even their acceptance into the League of Nations[446] and the Reich Conference of 1926 provided no clear evidence.[447] The practice of the League of Nations also permits no ultimate decision on whether the increase of votes to seven due to the addition of Ireland represented a political body that can also be classed juristically as a decision-making unit, or if these were independent votes and independent states in a confederation, or even a personal union. Dissent between the motherland and the Dominions on secondary issues in the League of Nations Assembly, incidentally, by no means provides a solution to the problem.

We believe we have demonstrated that sovereignty is constitutive for the concept of the international law person. Our theory of the universal territorial unit of decision-making and effect gains its most important rationale and proof from the emergence and termination of international law personality.

According to the dominant doctrine, the "existence of a state can only be based legally on its own will."[448] As substanceless as the dominant doctrine views this state will to be, and as wrong as its theory of the internally unconnected 'state elements' may be, this proposition remains indisputable. The international law fact of the 'state' owes its emergence solely to an act of will that constituted it, and to neither an international nor a state law legal rule. The fact that a universally decisive power unit asserts and establishes itself independently on a territory forms the starting point for all international law norms. In the dispute between France and England regarding the French King's recognition of the United States on February 6, 1778, which is fundamental to the problem of the emergence of states in international law, the French maintained that, because all the English efforts to subjugate the Americans had failed, it was enough for France that the former colonies "have established their independence, not only by a solemn act, but also as a matter of fact, and they have maintained it against the efforts of their mother country."[449] France did not have to verify the legitimacy of the territorial power.[450] For the emergence of a state, the issue is thus primarily a fact of power, unregulated and not to be regulated by law—simply the fact that the state is "able to *assert* itself on a delimited territory, internally and externally."[451]

Before the existence of such a territorial decision-making power, there can theoretically be no legal rules for it. Both state law and international law come about for this state only with and through its act of will. Therefore, theory and practice contradict the claim that "A legal rule must first be *presupposed*, so that a particular complex of behaviours can be stamped with the *fact* of having become a 'lawmaking

[446] See Schücking/Wehberg, *Satzung des Völkerbundes* (see note 353), p. 178 f.

[447] See Karl Löwenstein, "Das heutige Verfassungsrecht des britischen Weltreichs," in *Jahrbuch des öffentlichen Rechts*, 13 (1925), p. 404 ff.; especially, however, Karl Heck, *Der Aufbau des britischen Reiches. Der Verhandlungsbericht der Reichskonferenz von 1926*, Berlin 1927 (Beiträge zum ausländischen öffentlichen Recht und Völkerrecht, vol. 3), with extensive literature. Chamberlain's declaration in the League of Nations Council on March 9, 1927 is significant: "The seat which I occupy here and in the Assembly is attributed by the Covenant to the 'British Empire,' but the Dominions sit in the Assembly in their own name," League of Nations (ed.), *Official Journal*, 8 (1927), p. 377.

[448] Jellinek, *Staatslehre* (see note 3), p. 274.

[449] Charles de Martens, *Nouvelles causes célèbres du droit des gens*, vol. 1, Leipzig 1843, p. 484.

[450] Ibid. [451] Similarly, Verdroß, *Völkerrechtsgemeinschaft*, p. 131.

institution.' "[452] A state in the international law sense is not "one that is regulated by international law,"[453] but a fact that is presupposed by international law and entirely removed from its regulation. It is precisely there that the sovereignty of the state is expressed, in that, breaching positive law, it is able to make new law solely through the fact that it asserts and establishes itself as a territorial decision-making unit. To grasp this feature, which no jurist can ignore, the concept of capacity to act is insufficient; it is only satisfied by the concept of sovereignty, which for this very reason cannot be identified with "international law responsibility" or construed as "international law immediacy."[454]

The fact that the emergence of a state is a process that cannot be regulated by international law, and that even a universal territorial decision-making unit that has no connection to international law is still a sovereign state, must be the starting point for considering the recognition problem in international law. In the dispute over the declarative or constitutive significance of recognition under international law, we must first distinguish whether we mean recognition of a fact situation as a state or recognition of the same fact situation as an international law person. In the first case, recognition under international law is certainly not constitutive, as in the second case it cannot only be declarative. The emergence of a state must be accepted by international law as a *fait accompli*, which is not to be recognized or not recognized, but simply acknowledged. The only thing that can be recognized in this *fait accompli* within the scope of international law refers solely to its international law qualifications. Just as a slave is not born a legal person, and another legal person has nothing to recognize in this birth as such, so a state is not born into an international law community, nor can the fact of its emergence be recognized. Should the slave, as a legal person, be accepted into the legal community, this would require a specific act of will by the fellow members of the legal community. International law recognition of a new state therefore always refers only to its international law personality, and likewise requires an unambiguous act of will on the part of the recognizer, as well as the voluntary agreement of the recognized state. Before recognition is complete, the new state possesses no international law personality, and thus there can no more be a legal relationship between it and international law persons than there can be a legal relationship between a slave and a legal person. No legal rule exists that would oblige states to recognize a new state.[455]

[452] Verdroß, *Einheit* (see note 96), p. 58; Kelsen, *passim*.

[453] Verdroß, *Völkerrechtsgemeinschaft*, p. 129; Kelsen, *Problem der Souveränität* (see note 38), p. 228 ff. here, too, positivity, separated from sovereignty, takes its revenge; under the precondition of the norm "agreements are to be kept," says Verdroß (*Völkerrechtsgemeinschaft*, p. 127), "no *significant* difference" exists between the state of nature and the state of law based on contract. This brings us right back to Enlightenment natural law.

[454] See Verdroß, *Völkerrechtsgemeinschaft*, p. 118 f. John Fischer Williams, "Sovereignty, Seisin, and the League," in *The British Yearbook of International Law*, 7 (1926), p. 31, recently correctly pointed out that even if no conquest has taken place, "the consent of dispossessed state is not a condition *sine qua non* of a valid transfer of territory."

[455] See Anzilotti, *Corso* (see note 361), p. 91 f. The opposite view would remove the indispensable basis in will from international law and sovereignty from the international law persons, but it fails due to internal contradictions despite its fictions. Thus Verdroß (*Völkerrechtsgemeinschaft*, p. 128) allows states to be "legal organs" in international law even before their recognition, even though they are only

It is not a contradiction to understand states that are not yet recognized under international law as extra-international law facts, on the one hand, and, on the other, to allow their acts of state as such to have internal validity. Recognition under international law refers to nothing more than the international law personality of the new state; it doesn't have anything to do with its state law qualifications. Without recognizing a single one of the new state's legal rules as legal rules, I can still recognize them as the legal rules of the new state, as long as I establish the fact, still in no way normative as a matter of international law for the international law persons, that a universal decision-making unit has asserted itself on the territory as a new state. Acts of state of the non-recognized new state can never create international law, it is true, but of course they can have relevant state law effects for other states. For such effects, it is neither necessary for 'international law' to accept these acts as acts of state internally and externally, nor for the deciding state in the particular case to require that its act should be treated as the acts of a recognized state. Nowhere can such legal rules be shown to exist; if they did, they would be unnecessary. Acts of state need international law recognition only to the extent that they purport to be normative in international law. If a state act by a non-recognized state or government—cases that are the same in this regard—was to come before the court of an international law person, this court could not possibly deny the social fact that, on that territory, a system of unification of wills exists that has constituted a territorial decision-making unit, whose representatives are normally obeyed and whose commands count as legal precepts on that territory. All these social facts must be recognized by the court. They are addressed solely to its recognition function; a legal rule could not order its recognition. Without any legal rule, for example, it recognizes that A, who took possession of something from B against his will on the basis of a legal rule in force in that state, is not a thief, but carried out an expropriation. As long as the international law validity of the expropriation is not before the court, the issue is merely the recognition of social facts. That fact that the act of state of the non-recognized state has nothing to do with international law would be immediately clear if it were to claim immunity before a foreign court. Without at least preliminary recognition of the new state or revolutionary government, no international law person exists. The non-recognized state is "existent in international law" and a 'potential' international law person[456] in exactly the same sense as a slave exists as a potential legal person and a legally relevant fact.

These theoretical observations can be confirmed in their entire content by practice. The Supreme Court of the United States declared in 1808 that the sovereignty of a new state precedes the treaty of recognition; it is "anterior to and independent of the treaty." The new state can thus decide which persons possess its citizenship.[457] In a judgment of October 5, 1905, the Swiss Federal Court gave the opinion that, "in

"potential members" of the state community based founded on the fundamental norm of "agreements must be kept." This state community, however, as Verdroß himself admits (see above, note 401), is not yet a legal community; the non-recognized states are thus legal organs of a non-legal community.

456 Verdroß, *Völkerrechtsgemeinschaft* (see note 137), p. 140.

457 Moore, *Digest* (see note 361), vol. 3, p. 290 (McIlvaine v. Coxe's Lessee, 4 Cranch, p. 209 (214)).

case of the existence ... of a state power not founded in international law, even if it has been expressly denied recognition by all or some other states ... the internal state law acts of such a state power [are to be] treated equally to those of a lawfully existing government in the sense of international law, that is, the subjects of the institutions of the actual ruling polity are to be given their due, whether this polity is in conformity with international law or is in conflict with it."[458] The American decisions regarding acts of state of the non-recognized Soviet government are especially clear.[459] Thus, in the case of the Russian Reinsurance Company, the above-developed principle was clearly expressed: "The fall of one governmental establishment and the substitution of another governmental establishment which actually governs, which is able to enforce its claims by military force and is obeyed by the people over whom it rules, must profoundly affect all the acts and duties, all the relations of those who live within the territory over which the new establishment exercises rule. Its rule may be without lawful foundation; but, lawful or unlawful, its existence is a fact, and that fact cannot be destroyed by juridical concepts."[460] It is incomprehensible how Verdroß, who emphasizes the final words of this decision in boldface, can find evidence in them that non-recognized states and governments "are responsible under international law for implementing those acts of state that, under international law, are part of the state's internal sphere of activity."[461] It is these very decisions that show irrefutably that the emergence of states cannot be regulated legally, but that recognition under international law is constitutive for a new state's international law personality.

Just as a sovereign state can emerge as a pure fact of power vis-à-vis existing state and international law, it can perish in the same way, regardless of whether positive international law is violated by this or not, and regardless especially of what positive state law has to say about it. While the continuity of a state through a revolutionary change to its constitution is disputed in state law, in international law it can be considered indisputable that the fact of 'the demise of the state' is not the same as the end of the validity of a particular positive constitution. By virtue of customary international law, the state individuality of the same international law person remains, even if it radically revolutionizes its constitution and government.[462] This customary law rule is the most striking evidence for the fact that the problem of international law and the state can be understood as a relationship between will and norm, but not a relationship between two legal orders.[463] That legal rule would not be capable of

[458] *Zeitschrift für Völkerrecht und Bundesstaatsrecht*, I (1907), p. 280 (Entscheidungen des Schweizerischen Bundesgerichts, Amtliche Sammlung, XXXI 2 (1905), p. 828 (860)).

[459] See the good summary of cases in Verdroß, *Völkerrechtsgemeinschaft*, p. 134 ff.

[460] Verdroß, ibid., p. 136 note 1 (Russian Reinsurance Company v. Stoddard et al. (1925), 240 N.Y. 149, 147 N. E., p. 703 (705)).

[461] Verdroß, ibid., p. 137.

[462] Hall/Higgins, *International Law* (see note 430), p. 21; Verdroß, *Völkerrechtsgemeinschaft*, p. 145, with numerous good examples.

[463] See Kelsen and Verdroß (see above, p. 149); the latter, however, states that the demise of a state is legally always about the demise of the "state power" (op. cit., p. 149) and continuing validity of the same international law person, as long as the new constitution is established for the same "association of persons" (op. cit., p. 151).

being construed juristically if one dissolved the state into positive law and rejected a state will that is founded in a state people and is independent of a change in legal form, and whose identity and individuality is at stake in this case. What else but that state will did the French–Chilean arbitration panel mean, in its decision of July 5, 1901, when it spoke of: "The usurper who in fact retains power with the express or tacit asset of the nation acts and decides validly in the name of the state," with the result that the restored legitimate government had to give representation to its acts of international law.[464]

The sovereign decision-making unit thus emerges and disappears with its existence as a social fact of power. The emergence and demise of states is essentially not regulated by international law; they themselves regulate international law.

Thus, the discussion in this section has proven that sovereignty, as a universal territorial decision-making power that asserts itself even in opposition to international law, is a fundamental requirement for international law personality. Even if one were to identify one or another exception and admit to additional exceptions, it would be like studying the anatomy of international law on the basis of a pathological object if one were to construct the concept of the international law person on the basis of these exceptions. It is a banal fact that reality exhibits fluid transitions. Like all concepts based on social coexistence, juristic concepts are ideal-typical or representational, and not generic. The higher one climbs from civil law to public state law to international law, the narrower becomes the basis for abstraction. However, it also becomes clearer that the jurist's concepts do not permit total subsumption of examples under the genus, but, gained through logical isolation and idealization, represent individual phenomena in their typical similarity, but do not at all exhaust their scientific significance. Therefore, all juristic concepts are clear only at their center, but have an 'aureole' at the margins. Sovereignty forms the center of the concept of the international law person. To give it up because this concept, too, has an aureole would mean fundamentally confusing the formation of concepts in natural science and cultural science, and would render the concept of the international law person completely incomprehensible.

Sovereignty is thus not a completely superfluous term for a completely nonexistent purity of legal understanding, but the indispensable term for that property of a universal territorially decisive unit of will that allows it to assert itself even against positive law. Neither international law positivity nor legal personality can be construed without this concept of sovereignty.

[464] *Revue générale de droit international public*, 29 (1922), p. 279; further, ibid., p. 275 f.

# VIII

## The Claim of Sovereignty in International Law and against International Law

Where contemporary international law doctrine does not completely eliminate the concept of sovereignty, it attempts at least to minimize it. The attempt is made to draw its fangs by construing the nature of sovereignty as a kind of modest, legally normed capacity to act, as authority under international law, or as a discretionary sphere granted by international law. What an illusion! This operation can never succeed using the tools of international law. For international law is only possible as long as there are at least two absolutely independent territorial decision-making units. And only as long as this is true does sovereignty in the sense of conclusive law-making that violates international law remain possible, which cannot be imagined as authority delegated by an international law system.

Juristically, this fact is expressed first of all in the doctrine, which has not been seriously contested, that international law is addressed only to states, and that for it to be valid domestically, it requires transformation by a state act of will that is particularly directed to this end.[465] Nor can it be seriously contested that an act of state contrary to international law is law and remains law until a further act of state provides differently. All international law is realized only through acts of state! This proposition, however, would have already solved our problem. The possibility of law that violates international law and is conclusive can only be contested through the phrase 'for that which must not, cannot be.'

And it has been contested with this phrase. We already know that the *crux* of legal rationalism is the defective act of state. If legal rationalism is to remain consistent, it always faces "the logical impossibility of ascribing a wrong . . . to the personification of law—of letting the will of the law will illegality."[466] Because he can only imagine valid international law if "the individual state law norms and the international law norms form a unified system," Kelsen finds an international law delict "inconceivable," but an act of state that violates international law is "null and void . . . not only under international law, but also under state law."[467]

[465] As one of many, see Triepel, *Völkerrecht* (see note 166), p. 9, 111 ff.; Anzilotti, *Corso* (see note 361), p. 30 ff.

[466] Kelsen, *Problem der Souveränität* (see note 38), p. 147.

[467] Ibid., p. 147 f.

Now, Kelsen's view is such a slap in the face to the theory and practice of all nations that it has been rejected by international law experts of his own school.[468] But even Verdroß, as a legal rationalist, had to construe the 'state order' as a "spinoff" of 'the' international legal order, and sovereignty accordingly as a "bundle of international legal obligations," a discretionary sphere granted to the states by 'international law' that is "different in degree but not in kind from the discretion of domestic organs."[469]

Here and nowhere else is where the knot of the sovereignty problem is gathered. "Here is Rhodes, there I jump!" [*Hic Rhodus, hic salta*!] Certainly, it is the same legal phenomenon of defective acts of state in the domestic and international law arenas that constitutes the unified fact of sovereignty. But because there cannot be above the universal unit of decision-making and effect a similar unit, the problem of sovereignty is therefore the problem of effectively guarding the guard; sovereignty is therefore something fundamentally different from a domestic sphere of discretion. First of all, domestic discretion is indeed a spinoff of a universal legal order, which is not 'the' international law. Second of all, discretion "against the law" does not, in principle, become law. But where it becomes law as a defective act of state, this happens not on the basis of a positive legal norm, but as the expression of sovereignty that asserts itself against law and nevertheless makes law. All defective acts of state are only conclusively normative to the extent they do not revoke an act of state emanating from the same or a superior position. This revocation, however, presumes, first of all, the potential universality, and, second, the actual effectiveness of a decision. The two qualities are joined only in a sovereign state. Above it is neither a universal decision-making unit nor a unit of effect that would prevent the act of state that is asserting itself against that decision from maturing into law. As long as there is international law and no world state, there must be many sovereign states, and thus the possibility that an act of state creates conclusive and unappealable new law through the breach of state and international law. That world history here becomes an earthly world court, that here only war can ultimately decide, is not a discovery of faithless and amoral imperialism, but an idea from which the entire Middle Ages, especially Thomas Aquinas, determined the concept of the prince, that is, the state concept of the time: "It is not within the capacity of a private person to make war because he can seek justice in the judgment of his superior."[470]

Naturally there are and have also been, from the most ancient times, peaceful means of dispute settlement between states. Especially in recent decades, the states have created numerous international decision-making institutions suited to determine disputed law in numerous cases. But international law even today has no

[468] Verdroß, *Einheit* (see note 96), p. 166 f.; Verdroß, *Völkerrechtsgemeinschaft* (see note 137), p. 34 ff. (36); Fritz Sander, *Staat und Recht. Prolegomena zu einer Theorie der Rechtserfahrung*, Leipzig and Vienna 1922 (Wiener Staatswissenschaftliche Studien, Neue Folge, vol. 1), vol. 1, part ii, p. 1138.

[469] Verdroß, *Völkerrechtsgemeinschaft*, pp. 118, 182, 35.

[470] Thomas Aquinas, *Summa theologiae*, secunda secundae, qu. XL, art. 1.4 (quoted in Verdroß, *Einheit*, p. 19). On this, see Kant (see above, note 355).

general decision-making units, and cannot have any universal ones as long as international law exists and states remain sovereign.

Until the World War, the international arbitral panels were such interstate decision-making institutions, based on voluntary agreement between two sovereign states, appointed for each individual case, terminable by one side, and functioning through judges who made their decisions in the name of the parties that freely chose them. Only second-tier cases were submitted to them for decision. It is clear that this type of dispute settlement in no way derogates from the states' sovereignty.

The sovereignty problem has become more complicated for members of the League of Nations and its Permanent International Court in The Hague. The principles of a treaty order free of domination on which these institutions rest have not fundamentally changed; voluntariness and unanimity are preserved under these principles. The League of Nations and the Court unquestionably do not form a universal decision-making unit; the sovereignty of the states is guaranteed under this principle.[471]

The League of Nations, together with the international courts, is not a universal decision-making institution primarily because the so-called *obligatorium*, the absolute duty to settle disputes peacefully, does not exist and—as will be discussed shortly—cannot exist. All that is obligatory is the attempt to achieve a peaceful settlement. War, including aggressive war, is expressly envisaged, even though numerous conditions have been placed on its lawfulness. A lawful war is—if we do not take into account warlike actions that are termed execution—envisaged first of all for cases in which the Council, in a non-justiciable dispute, comes to a non-unanimous advisory opinion, of course irrespective of the objections of the parties to the dispute. Second, for cases in which both parties fail to acquiesce in the opinion. Third, when the Council fails to submit its report within six months or the arbitral judges do not submit their decision within a reasonable period.[472]

Above all, however, war is expressly envisioned in Article 15(8) of the Covenant: "If the dispute between the parties is claimed by one of them, and is found by the Council, to arise out of a matter which by international law is solely within the domestic jurisdiction of that party, the Council shall so report, and shall make no recommendation as to its settlement."[473]

[471] See also Schücking/Wehberg, *Satzung des Völkerbundes* (see note 353), p. 88; see above, note 429 and Leon Bourgeois's statement on January 24, 1924 in the French Senate, quoted in Carl Schmitt, *Die Kernfrage des Völkerbundes*, Berlin 1926 (Völkerrechtsfragen, vol. 18), p. 10; see also the discussion in the 6th session of the First League of Nations Commission of September 20, 1926, between Hurst, Barthelemy, Scialoja, and Latham; the last explained, in support of Hurst, that he believed that if one could not from the beginning limit "the future activity of the League, one should not forget that each country desires to be master of its internal affairs, and believes that it would be to the advantage of the League never to forget this," Sociètè des Nations (ed.), *Journal officiel*, Supplément spécial (Séances plénières et Commissions), no. 45, Geneva 1926, p. 19 ff. (22).

[472] See Schucking/Wehberg, *Satzung des Völkerbundes*, p. 92 ff.; 596. Against this interpretation (ibid., p. 589 f.) of Art. 15(8), which contradicts its meaning and wording as well as its international interpretation, see the text above.

[473] (Friedensvertrag von Versailles, June 28, 1919, Part 1, *RGBl.* 1919, p. 687 ff. (730).)

This provision is crucial to the nature of the League of Nations and the sovereignty of its members. The case provided for here is correctly called the sovereignty case; the first draft of Article 15(8) described it using the words "a question that is, in public law, the exclusive portfolio of the national legislative jurisdiction of one of the parties." The same set of facts is also called a "domestic affair" [*affaire domestique*] or "reserved domain."

If we try to understand this sovereignty case using the concepts we have developed, we must first determine its extent. In regard to form, it is indicated by the fact that non-arbitrable and non-judiciable issues are counted as part of it. According to dominant, though in places disputed, doctrine, substantively included in its ambit are vital interests, honor and independence, as well as the state's constitutional law. In the nature of things, as we will soon see, the substance belonging within this area is highly indeterminate. The authors of the League of Nations Covenant, who adopted Article 15(8) into the Statute at the urging of Wilson and some neutral powers, were probably thinking primarily of the issue of the immigration of alien races, which was at that time a particularly important issue in American politics, of the Monroe Doctrine, customs tariffs, and citizenship.[474] The draft law on ratification of the Versailles Peace Treaty, rejected by the United States Senate on March 19, listed, in addition to the above-mentioned matters, the issues of labor, coastal trade and trade in general, trafficking in women and children, and trafficking in opium and harmful drugs, and finally added the very typical wording, "and all other domestic questions."[475]

There is an astonishing lack of clarity in the literature on the significance of the "exclusive competence" [*compétence exclusive*] in Article 15(8) of the Pact; but such astonishment is justified only to the extent that this lack of clarity was not politically intended. A large number of writers treat this "exclusive competence" as analogous to the jurisdiction of a state organ of the rule of law state, and the relationship between international law and the League of Nations, on the one hand, and the state, on the other hand, is discussed in such a manner as if it were a dispute over authority between two local tax offices in the same state province. Behind these kinds of conceptions is always the skewed idea of a universal international law order of decision-making and authority, a universal international law system that normalizes international law acts. Even the creation of international law that violates international law must ultimately be seen as being 'normed' by international law. This can easily be achieved by a juristic idealism, satisfied with value-free logical construction of the facts, through the theory of the "metamorphosis of the factual into the normative."[476] If one then accepts a contentless basic international law norm, the claim may indeed be made that "domestic law is also [dependent] on that basic norm,

[474] Schücking/Wehberg, op. cit., p. 591 f.; Politis, "Limitations de la souveraineté" (see note 98), p. 49; on the issue of citizenship, see the advisory opinion of the Permanent Court of International Justice of February 7, 1923, Société des Nations (ed.), *Publications de la Cour permanente de Justice Internationale*, Série B (Recueil des avis consultatifs), no. 4, Leiden 1923, p. 24.

[475] Henry Cabot Lodge, *The Senate and the League of Nations*, New York 1925, p. 185 (see *Congressional Record*, no. 59, pt. 5, p. 4599, Resolution of ratification, Art. 4).

[476] Kelsen, *Problem der Souveränität* (see note 38), p. 241.

since the limits within which states may move and develop freely are likewise set by international law norms."[477] Now the problem of making law in violation of international law vanishes, and sovereignty is an authority no different from the independent sphere of activity of any mayor. We find similar reasoning in Politis in interpreting Article 15(8). He would like to avoid answering the question whether the state's decision-making power is "recognized or merely tolerated" by international law, by using the phrase: "It would be most embarrassing to have to choose between the two." But his opinion becomes clear in his statement that he finds it "in effect inconceivable that the law itself decides that such a human activity remains beyond its grasp."[478] This 'law' of Politis is identical to Kelsen's universal system of law, through which the sovereignty of states is merely delegated as authority. Politis even assures us that the "reserved domain" is only "comprised of the sum of gaps in the law."[479] But to the "objective question" of who determines the limits of this "reserved domain," we receive the answer: "In case of controversy ... through international means"[480]—an all in all somewhat questionable decision-making unit, if one considers that conflicts tend generally to arise from the antagonism of public opinion.

All this reasoning fails to recognize that while the League of Nations is not a universal decision-making unit, the state is. It is not international law that delegates sovereignty, but the state that, through its acts of will, delegates certain powers to the League of Nations. Thus, we can enumerate the cases that represent a sovereign person's obligations to international law, but not the substance of an "exclusive competence," that is, a universal decision-making unit. One may speak of a competence-competence on the part of the state, a not very nice and not very clear phrase, which implies something similar to what our universality of decision-making means; the identification of competence and sovereignty is, however, the expression of a view that makes the state a fiction, in order to be able to make the fiction of a "world state."

Any limitation on a universal territorial decision-making unit is only possible by treaty, and only in particular expressly normed areas. Any decision-making institution brought into being by treaty, be it an arbitral panel, a court, or even just political mediation, possesses clear limits drawn by the sovereignty of the delegating states. If a state has not subjected itself by treaty to any decision-making institutions, it is solely itself that decides on the limits of its activity, within the bounds of fundamental legal principles. The Senate of the United States was therefore fully empowered under international law to make the resolution of March 13, 1920 in which it declared, "The United States reserves to itself exclusively the right to decide what questions are within its domestic jurisdiction."[481]

[477] Verdroß, *Völkerrechtsgemeinschaft* (see note 137), p. 35. [478] Politis, op. cit., p. 47 f.
[479] Ibid., p. 56. [480] Ibid., p. 51.
[481] Lodge, op. cit., p. 185 (Reservation no. 5 Senator Kellogg, see *Congressional Record* (see note 475), ibid.).

# IX

# The Juristic Limits of and the Absolute Character of Sovereignty

This study results in the following thesis: *sovereignty is the characteristic of a universal territorial unit of decision-making and effect, by virtue of which, for the sake of law, it sometimes asserts itself absolutely against law.*

The fact that sovereignty preserves its absolute character despite highly developed international law, regardless of the great economic and other dependence of states, seems to many jurists to be an insoluble logical contradiction. Its juristic solution is simply enough.

A large number of the misunderstandings that one encounters with particular frequency in the French and Anglo-American literature are eliminated in a moment if the juristic character of the concept of sovereignty is emphasized.[482] All the states' social interdependence does not itself negate their juristic independence. In fact, however, to this day, international social integration corresponds with the particularity of the nation state. Even the peace treaty forced upon the conquered state by the victor does not, as has recently been emphatically claimed,[483] negate the sovereignty of the conquered, but only confirms it. The force of war is extra-legal in nature. The martial superiority of the victor, if it does not end with the utter conquest of the defeated, does not then create any 'command authority' on the part of the victor, who, precisely because it chooses the form of a treaty to establish peace, recognizes the defeated not as conquered, but as a continuing international law person. International law does not take cognizance of the force preceding the peace treaty to the extent it is aimed at the state. As long as international law does not prohibit belligerent self-help, it cannot prohibit threats of forced self-help against a state.

Nor does the concept of sovereignty lose its absolute character as a result of any international law obligations. Even the extensive decision-making powers of international courts and arbitral panels cannot eliminate it. As Pillet, to whom we owe the best study of our problem, correctly noted: "International law does not and cannot exist apart from distinct nations, separate, and living their own lives. So it

[482] See above, p. 140 f.

[483] Jahrreiß, *Rechtliche Liquidation* (see note 126), p. 53 f. Against this, see Friedrich Karl Neubecker, *Zwang und Notstand in rechtsvergleichender Darstellung*, vol. 1, Leipzig 1910, p. 134 ff., with comprehensive literature. See also Williams, "Sovereignty" (see note 454), p. 30 ff.

must therefore write on the pediment of its edifice that nations have the right to preserve themselves and to freely take the measures that serve this objective."[484] This absolute right of self-preservation demanded by international law is the basis for the absolute character of sovereignty.

Given the necessary linkage, as shown, between the positivity of law and state sovereignty, the absolute right of self-preservation of the latter is a self-evident and unavoidable requirement of a clearly thought out positivism. The hierarchical structure of law theoretically ends where the universal territorial decision-making unit that positivizes law stands. This unit, which we would initially like to imagine as a "world state," must be imagined as a will, and cannot be construed as a normative order, because the individual and his history cannot be definitively rationalized; there will always be situations where the predictions of that positive legal order fail, and a will "according to the demands of the case, of the times and of persons" has to decide even without and against positive law. But that universal decision-making unit must also be recognized by jurists as a will and not as a norm, because only a vital unit of effect could prevent lawmaking by lawbreakers. Positivity of law means both decisiveness and effectiveness of law, but both are absolutely dependent upon the existence of a unit of will that, in the modern centralization of lawmaking, means a state. And this is why the absolute self-preservation of the state is the highest fundamental legal principle. It is the necessary legal prerequisite for both the state legal order and all international law norms, which are always positivized only by state or state-delegated acts of will. If even the most radical legal rationalism has to admit that international law "becomes a meaningless fragment without the simultaneous supplemental validity of the state legal order,"[485] then anyone who does not identify the state and law must, as a jurist, honor the state's absolute right to self-preservation.

In substance, this is as good as undisputed in literature[486] and practice. However, first of all, the character of the right to self-preservation, its prerequisites and its effects are contested in the literature. Most recently, Strupp has shown beyond question, on the basis of extensive historical material, that international law practice recognizes this right.[487] Yet it is theoretically irrelevant whether a statesman in a given case has, correctly or incorrectly, pleaded the presence of the existential case; all that matters is whether the absolute right of self-preservation is recognized as such. On this condition, Lord Wellesley's remark at a session of the English upper house on February 8, 1808 is quite significant: "The great maxims of the law of nations were founded on the law of nature; and the law of security or self-preservation was,

[484] Antoine Pillet, *Recherches sur les droit fondamentaux des états*, Paris 1899, p. 5.

[485] Kelsen, *Problem der Souveränität* (see note 38), p. 122.

[486] One would have to offer as good as the entire international literature of international law as positive proof. See the literature citations in Erich Kaufmann, *Wesen des Völkerrechts* (see note 283), p. 192 ff.; Strupp, *Völkerrechtliches Delikt* (see note 444), p. 122 f.; Sigmund Cybichowski, *Studien zum internationals Recht*, Berlin 1912, p. 21 ff.; A. V. Kirchenheim, "Grundrechte der Staaten," in Karl Strupp, *Wörterbuch des Völkerrechts und der Diplomatie*, vol. 1, Berlin 1924, p. 440; Hall/Higgins, *International Law* (see note 430), p. 264; Pillet, op. cit.

[487] Strupp, op. cit., p. 122 ff.

among those, the most important and sacred."[488] In 1916, in the *Zamora* case, the English Privy Council declared that there were "cases of necessity in which the right of self-defence supersedes and dispenses with the usual modes of procedure."[489] Besides these statements by national institutions, there is Metternich's declaration on the Krakow affair of January 9, 1847, appealing to "the first law of each state, the right of self-preservation and of the protection of its subjects";[490] a principle that England and France recognized in principle, in that the former only denied an "adequate necessity,"[491] and the latter raised the question whether there was any other means (*d'autre moyen*) to achieve the purpose.[492] In the *Virginius* case (1873), Spain's actions were attacked by the United States only to the extent that they were not backed by any "imminent necessity of self-defence."[493] In the *Caroline* case, the two participants most clearly acknowledged a "necessity, which controls all other laws,"[494] a "great law of self-defence,"[495] the prerequisites for which were recognized by Secretary of State Webster, in a note on August 6, 1842, as being present in cases in which the "necessity of that self-defence is instant, overwhelming, and leaving no choice of means, and no moment for deliberation."[496]

If we add to this summary overview Article 23(g) of the Hague Rules of Land Warfare, in the version of 1907, which forbids "the destruction or seizing of enemy property" but then continues "except in cases where this destruction or seizing would be imperiously commanded by the necessities of war,"[497] there should be sufficient evidence to support the claim that international law practice is acquainted with the state's absolute right of self-preservation.

For the controversial juristic construction of this right, its absolute character is crucial. Here, too, jurisprudence attempts without success to provide a minimizing relativization by construing this absolute right as analogous to self-defense or state of emergency in civil and criminal law. But this overlooks the fact that it blurs exactly that fundamental difference between the sovereign state's absolute right of self-preservation and the merely relative right of self-preservation of all other legal persons without exception, which is of crucial importance for concept formation in state law and international law. But how can one determine the bearer of this right without enlisting the concept of sovereignty, and in fact absolute sovereignty? It is

[488] T. C. Hansard, *The Parliamentary Debates from the Year 1803 to the Present Times*, vol. X, London 1812, col. 348.

[489] *Prize Cases heard and Decided in the Prize Court During the Great War*, vol. 2 (ed. Albert Wallace Grant), London 1918, p. 22.

[490] Metternich to Dietrichstein, January 9, 1847, in Georges Fréderic de Martens, *Nouveau Recueil général de Traités*, 10 (1847), Göttingen 1852, p. 125.

[491] Palmerston to Ponsonby, November 23, 1846, in Martens, ibid., p. 111.

[492] Guizot to the Austrian cabinet, December 4, 1846, in Martens, ibid., p. 118.

[493] Moore, *Digest* (see note 361), vol. 2, p. 903.

[494] Lord Ashburton to Webster, July 28, 1842, in Moore, ibid., vol. 2, p. 411.

[495] Webster to Ashburton, August 6, 1842, in Moore, ibid., vol. 2, p. 412.

[496] Moore, Digest, vol. 2, p. 412. On the also juristically confused declaration by Bethmann-Hollwig regarding Belgium on August 4, 1914, correctly, see Strupp, *Völkerrechtliches Delikt* (see note 444), p. 141, no. 10 [143]; 158 f.

[497] (Annexe à la Convention IV, concernant les lois et coutumes de la guerre sur terre, in *Recueil international des traités du XXe siècle*, Paris 1907, p. 262.)

clear that an absolute right of self-preservation cannot be attributed to either some private legal person or a municipality. But what about a vassal state, a genuine protectorate relationship, or above all the member states of a federal state? In seeking to determine the international law person's 'emergency law' according to its delictual liability under international law, one merely shifts the question onto another track. One likewise avoids the answer when one refers to the "state law and not international law" nature of the question in regard to 'emergency law' in member states and 'semi-sovereign' states.[498] That neither an independent state nor a member state can be attributed an absolute right to self-preservation arises from the necessary sovereignty of the supreme state. There are cases in which the supreme state makes decisions about the existence of the legal persons integrated into it, without them being able to call upon a right to emergency law or self-defense. The sovereign state always ultimately decides on the behavior of all legal persons without exception on its territory, and its right of self-preservation is alone absolute, just as, where its existence is at issue, it alone can violate the interests of other international law persons that are protected by international law.[499]

Because of its absolute character and character as a legal presupposition, we refuse to construe the state's right of self-preservation as analogous to the state of emergency of other legal persons.[500] We must see in this claim by a sovereign state the subjective correlate of a supreme fundamental legal principle, which, as a prerequisite to a law, should in fact be described as a basic norm, but in a subjective respect must be called a basic right of states. The old doctrine of a state's multiple basic rights has more recently been vehemently criticized and certainly cannot be upheld in its traditional form. Indeed, the basic rights to equality, respect, independence, intercourse, judiciary, and so on convey too much and too little; what is essential and also indispensable about them implicates the basic right to self-preservation.[501] But how indispensable this basic right is, is shown by the practice of the Catholic Church, which is no longer bound by its Concordat once its highest interests are at stake.

Because the sovereign state's right of self-preservation is the prerequisite for any legal validity, it is also an immanent limit to the validity of any law. The doctrine of "as long as these conditions persist," which has become "general opinion" [*communis opinio*], curiously wishes to develop this thinking only for international treaty law,

[498] Strupp, op. cit., p. 150. See above, note 445.

[499] That the federal state is authorized in extreme cases, if danger threatens it through the international law-violating behavior of the member states, to force the member states to act in accordance with international law even if no legal rule empowers it to, was already emphasized by Haenel, *Staatsrecht* (see note 301), vol. 1, p. 355, and Triepel, *Völkerrecht* (see note 166), p. 379.

[500] Most recently, in particular detail, see Strupp, who, however, presumes "emergency law"; but there is no emergency law because there is no "counter right" (Strupp, op. cit., p. 144; 148).

[501] See the critique in Heilborn, *Das System des Völkerrechts*, Berlin 1896, p. 279 ff., and Georg Jellinek, *System* (see note 168), p. 316 ff.; if the catalogue of basic rights conveys only that "the state has the right to be a state" (Jellinek, op. cit., p. 316), it still conveys a great deal, assuming a resolved concept of the state. Pillet, too, *Recherches* (see note 484), p. 4, reckons that the right to self-preservation is one of the "incontestable rights and of capital importance" and because it recognizes its objectively norming character, can ultimately (ibid., pp. 41, 47) identify with its "right to mutual respect of their sovereignty." As above, see Kauffmann, *Wesen des Völkerrechts* (see note 283), p. 196; v. Kirchenheim, op. cit., p. 438.

but within it always makes use of a sphere of rule to an extent that it certainly does not deserve. According to Erich Kaufmann, international law treaties only bind "as long as the situation of power and interests obtaining at the time they are concluded does not change so much that essential provisions of the treaty become incompatible with the right of self-preservation of the contracting states."[502] The provision thus formulated must be unreservedly endorsed. It is to this extent merely an application to treaties under international law of the state right of self-preservation, and signifies nothing more than this right.

Of course, the state's absolute right of self-preservation does not mean its absolute implementation in every single case. Such a concept of sovereignty, which incidentally neither Bodin nor anyone else has advocated, would radically preclude any international law. Pillet has already correctly pointed out that an objective element appertains to the right of self-preservation, which, through its unambiguous objective, the assurance of the state's existence, permits the setting of limits and the detection of its misuse.[503] One must be careful, however, of setting the limits too narrowly. It is a very questionable political view that believes that, in contrast to individual self-defense, the dangers to the state are "much less urgent and permit more time for defence and rescue, as the great 'person,' the state, cannot be ruined as quickly and easily"; therefore the scope of self-defense in international law is small—in fact it is "as good as totally" absent.[504] It cannot, certainly, be precisely calculated when an attack on the territorial and personal existence of a state or on its honor affects its vital interests. The smallest spark is often enough to cause the greatest fire. Precisely because these situations and acts do not allow an individualized normative control, we are dealing with a fundamental legal principle and not a legal rule of self-preservation. The question of whether an existential case is present that overrides any legal limits, whether a present or imminent danger, avoidable in one way or another, seriously threatens the existence of the state or not, can only be answered on the basis of the highly individual overall political situation.[505] Even after a danger is overcome, as we know, the assessment of all of these prerequisites to the existential case fluctuate within broad limits—though within objective limits whose violation doubtless represents a renewed breach of the law.[506] But because the sovereign state can make new law by breaching law, every state must be entitled to the responsible decision on the existential case. The decision whether this existential case is present or not can only be reserved to the sovereign decision-making unit itself. It is the indispensable correlate of the ever-present danger of "complete

[502] Kaufmann, *Wesen des Völkerrechts*, p. 204. Anzilotti, *Corso* (see note 361), p. 256, expands the clause to all of international law. Basically, even Heinrich Lammasch, "Vertragstreue im Völkerrecht," *in Österreichische Zeitschrift für öffentliches Recht*, 2 (1915/16), p. 25, cannot deny the validity of the clause; he admits, after all, that the common wording for territorial secession, "for all time," is only a 'standard formulation' [*clause de stile*], since reconquest is permitted under international law, and, on the other hand, himself cites cases of emergency (op. cit., p. 28 f.) that allow a formal break with the sanctity of treaty; here, where the right of self-preservation is conceded as against treaty obligations, one unfortunately notes too much the Austrian intent of 1915.

[503] Pillet, op. cit., p. 15. [504] Cybichowski, *Studien* (see note 486), p. 70; 31.

[505] See Strupp, *Völkerrechtliches Delikt* (see note 444), p. 160 ff., and those named therein.

[506] Unclear in Kaufmann, *Wesen des Völkerrechts*, p. 231.

destruction," the expression for the necessity of international law self-help, which could only disappear if there were a "world state."[507]

I cannot imagine a more fundamental misunderstanding of international law than the claim that the self-preservation clause is 'dispositive international law'[508] and could be eliminated by treaty. Perhaps we might imagine a legal rule that obligates individuals to commit suicide; but no legal rule is conceivable that expects the same from the state. Such a treaty would have as its content a type of conditional state founding. We need not address the question, which we would obviously answer in the negative, of whether a state can even emerge from a treaty at all. But it should not be contested that no treaty that does not provide for the immediate joining of two or more states into a new state, but unquestionably intends the continuity of its international law persons, can eliminate the self-preservation clause as "a right of necessity" [*ius necessarium*].

Even a treaty that has as its content the unconditional judicial settlement of all disputes between two states would not contain a renunciation of the reserved right of a minimum of self-preservation. The Federal Council of the Swiss Federal Assembly affirmed with justified pride of the treaty concluded on September 20, 1924 between Switzerland and Italy on the settlement of disputes through conciliation or judicial proceedings[509] that in this treaty, for the first time, the principle of obligatory, general, and unconditional judicial settlement had been established by treaty. The Federal Council explained, among other things, that the treaty lacked "completely the cautious and often perhaps unjustified reservations that had heretofore, in conformity with almost unanimous legal science, tended to be incorporated into arbitral treaties; thus it tacitly demonstrated that the complete application of the principles of law and equity to interstate relations in no way impaired national sovereignty, but on the contrary spelled their best guarantee."[510] These words already contain, willy nilly [*nolens volens*], the inviolability of the case of sovereignty. Through the conclusion of the unconditional treaty, Switzerland merely expressed its trust that the arbitral or legal decisions made on the basis of this treaty would not endanger its sovereignty, but would instead guarantee it. The fact that this is really Switzerland's view can be seen in a message from the Federal Assembly issued on the same day concerning the arbitration agreement concluded with Brazil on June 23, 1924.[511] Here it is rightly noted that obligatory arbitration is not a weapon "that is aimed *a priori* against a state for the benefit of another. From the standpoint of strict international justice, it would be impermissible to connect a court or arbitral decision with the idea of profit or loss; as a manifestation of interstate administration of justice, it cannot, as the name implies, desire anything unjust, and since it is only equipped with considerations of legal right or equitable

[507] See also Jellinek, *System* (see note 168), p. 323.

[508] Ernst Radnitzky, "Dispositivises Völkerrecht," in *Östereichische Zeitschrift für öffentliches Recht*, 1 (1914), p. 656 ff.; Strupp, op. cit., p. 131.

[509] (Reprinted in Société des Nations (ed.), *Recueil des Traités*, XXXIII (1925), p. 91).

[510] Federal Council of the Bundesrat of October 28, 1924, in *Bundesblatt*, Bern, 76 (1924 III), p. 668.

[511] (Reprinted in Société des Nations (ed.), *Recueil des Traités*, XXXIII (1925), p. 415).

discretion, it is difficult to understand how the sovereignty or the existence of a state could be threatened without violating the principles of international law, which must be respected. . . . This allows the problem to be ascribed to a matter of trust."[512] This first of all establishes the fundamental international law principle of state self-preservation, which cannot be touched by any institution, and, second, expresses the hope that—as the Federal Council says—"the uncertainty arising from application of fragmentary law by arbitrators or judges, whose judgments are obviously not immune to errors due to the lack of a foundation of fully established legal rules" would not lead to violations of sovereignty.[513]

The Swiss–Italian treaty cited earlier is the most far-reaching attempt at peaceful dispute settlement known in the history of international law—and it, too, implicates the case of sovereignty!

The unconditional obligation of the Geneva Protocol submitted to the League of Nations Assembly on October 1, 1924 never went beyond an attempt.[514] Nevertheless, the Protocol is significant for the theory of the state and for the sovereignty dogma because of a legal philosophy monograph. Drafted under the direction of Politis and Beneš, it was meant to expand the law of war prevention in Article 15(8), and in particular to contribute to reducing national armaments. It did not fail, as one generally hears, primarily because the development of international law cannot be forced, but mainly because of some of its internal contradictions. In a slogan, the Protocol wanted to shape the League of Nations into a semi-universal or semi-sovereign decision-making unit.

It must by rights, however, be stated that the Protocol's internal contradictions are merely the enhanced expression of those antinomies that inhere perhaps not necessarily in the idea, but certainly in the concrete embodiment of this League of Nations. The Pact itself, and to an enormously increased measure the Protocol, imagine international law as a universal legal order, which makes it possible for the League of Nations institutions, or rather the arbitral tribunal of first or second instance provided for in the Protocol, to reach decisions, even in cases involving sovereignty, that are legally binding on both parties—even, under the Protocol, against the will of both parties. This intrusion into state sovereignty would have corresponded to semi-sovereignty on the part of the League of Nations Council, whose unanimous decisions would have been accompanied by the full effect of the judgment, or in case of violation, by the enormous penal sanctions of Article 10 ff. of the Protocol. Based on this imagined universal legal order, the Council would be granted the right to decide in every case whether a state was guilty of the 'international crime' of aggressive war. The "right of war" [*ius belli*] within the League would be transferred exclusively to the League of Nations; the signatory states would have

512 Federal Council of the Bundesrat of October 28, 1924, in *Bundesblatt*, op. cit., p. 653 f.

513 Ibid., p. 654; see the assessment of the treaty by Walter Simons in *Mitteilungen der Deutschen Gesellschaft für Völkerrecht*, 6 (1925), p. 25 f.

514 *Protocole pour le règlement pacifique des différends internationaux*, in Société des Nations (ed.), *Journal officiel*, Supplément spécial (Séances plénières et Commissions), no. 26, Geneva 1924, p. 189 ff.; reprinted in Liszt/Fleischmann, *Völkerrecht* (see note 367), p. 691 ff.

not only the right but also the duty of legitimate self-defense. Thus, decision-making on the existential case would be removed from the League of Nations members once and for all.

It follows unquestionably from Article 4, no. 4 of the Protocol that a majority of the League of Nations Council would be clothed with this right; for an arbitral tribunal whose membership, powers, and procedure are determined by a Council majority is a political instrument of the Council majority. Now, our allegation of internal contradictions in no way coincides with that of almost all the opponents of the Protocol on the point that, ultimately, a political, non-judicial form of dispute settlement is being proposed. Even in state legal orders, non-justiciable cases that are not regulated by legal rules must also lead to more or less political decision-making. It is by this very characteristic that we recognize the nature of the sovereign state. Rather, the internal instability of the Protocol lies in its halfway measures, in the compromise it has reached between its juristic fictionalism and the political-juristic realities. Its aim was the grotesque idea of a state power that would have had to execute a "natural order." The vilified sovereignty dogma, however, presents its theoretically and practically irrefutable demands! Politis, at least, was aware that the fundamental legal principles shared by the signatory powers were not enough to constitute a universal decision-making unit capable of developing positive law. As he said in Geneva, "There will be grounds for war, because certain conflicts can still not be regulated by the application of legal rules. It will not be until law is enriched, until it will have rules for every situation, until one is sure that all the disputes could be regulated, not only in a peaceful manner, but also in a juridical manner, that one will have a true preventative safeguard against war."[515] However, this juristic idealism, as we have seen often enough, achieves a "peaceful manner" [*manière pacifique*] without a "juridical manner" [*manière juridique*] by pronouncing the "brute fact" [*brutum factum*] of existing power relations to be the "natural order." This is exactly what the Geneva Protocol does in removing review of international treaties and territorial rights from the Protocol's arbitral jurisdiction. This legal rationalism, which elsewhere also confuses legal rules with fundamental legal principles, need not differentiate between legality and legitimacy. It apparently does not worry this jurisprudence that, despite its admitted inability to distinguish, in terms of substantive law, between a war of aggression and one of defense, this attempt at an absolutely definitive legalization of the last successful war in recent times would mean a futile bid to bind the future to fundamental legal principles.

Even Kelsen teaches that, for the nature of the legal order, it "does not matter whether it can be changed or not."[516] The *status quo* as a legal ideal, and the majority of the League of Nations Council as the semi-sovereign executor of the "natural order"—that is the meaning of the *Geneva Protocol*.[517] But its internal contradictions

[515] Nicolas-Sokrate Politis at the 25th session of the League of Nations Assembly on October 1, 1924, in Société des Nations (ed.), *Journal officiel*, Supplément special (Séances plénières et Commissions), no. 23, Geneva 1924, p. 200. Cf. Politis, "Limitations de la souverainete" (see note 98), p. 41: "without formulating and applying a criterion of the legitimacy of war."

[516] Kelsen, *Problem der Souveränität* (see note 38), p. 258.

[517] I am speaking here as a juristic theoretician, not as a German affected by the Versailles Peace Treaty. One can completely understand that the French, Poles, and Czechs recognize the current *status*

result from the division of sovereignty between the League and its members. It was clear that the League of Nations did not represent a universal lawmaking institution acceptable to all its members. It could not be given the universal "power for the giving and abrogation of the law," in the absence of sufficient commonality of fundamental legal principles. On the other hand, however, a military action, too, is only an execution, and not an arbitrary war that cannot be judged legally, if it occurs to implement a decision based at least in generally accepted fundamental legal principles, if not in legal rules. Where such fundamental legal principles are not sufficient to constitute a common sovereign lawmaking institution, then they are not sufficient, "by themselves" [*eo ipso*], to create an institution that makes decisions on war and peace, that is, on the most serious of all issues. This divided sovereignty constitutes the juristic-technical half-measure in the Geneva Protocol.[518] The enormously exaggerated, coercive idea of the Protocol, backed by no fundamental legal principles, let alone legal rules, leads inevitably "either to the collapse of the international community or to imperialist super-states."[519]

We have enlisted all our examples only to ground our theory; they should suffice. A detailed discussion of the problem of the League of Nations and sovereignty lies outside the scope of this study; given the current circumstances, it is also best avoided.

Only the question of the extent to which the League of Nations constitutes a limit to the state's absolute right of self-preservation will be answered, through an example. The League of Nations can only make this claim if it offered a sufficient guarantee that acts contrary to international law by a state could mature into law. Anyone asking this question must keep in mind, regarding the League of Nations, that an institution so young and functioning under such difficult circumstances is often well advised not to subject itself to great tests of strength. On the other hand, however, this psychological-political insight should not prevent jurists from determining that the practice of today's particular League of Nations does not rule out international lawmaking through international lawbreaking, not even among League members. When Lithuania requested in October 1920, due to the incursion into Vilna by Polish troops under the command of Polish General Želigowski, that

*quo* as a national-political legal ideal—but they too cannot claim the *status quo* as a permanent international legal ideal. Just as I cannot ask the working class to see bourgeois security and its present form of order as binding for the sake of order as an ideal, so too can I not concede the categories of legitimate and criminal war, based solely on the current *status quo*. See also Philip Marshall Brown, "The Geneva Protocol," in *The American Journal of International Law*, 19 (1925), p. 338 f.

[518] Yet Politis's intellectual agility is able to master all of these contradictions. In 1923 he said, in regard to the "obligation" (*La justice international*, Paris 1924, p. 168): "The notion of obligation rests on reciprocal confidence. If this confidence is not shared by all, one should not recommend obligation, because, if it is stipulated in the absence of conviction, it risk in practice remaining a dead letter, which is worse than denying it entry." In 1924 he wrote and defended the Geneva Protocol, and in 1925 explained that the English government, which had caused the failure of the Protocol, should be "thanked for their frankness, for it permitted a full apprehension of reality, without which the effort to achieve peace would not only be a chimera, but also dangerous." Nicolas Politis, "Les Accords de Locarno," in *Revue de droit international*, 52 (1925), p. 716.

[519] Simons (Thesis 7), in *Mitteilungen* (see note 513), p. 29.

Article 16 of the Pact be applied to Poland, its request was not met. Poland, which first tried to deny any responsibility for Želigowski, today enjoys sovereignty over the Vilna region.[520]

But as long as the state's absolute right to self-preservation is only ensured by international law, and no international law eliminating world state, as a universal territorial unit of decision-making and effect, prevents world history as a world court from finding in favor of international lawbreakers by allowing them to prevail—as long as this is the case, the sovereignty of every state must in the existential case remain a "legally unlimited authority" [*legibus soluta potestas*] vis-à-vis international law and the League of Nations.

The nature of all law plainly consists in the fact that it can be misused; this is how logical validity differs from juristic validity, a "natural order" independent of our will from positive law and from any norm that appeals to our will. If one therefore admits that a state can only fulfill its indispensable ordering function through the universality of its decisions, but that this universal decision-making unit is only possible if it asserts itself existentially even against law, then the allegation against sovereignty, made by numerous authors, that it makes arbitrary misuse possible is at least not a juristic refutation. Furthermore, as long as positive law is made valid and maintained by human will, the catchword of legal sovereignty denotes a juristically vague wishful thinking, which is in no way realizable even through the "world state." It is certainly true that the multiplicity of sovereign units of will, considered abstractly, means a quantitatively greater number of possible arbitrary actors than the unit of will of the "world state." But aside from the fact that the scope of each arbitrary act by a world state would be proportionally larger and more consequential, even in a world state one could not speak of legal sovereignty. Any attempt to eliminate arbitrariness once and for all ends with the elimination of the will and would mean, in the current state of the world, which has no universal legal order, the perpetuation of the *status quo* as a surrogate for the "natural order." But should a 'legal form' be found "in which modifications occur when they are based in the evolution of nations,"[521] should this goal be linked with a change "that the concept of sovereignty of Roman law experienced in the contemporary system of coordinated states and through the development of international intercourse,"[522] then the juristically necessary concept of sovereignty would in turn fall victim to an unjuristic mindset. For as certain as it is that international intercourse has enormously developed the economic and general social interdependence of states, it is equally certain that it did not eliminate their political and legal independence and did not fundamentally change the concept of sovereignty. Yet even if the coordinated states were to be eliminated, and in this way, the only way possible, the postulated legal form, in the guise of the world state, was to exist, nothing would change in the fundamental relationship between will and legal norm, sovereignty and positivity.

[520] Société des Nations (ed.), *Journal officiel*, Supplément spécial, no. 4, Geneva 1920, p. 135 ff. Cf. Schücking/Wehberg, *Satzung des Völkerbundes* (see note 353), p. 472 f.

[521] Lammasch, "Vertragstreue" (see note 502), p. 25.

[522] Ibid., p. 34.

# X

# Political and Ethical Evaluation of Sovereignty

Every juristic theory and construct of state law phenomena is at the same time, of necessity, a political value judgment, if only because both must be positively related to the unity of territorial decision-making. The attempt to completely undo this political connection must necessarily remain a self-deception, resulting in a state law doctrine without law and without a state.

Every juristic theory and construct also remains rooted in political contradictions and can only relatively, but never absolutely, escape value judgments. True objectivity can only be achieved by a jurist if he is aware of his own value judgments, but never if he leads himself and others to believe that his research is completely without presuppositions.[523]

The 'pure juristic' doctrine that has been dominant in Germany since Gerber and Laband is therefore nothing but, at best, a grandiose self-deception. Its supposedly conceptual, juristic-logical imperatives, especially its unreal state, reveal themselves today to be the very relative political judgments of liberalism. Its latest offshoot, the 'pure theory of law,' is the methodological absolutisation of liberalism and its 'freedom from the state,' and thus at the same time the juristic mask of liberal opposition to the dogma of state sovereignty.

A logically steadfast liberalism ends in anarchism. The fundamental rejection of state sovereignty is therefore just as consistent from a liberal and anarcho-syndicalist position as it is internally contradictory on the basis of a socialist assessment. The tactical necessity of socialist agitation against the sovereignty of the modern nation and class state is politically understandable. The phraseology of the death or slumber of the state in socialism can also be historically explained by the competition with anarchism in which Marx and Engels found themselves.[524] But that a political movement whose programmatic core is the "rule of popular will, organized in a free people's state, over the economy,"[525] would strive as a matter of principle for an enormous expansion of the content of sovereignty—this can only be the misjudgment of a socialism that, in its political mindset, is still sailing completely in the wake of liberalism. But to the extent that socialist syndicalism wishes to be

[523] See Heinrich Triepel, *Staatsrecht und Politik* (rectorate's lecture), Berlin 1926, p. 38 f.

[524] See Hermann Heller, *Sozialismus und Nation*, in *Gesammelte Schriften*, vol. 1, p. 488 ff., and Heller, *Die politischen Ideenkreise der Gegenwart*, in ibid., vol. I, p. 384 ff.

[525] (*Protokoll über die Verhandlungen des Parteitages der Sozialdemokratischen Partei Deutschlands* (September 18–24, 1921 in Görlitz), Berlin 1921, p. 111 ff.)

not chiliastic prophecy but politics, it must see its task as that of replacing the atomistic constitution of sovereign territorial decision-making units with its syndicalist structure. The struggle of syndicalism against state sovereignty in principle is either a misunderstanding or a technique of agitation.

The confusion between demo-liberalism and democracy also forms a rich source of internally contradictory evaluations of sovereignty. It is the Anglo-American literature in particular that, by not separating state and organ sovereignty, places democracy and sovereignty in necessary contradiction. The German doctrine of state sovereignty may easily seem to be an expression of absolutist monarchism if one accepts the theoretically false claim that "The limitations of sovereign power in any one state characterize the conditions of its political development. The greater the limitations, the more democratic the government."[526]

If the struggle against sovereignty, which is logical in liberalism, is an expression of the immanent utopia that the idea as such wishes to achieve—that is, to realize the legal idea without the intervention of a will—then state-theoretical nationalism is characterized by the fact that it raises the reality of the contemporary nation state and its sovereignty to the level of an idea. This Hegelian method, even when it claims a prestabilized harmony between the pursuit of power and moral efforts, arrives at a "cultural individualism"[527] that absolutizes current nation state sovereignty as the founding idea of the world spirit. Since such historicism must make the political will believe that it has nothing better to do but to "enforce past history"—as the professor concerned understands it—then the conclusion may be drawn from the "nature" of the current European nation states, which must simply "rub and bump," that "not only the world state, but also the empire of Europe is a utopia that one cannot seriously desire, and which one must not desire if one wishes not to betray the spirit of the Occident."[528] To this image of history, papal world rule, which is after all Occidental, represents only a "pathological phenomenon," and the world state is an impossibility because, by developing its power externally, it would lack "the necessary life principle."[529]

In contrast, the question may well be posed as to whether the existence of the cultural individualism of the European nations is threatened today precisely by their political individualism, and can only be saved by a sovereign European federation.

Because the achievement of this goal is contingent on political agitation that starts with the dissolution of nation state sovereignty, neither a positivist jurist nor a legal expert should delude himself that the dissolution of nation state sovereignty is only possible through integration into a more comprehensively sovereign state. That jurisprudence deceives itself regarding this situation and speaks of a change in the sovereignty concept in principle, of the dissolution of the sovereignty dogma, being due, in terms of the history of ideas, to the fact that it juridifies ethics and moralizes law, in the tradition of Enlightenment natural law, or that it revives this tradition. This violates both spheres, the legal field as well as the ethical world. It is this failure

[526] W. R. Bisschop, "Sovereignty," in *The British Yearbook of International Law*, 2 (1919/20), p. 123.
[527] Kaufmann, *Wesen des Völkerrechts* (see note 283), p. 153; 135.
[528] Hans Freyer, *Der Staat*, Leipzig 1925, p. 212.
[529] Kaufmann, op. cit., p. 136.

to recognize the autonomy and relative independence of law that leads to a failure to recognize the sovereignty problem. It is no accident that the father of the "world state" in international law, Christian Wolff, was the one who maintained that "Every nation must manifest affection for the others and love them as it does itself, even if it is also to be a hostile nation."[530]

Only those who take seriously the Christian commandment to love and do not sentimentalize it know that this commandment always requires us to get to the point of decision, but that our decisions never fulfill this commandment, even if we ourselves are saints; indeed, our decisions always violate it. The moral commandment is valid, notwithstanding the fact that we never fulfill it. The validity of the legal commandment, however, is only possible through constant observation. Law requires a specific minimum amount of legal certainty. The moral decision knows no earthly security; it is the deepest, most unsettling uncertainty. Only for those who believe that they have been mercifully decided upon before they decide themselves—only in heavenly mercy is there security. But this final certainty exists only for the highly individual, devout soul.

The certainty of law, in contrast, is necessarily earthly, predictable, the certainty of intersubjective normative will creation. In order for there to be orderly coexistence, physical and metaphysical self-preservation, an authoritative common will must effectively decide on our social acts of will, before we decide individually on these questions that are necessary for the unity of territorial–social interaction. We can be sure that the state is never the highest authority. It is, however, the highest legal authority; that is, it is sovereign, it is the potential universal unit of decision-making and effect on its territory.

Modern natural law was secularized theology. Its "natural order" was supposed to take from us the moral and legal responsibility for decision-making, and thus our sense of guilt; it was a surrogate for Christian mercy and seemed suited to guarantee with mathematical certainty at least the security of social organization. The belief lasted as long as this "natural order," filled with the substance of its Christian heritage, had at its disposal certain substantive legal postulates as generally acceptable "natural order." We do not have this security of fundamental legal principles that constituted our grandfathers' bourgeois security. In social organization, too, we are once again faced with a mortally dangerous decision. However it may turn out—should it become intersubjective, normative binding of wills, or positive law—it must be the decision of a sovereign state. No "natural order" is capable for all eternity of taking from us the either–or of a decision. Therefore, as long as human acts of will constitute the state, they will with sovereign force constantly break legal rules, whether they thereby violate fundamental legal principles or lead them to victory.

[530] Christian Frh. v. Wolff, *Grundsätze des Natur- und Völkerrechts*, Halle 1754, IV, 810; on this, see Kelsen, *Problem der Souveränität* (see note 38), p. 250 ff.

# *Index*

The manufacturer's authorised representative in the EU for product safety is Oxford University Press España S.A. of El Parque Empresarial San Fernando de Henares, Avenida de Castilla, 2 - 28830 Madrid (www.oup.es/en or product.safety@oup.com). OUP España S.A. also acts as importer into Spain of products made by the manufacturer.
Printed and bound by CPI Group (UK) Ltd, Croydon, CR0 4YY
14/09/2026
02216308-0004